TWENTIETH CENTURY VIEWS

The aim of this series is to present the best
in contemporary critical opinion on major
authors, providing a twentieth century
perspective on their changing status in an
era of profound revaluation.

Maynard Mack, *Series Editor*
Yale University

THACKERAY

A COLLECTION OF CRITICAL ESSAYS

Edited by
Alexander Welsh

Prentice-Hall, Inc. A SPECTRUM BOOK   *Englewood Cliffs, N. J.*

Contents

Introduction

by Alexander Welsh

Modern criticism, in spirit committed to analysis and discovery rather than intelligent general responses, apparently faces special difficulties in treating some of the great prose artists of our literature. Thackeray is an artist not only careless and amateurish in part, but, for complex personal and social reasons, sometimes defiantly so. A brilliant master of language, he nevertheless makes it hard for us to hold him at his word. For example, in the paragraph immediately preceding the text from *The Adventures of Philip* that I shall present in a moment, occurs a typically puzzling parenthesis:

> Mamma, I say, has left the room at last, bowing with a perfect sweetness and calm grace and gravity; and she has slipped down the stairs, scarce more noisy than the shadow that slants over the faded carpet (oh! the faded shadow, the faded sunshine!)—mamma is gone, I say, to the lower regions, and with perfect good breeding is torturing the butler on his bottle-rack—is squeezing the housekeeper in her jam-closet—is watching the three cold cutlets shuddering in the larder behind the wires . . .

That the apostrophe to "the faded shadow, the faded sunshine!" is merely one of Thackeray's nostalgic calls to the past seems incredible. The treatment of mamma's descent into the lower regions of the house is too sarcastic. Each reference in the paragraph to her calculation in the management of her house reflects her unspoken calculation that the young lovers, whom she "with a perfect sweetness and calm grace and gravity" has left to themselves upstairs, will contract a profitable marriage. Even the choice of "mamma," the sweet diminutive that Thackeray typically uses in this mercenary context, is clothed with sarcasm. Then what can be the logical import of the apostrophe to the shadow and the sunshine? Either it is the nostalgic call, irrelevant and disturbing in this context, or it is the writer's self-mockery for having written—though as sarcastically as he could please—"scarce more noisy than the shadow that slants over the faded carpet." With

Thackeray we are in the presence, not of a conscious artistry, but of a terrible self-consciousness of language—and of fiction.

A case for the late, "bad" novels of Thackeray can obviously be made: the puns on the domestic "rack," "jam-closet," and "wires" in *Philip* ingeniously spell out the implications of a house with "lower regions" or dungeon; the "three cold cutlets shuddering in the larder" symbolize the meanness of the Talbot Twysden family; Mrs. Twysden's hypocritical "gravity" derives from the satire of Fielding, who attributed the exposure of "gravity" to Shaftesbury, who borrowed it from Hobbes (in *Leviathan*, I, x). On the other hand, merely to cite the rest of the sentence from this last completed novel of Thackeray would display some of his weaknesses. The received opinion that Thackeray's achievement diminishes after *The Newcomes* is essentially sound. My object is rather to concentrate attention on one segment of a little-known novel—a segment that is not in any way memorable—in order to show the characteristic nature of Thackeray's fiction. At this point in the narrative the hero, Philip Firmin, is courting his cousin Agnes, the daughter of those tight Twysdens, and the purpose of the narrative is to display her falseness and inferiority:

> . . . A wretched maid, who has been ironing collars, or what not, gives her mistress a shuddering curtsey, and slinks away with her laces; and meanwhile our girl and boy are prattling in the drawing-room.
>
> About what? About everything on which Philip chooses to talk. There is nobody to contradict him but himself, and then his pretty hearer vows and declares he has not been so very contradictory. He spouts his favorite poems. "Delightful! Do, Philip, read us some Walter Scott! He is, as you say, the most fresh, the most manly, the most kindly of poetic writers— not of the first class, certainly. In fact, he has written most dreadful bosh, as you call it so drolly; and so has Wordsworth, though he is one of the greatest of men, and has reached sometimes to the very greatest height and sublimity of poetry; but now you put it, I must confess he is often an old bore, and I certainly should have gone to sleep during the 'Excursion,' only you read it so nicely. You don't think the new composers as good as the old ones, and love mamma's old-fashioned playing? Well, Philip, it is delightful, so lady-like, so feminine!" Or, perhaps, Philip has just come from Hyde Park, and says, "As I passed by Apsley House, I saw the Duke come out, with his old blue frock and white trousers and clear face. I have seen a picture of him in an old *European Magazine*, which I think I like better than all—gives me the idea of one of the brightest men in the world. The brave eyes gleam at you out of the picture; and there's a smile on the resolute lips, which seems to ensure triumph. Agnes, Assaye must have been glorious!"

"Glorious, Philip!" says Agnes, who have never heard of Assaye before in her life. Arbela, perhaps; Salamis, Marathon, Agincourt, Blenheim, Busaco—where dear grandpapa was killed—Waterloo, Armageddon; but Assaye? *Que voulez-vous?*

"Think of that ordinarily prudent man, and how greatly he knew how to dare when occasion came! I should like to have died after winning such a game. He has never done anything so exciting since."

"A game? I thought it was a battle just now," murmurs Agnes in her mind; but there may be some misunderstanding. "Ah, Philip," she says, "I fear excitement is too much the life of all young men now. When will you be quiet and steady, sir?"

"And go to an office every day, like my uncle and cousin; and read the newspaper for three hours, and trot back and see you."

"Well, sir! that ought not to be such very bad amusement," says one of the ladies.

"What a clumsy wretch I am! my foot is always trampling on something or somebody!" groans Phil.

"You must come to us, and we will teach you how to dance, Bruin!" says gentle Agnes, smiling on him. I think when very much agitated, her pulse must have gone up to forty. Her blood must have been a light pink. The heart that beat under that pretty white chest, which she exposed so liberally, may have throbbed pretty quickly once or twice with waltzing, but otherwise never rose or fell beyond its natural gentle undulation. It may have had throbs of grief at a disappointment occasioned by the milliner not bringing a dress home; or have felt some little fluttering impulse of youthful passion when it was in short frocks, and Master Grimsby at the dancing-school showed some preference for another young pupil out of the nursery. But feelings, and hopes, and blushes, and passions now? Psha! They pass away like nursery dreams. Now there are only proprieties. What is love, young heart? It is two thousand a year, at the very lowest computation; and, with the present rise in wages and house-rent, that calculation can't last very long. Love? Attachment? Look at Frank Maythorn, with his vernal blushes, his leafy whiskers, his sunshiny laughing face, and all the birds of spring carolling in his jolly voice; and old General Pinwood hobbling in on his cork leg, with his stars and orders, and leering round the room from under his painted eyebrows. Will my modest nymph go to Maythorn, or to yonder leering Satyr, who totters towards her in his white and rouge? Nonsense. She gives her garland to the old man, to be sure. He is ten times as rich as the young one. And so they went on in Arcadia itself, *really*. Not in that namby-pamby ballet and idyll world, where they tripped up to each other in rhythm, and talked hexameters; but in the real downright no-mistake country—Arcadia— where Tityrus fluting to Amaryllis in the shade, had his pipe very soon put out when Meliboeus (the great grazier) performed on his melodious, exquisite, irresistible cowhorn; and where Daphne's mother dressed her up with ribbons and drove her to market, and sold her, and swapped her, and bartered her like any other lamb in the fair. This one has been trotted to the market so long now that she knows the way herself. Her baa has been heard for—do not let us count how many seasons. She has nibbled out of countless hands; frisked in many thousand dances; come quite harmless away from goodness knows how many wolves. Ah! ye lambs and raddled innocents of our Arcadia! Ah, old *Ewe!* Is it of your ladyship this fable is narrated? I say it is as old as Cadmus, and man-and-mutton-kind.

So, when Philip comes to Beaunash Street, Agnes listens to him most kindly, sweetly, gently, and affectionately. . . . (ch. ix)

The Victorian female is properly in the same relation to her lord, or future husband, as a minister of state is to the king in the Elizabethan imagination. Agnes betrays her high office when she flatters Philip in his shallowness, and leaves "nobody to contradict him but himself." When she accedes to his glib disparagement of those cultural heroes, Scott and Wordsworth, she permits him to be false to his better self. Since she cannot understand Philip's sentiment about dying after the victory of Assaye (if he were the Duke of Wellington), she has no conception of honor; she is mystified when he speaks of battle as a game. Her misunderstanding is predictable, of course, because her father and brother are not really gentlemen but persons who "go to an office every day." The most subtle charge of all that Thackeray brings against this sacrificial lamb is that she thinks of the great Duke, "that ordinarily prudent man"—the "moderate, resolute" Wellington of Tennyson's funeral ode—as a mere European or Englishman, not as the great Anglo-Indian who made his significant impact on world history in the Mahratta War of 1803.

To bring his indictment against Agnes Twysden the novelist constructs his narrative with an apparently chaotic, typically Thackerayan, logic. For the simple transition between the conversation on great poets to that on the great Duke, for example, a new and separate fiction is invented: "Or, perhaps, Philip has just come from Hyde Park, and says . . ." The whole conversation on the Duke, together with the estrangement of the lovers and their cross-purposes, are governed by this speculative and even doubtful "perhaps." The continuing present tense of the narrative permits the interpretation that the conversations on the poets and the Duke took place on different days. But the logic of the transition equally permits the interpretation that only one of these conversations took place. Then it appears that neither conversation is definitely asserted to have occurred, for the conversation on poets is also introduced with a speculative turn: Philip and Agnes are talking—"About what?" We expect a novelist to tell his lies (narrate his story) directly: One day Philip said . . . Another day he said . . . and Agnes replied. But Thackeray keeps refusing to disguise his fiction as fact. If we thread back through several pages of *Philip* to discover how and when the action arrived at Beaunash Street, we find only the general invitation, "Look into that grave [note the gravity], solemn, dingy, somewhat naked, but elegant drawing-room, in Beaunash Street, and with a little fanciful opera-glass you may see a pretty little group or two engaged at different periods of the day." Look in at different periods of the day? At one little group or two? The normal temptation to fix the time of action, to imagine a definite action, is forestalled immediately, both by the indefinite invitation and by a series of alternative possibilities that anticipate the alternative conversations on poets and Duke: "a fair-haired young fellow with large feet [Philip] . . . breaks out regarding the debate of the previous night, or the pamphlet of yesterday, or the poem of the day previous, or the scandal of the week before, or upon the street-sweeper at the corner, or the Italian and monkey before the Park." The novel that purports to narrate the adventures of a young man so remarkably like Thackeray himself asserts only their main outline, filled in which a series of alternatives, possibilities, fictions that experimentally present the experience of those adventures. This method is thoroughly consistent with Thackeray's habit of employing an intrusive narrator, to conduct the experiments, invent the scenes, pose the alternatives—to speculate, reconstruct, and generalize. The method is thoroughly consistent also with Thackeray's habit (or Arthur Pendennis's habit) of generalizing his invented fiction in terms of the still more obviously fictitious parable of "Frank Maythorn" and "General Pinwood," with its further extension in terms of the fictitious shepherds of Vergilian pastoral— and, oddly enough, with the persistent claim that the general phenomenon that he is describing is factual, ordinary, *"really"* the case.

The run-away development of a narrative of fragmentary possibilities has no logical stopping point. The spiralling fictions are finally unable to elucidate further the primary imagined experience of the courtship of Agnes and Philip, and the narrative suddenly leaps out of fiction altogether with an insult to the reader, "old *Ewe!*" The leap is rather desperate, but a reader, presumably, has existence independent of the novelist, who thus escapes from his tangle of fictions. Because the scenes are exploratory and fictitious analogues theoretically

unlimited in number, the narrative can only be checked by throwing
it into reverse or arbitrarily giving it up. In *Vanity Fair,* much more
conventionally narrated than *Philip,* the most famous of all Thackeray's reversals—"Oh, Sir Pitt! . . . I'm *married already*"—is carefully made consistent with the imagined reality by means of a secret
marriage. But at the end of *The Newcomes,* Thackeray suddenly
throws over the entire masterfully created world of his novel by with-
drawing the narrative from Arthur Pendennis and stating in a new
voice that you may believe in that world if you care to—if you
happen to like fairy tales. Thackeray's use of fiction is both daring
and necessarily self-conscious. By the writing of *Philip,* not only is
it nearly impossible to sustain the continual advance and retreat of
this method for hundreds of pages, but Thackeray has said most of
what he has to say, conducted most of these experiments before. The
increased self-consciousness is further compounded by the note of
personal betrayal, Thackeray's famous cynicism, hand in glove with
his sentimentality: "Agnes listens to him most kindly, sweetly, gently,
and affectionately."

The non-sequiturs of Agnes's speech, as she skips from poets to
new composers to mamma's playing, do not prove that she is scatter-
brained. As a Twysden she is too mean to be scatter-brained. Thackeray is actually characterizing her by means of a dramatic mono-
logue, in which the apparent gaps in her flow of thought may be
understood as responses of her interlocutor. This particular use of
direct discourse—of which Thackeray's contemporary Robert Browning is the great master—implies that Agnes must always behave this
way in this kind of situation. Thackeray and Browning are renowned
as portrayers of character, but it can be as readily said of them, as
Pater said of Browning,[1] that they are pre-eminently poets of situation. They are able to construct brilliant "true-to-life" characters by
testing their personages, who often have real-life counterparts, in
concrete fictitious situations. Their great successes are not precon-
ceived characters but genuine creations of narrative experiments;
and there is much practical truth in Thackeray's defense that he did
not marry Henry Esmond and Lady Castlewood because, "They
married themselves." [2] Moreover, in *The Ring and the Book* Browning states a theory of fiction that is highly applicable to Thackeray:

---

[1] "Winckelmann," in *The Renaissance.*

[2] Gordon N. Ray, *Thackeray: The Age of Wisdom, 1847–1863* (New York, 1958),
p. 188.

> Is fiction which makes fact alive, fact too?
> The somehow may be thishow. (I, 706–07)

Historical knowledge of the past, even the immediate past, is bound to be fragmentary. But something happened, there are such things as facts. How it happened, and in some cases whether anything happened, can be determined by reconstructing the event in one or more fictions. The unlikely courtship of Agnes and Philip did take place, Thackeray posits, and the somehow may be thishow—or perhaps thishow. Even where the assertion of Thackeray's fiction is much firmer, as in *Vanity Fair,* which from the first sentence fixes in more conventional manner a time and place for the action—even here Thackeray's use of fiction is heuristic. Becky Sharp could not have carried on her affair with Lord Steyne on the grand scale without discovery: the discovery occurred, argues Thackeray, and the somehow may be thishow—the since famous confrontation of Steyne and Rawdon Crawley.

Thackeray's serious use of fiction as a means of investigation, even in comic and satiric modes, comes very close to the broad effort of Henry James as an artist, especially as we trace this effort in James's notebooks, from the *donnée* in fact or story to the selected thishow. The main disagreement between James and Thackeray, a difference amplified by Percy Lubbock, concerns a separate issue—the importance of maintaining the illusion of reality throughout the experiment. But Thackeray, who is careless of this illusion, is left free to apply multiple fictions to his *donnée,* as in the passage from *Philip,* and in general to communicate the nature of his experiments to the reader by performing them on the surface of his narrative. For better or worse, his self-consciousness contributes to this transparency. What must be stressed is the important, heuristic use of fiction, which may truly be regarded as scientific. In *The Newcomes* the novelist compares his method to that of paleontology, the most influential science of Thackeray's time:

> How can I tell the feelings in a young lady's mind; the thoughts in a young gentleman's bosom?—As Professor Owen or Professor Agassiz takes a fragment of a bone, and builds an enormous forgotten monster out of it, wallowing in primæval quagmires, tearing down leaves and branches of plants that flourished thousands of years ago, and perhaps may be coal by this time—so the novelist puts this and that together: from the footprint finds the foot; from the foot, the brute who trod on it; from the brute, the plant he browsed on, the marsh in which he swam—and

thus, in his humble way a physiologist too, depicts the habits, size, appearance of the beings whereof he has to treat;—traces this slimy reptile through the mud, and describes his habits filthy and rapacious; prods down his butterfly with a pin, and depicts his beautiful coat and embroidered waistcoat; points out the singular structure of yonder more important animal, the megatherium of his history. (ch. xlvii)

The analogy, like so many passages in Thackeray, is both brilliant and facetious—including the self-conscious comparison of Clive Newcome and other heroes to the genus *Megatherium*. In the mid-twentieth century, when not only the natural sciences but economics and the social sciences rely so heavily on constructing heuristic fictions or "models" of given data, the nature of Thackeray's practice in literature and the appositeness of his scientific analogy deserve to be taken quite seriously.

Past literature, furthermore, has already constructed a vast store of fictions on which the experimental novelist can draw. Thackeray's early career as a writer was largely devoted to burlesque and parody, and the surface of most of his writing is cluttered with literary allusion. As John Loofbourow's pioneering study seeks to demonstrate,[3] virtually all his work engages in a play on literary forms and styles. On the one hand, this play exacerbates Thackeray's self-consciousness as a writer. He cannot adopt a style or form without mixed feelings, as if he were caught doing something silly, something he has laughed at others for doing. On the other hand, each conscious sally against a style or form is conducted on behalf of realism. For by making his readers aware that he is anti-literary in spirit, by stressing the differences between literature and life, Thackeray intends to bring the real world vividly before us. He scorns the "namby-pamby ballet and idyll world" of literature, in the passage from *Philip,* and exposes the "real downright no-mistake country" of mercenary marriages. In his awareness of the interplay between reality and the literary distortions of reality he is like no other English novelist so much as Fielding—with whom he closely identified, despite his rather smug Victorian strictures and misunderstandings of Fielding in the lectures on *The English Humourists.* Yet the literary awareness that inspires both novelists leaves Thackeray uneasy. For one thing, the determination to be a gentleman is much more defensive in the nineteenth century than in Fielding's time, and Thackeray, like Scott, is not quite sure that writing fiction is a gentlemanly vocation. For another, a certain evangelical fervor for truth weighed heavily on the

[3] *Thackeray and the Form of Fiction* (Princeton, 1964).

nineteenth century. Macaulay, for example, wrote that "We cannot unite the incompatible advantages of reality and deception, the clear discernment of truth and the exquisite enjoyment of fiction."[4] For all his insight and literary sophistication, Thackeray could not escape the serious doubts about fiction of his class and period.

One anti-literary stance of Thackeray is so broad that we tend to undervalue it: his determination to explore the married lives of his characters. In the English novel marriage is very emphatically enshrined as the end of life—in both senses of "end." Thackeray complained in *Vanity Fair* that, "As his hero and heroine pass the matrimonial barrier, the novelist generally drops the curtain, as if the drama were over then: the doubts and struggles of life ended" (ch. xxvi). Consulting his own unhappy experience, he courageously explored the other side of the barrier in more than one novel. His full-scale treatment of mothers, particularly Helen Pendennis and Lady Castlewood, is even more unconventional in English novels. Here Thackeray stands almost alone. Though Jane Austen poked fun at the absence of mothers in novels in the opening of *Northanger Abbey,* she nevertheless tends to caricature mothers in her own work. As for Dickens, among the extant mothers in his work the most prominent are Mrs. Nickleby, Mrs. Micawber, and Mrs. Wilfer. Only occasionally, as in Lawrence's *Sons and Lovers,* has an English novelist gone further than Thackeray in exploring the maternal relationship. In the four major novels beginning with *Vanity Fair* he took still another literary convention of his time, a pair of morally contrasted heroines, and, after first exaggerating it, progressively rehandled the convention until he emerged with Ethel Newcome, a single heroine who is genuinely complex—or so I have argued in another connection.[5] Finally, Thackeray was uncommonly aware of the part wish-fulfillment plays in the distortion of reality in novels. Embarrassment at wish-fulfillment in his own work is always likely to arrest Thackeray. Witness the ambiguous remarks about the marriage of Dobbin and Amelia at the end of *Vanity Fair,* or the wholesale repudiation of the narrative at the end of *The Newcomes.* The perplexed quality of these endings seems almost unnecessary: the novelist has already done battle with the convention of the happy ending by permitting his protagonists unhappy first marriages. Why qualify their second chances? Yet Thackeray cannot bring Dobbin and Amelia together without passing a remark about the "tender little parasite"

---

[4] *Edinburgh Review,* XLII (1825), 309.
[5] "The Allegory of Truth in English Fiction," *Victorian Studies,* IX (1965), 9–12.

and hinting of the failure of Dobbin's love. In *The Newcomes,* after his savage portrayal of Clive's wretched marriage—doubly wretched because the hero has married to please a father who is trying to please his son ("the boy's evident unhappiness was like a reproach to his father")—Thackeray dutifully works the action around to the point where his hero can finally marry the right heroine but then throws up the whole business as a bad job. Though he conjectures that "in Fable-land somewhere Ethel and Clive are living most comfortably together," the experiments conducted by his narrator in the body of the novel have actually led to a different conclusion. Thackeray, fabulist extraordinary, is a poor liar. His failure to complete *The Newcomes* in form is very moving, his struggle not merely with sentiment but with the conventions of the novel. The failure is something of an event in literary history, foreshadowing the different concept of plot, especially in regard to endings, of Henry James, E. M. Forster, and others.

It no longer seems necessary to defend Thackeray in principle against the Jamesian criticism that stresses a controlled point of view and scorns a talkative narrator. Geoffrey Tillotson's study of Thackeray's unity,[6] written not many years ago, already strikes one as unnecessarily defensive. The critical hold of so-called Jamesian criticism has been broken during the last decade, and the "great tradition" of English novelists defined by F. R. Leavis has been judged too narrow. The "large loose baggy monsters" of the nineteenth century are even admired for their bagginess. To be sure, this minor revolution in critical opinion has been fought chiefly on behalf of Dickens and George Eliot rather than Thackeray—so much so that many students and some writers on the novel seem under the impression that by "large loose baggy monsters" James referred to *Bleak House* or *Middlemarch* instead of honoring with this term, as is actually the case, *The Three Musketeers, War and Peace,* and *The Newcomes.*[7]

But there is another issue, one that goes to the substance of Thackeray's art, on which critical opinion continues to differ. The scholar who has studied Thackeray and his work more thoroughly than anyone else, Gordon N. Ray, argues that the novelist "attained [his] high position among his contemporaries chiefly by redefining the gentlemanly ideal to fit a middle-class rather than an aristocratic context." [8] No one can readily quarrel with this judgment, either with respect to Thackeray or to the importance of the ideal of the gentle-

---

[6] *Thackeray the Novelist* (Cambridge, England, 1954).
[7] Preface to *The Tragic Muse.*
[8] *Thackeray: The Uses of Adversity, 1811–1846* (New York, 1955), pp. 13–16.

man in modern British history. But it is possible to debate the implication that Thackeray succeeded in this redefinition, or that such a redefinition was indeed possible by the mid-nineteenth century. The problem is not confined to a selection of qualities or styles of behavior befitting a gentleman. The real thrust of Professor Ray's judgment is that Thackeray (and others) urged that gentlemanliness is not a class concept. But is it not? The theory that gentlemanliness is not the monopoly of a social class derived precisely from the effort to wrest the ideal away from the aristocracy. Victorian novels are therefore full of aristocrats who do not behave like gentlemen and some lower-class individuals who do. This proved that there are some gentlemen and some non-gentlemen at every level of society, but did not eliminate class-consciousness from the concept, which would have had little vitality in the first place if it were merely the collective name for certain values. Historically, English gentlemen had come to regard themselves as a class, and pride of class depends on the principle of exclusion, or the identification of non-gentlemen. Thackeray and other English novelists were preoccupied with sorting gentlemen from non-gentlemen, whether on frivolous or moral grounds, because they were engaged in defining a social class. If this task was more often than not accomplished with tact or kindness, it was owing to fear of class conflict or to Christianity rather than to gentlemanliness per se. The name for a non-gentleman posed a delicate problem: "clown," "churl," and (for a fallen gentleman) "cad" were never thoroughly accepted. It was Thackeray's happiness to hit upon the word "snob," the word used at Cambridge to signify non-gentleman. He inverted it and gave it its modern meaning in his first really popular work, *The Book of Snobs*. *"He who meanly admires mean things"* (ch. ii) was Thackeray's definition, but the word as he used it, and as it has been used since, means approximately, he who adheres too slavishly to the principle of exclusion in social groups. Thackeray subtitled his book on snobs, "By One of Themselves," and he helped confirm the Victorian paradox of the gentleman who prides himself on not being proud, who depends for his self-respect on a principle of exclusion that he does not believe in, and who is, in short, both snob and anti-snob. Thackeray's honesty cannot resolve the paradox. His protagonists all ultimately depend on being gentlemen in class as well as morals or manners. His most famous gentleman, Colonel Newcome, Thackeray deliberately construed as a quixotic character: the much loved Colonel is not really at home in the nineteenth century.

The concept of the gentleman is also bound up historically with that of an "independence"—an unearned income. That a gentleman does not work for a living is, in fact, the most tangible feature of the ideal, and the fundamental economic reason that it takes more than one generation to make a gentleman. Obviously, in the nineteenth century this qualification of the gentleman was becoming untenable, not only because of changing economic relationships but because of the intense resurgence of the puritan ideal of work—as the very reason for existence or means of salvation in an age of religious doubt. Thackeray himself found that he had to work for a living, and he requires Arthur Pendennis, Clive Newcome, and Philip Firmin to face similar challenges. But to see that Thackeray has not succeeded in redefining the gentlemanly ideal in this respect, one only has to observe that, for these heroes, to work is an act of courage, and the necessity of work a condition of adversity. This is not to make light of Thackeray or to diminish Professor Ray's shrewd insistence that the condition of a gentleman is Thackeray's central theme—quite the contrary. As far as the criterion of work is concerned, one can examine a similar discrepancy between work as a moral value and the actual career of the hero in the novels of Dickens. The two novelists, Pendennis and David Copperfield, are the only gentleman heroes with clearly specified vocations. The true workers in memorable Victorian novels, the occasional Caleb Garths or Daniel Doyces or J. J. Ridleys, belong to a class distinct from that of heroes. In Thackeray the ideals of work and gentlemanliness clash with a staggering ambivalence.

There is another important ambivalence that can be studied with profit in his work. Again, the difficulty is not to be attributed to Thackeray alone; rather, it goes to the heart of Christianity itself. I mean the conflict between the ideals of Christian forgiveness and of instinctive moral revlusion—the latter sometimes called "Christian indignation," but also an aspect of the code of gentlemen. George Warrington, whose stabilized moral views Thackeray generally endorses, puts the case for moral revulsion this way in *The Newcomes:* "Why should we overcome such instincts? . . . Why shouldn't we hate what is hateful in people, and scorn what is mean?" (ch. liv). The principle is very freely exercised in Thackeray's novels: that is, not only are appropriately hateful people introduced, but a significant pleasure is derived from their chastisement. One of the qualifications of being a gentleman is the ability and inclination to administer chastisement in a satisfying fashion—not excluding caning, punching, or even kicking a sufficiently detestable object. Apart from the problem of determining what is hateful and what is not, it is the emotion accompanying this chastisement that sits so uneasily with the ideal of forgiveness. The two ideals—or perhaps impulses—are unresolved in Thackeray. But are they resolvable?

In one respect Thackeray's Christianity differs from that of most Victorian writers, including Dickens and George Eliot: he believes more strongly in the possibility of repentance. For most Victorian writers no conviction is more stubbornly held than that of the finality of moral acts and their consequences: the thought of remission of sins is virtually an anathema. And this conviction cuts across a wide spectrum of moral and political opinion. Herbert Spencer, for example, was perfectly confident that he could construct a "system of pure Ethics," but was dumbfounded by the problem of what to do about anyone who sinned against such a system: "whether it is possible to develop scientifically a Moral Therapeutics seems very doubtful." [9] But Ruskin, too, so unalterably opposed to Spencer on most issues, finds exactly the same difficulty, as in this lecture to young girls:

> *Lecturer.* . . . All doubt and repenting, and botching, and retouching, and wondering what it will be best to do next, are vice, as well as misery.
>
> *Mary (much wondering).* But must not one repent when one does wrong, and hesitate when one can't see one's way?
>
> *Lecturer.* You have no business at all to do wrong. . . .[10]

Thackeray, however, is a veritable student of human botching and repenting, and rather likes to portray his heroes in a state of moral misery. He seems to feel, moreover, that repentance offers a tolerable moral therapeutics. One can only complain that repentance and forgiveness in his novels may operate selectively, as if the therapy were available primarily to heroes and other gentlemen. Still, as usual with Thackeray, the anomaly is instructive: it may be that novels in general treat their heroes solicitously rather than objectively. If one had to pick out a single forebear of the Thackerayan hero, it would be the undeserving Captain Booth of *Amelia,* the novel of Fielding that Thackeray could most warmly endorse:

> The prodigal Captain Booth is a better man than his predecessor Mr. Jones, in so far as he thinks much more humbly of himself than Jones did: goes down on his knees, and owns his weaknesses, and cries out, "Not

[9] *Social Statics* (London, 1851), p. 58.
[10] *Ethics of the Dust* (1866), in *Works,* ed. E. T. Cook and Alexander Wedderburn, 39 vols. (London, 1903–12), XVIII, 264.

for my own sake, but for the sake of my pure and sweet and beautiful
wife Amelia, I pray you, O critical reader, to forgive me." [11]

In the present collection of critical essays I have tried to represent
the best twentieth-century criticism of Thackeray. But I have not tried
to conceal that the twentieth century has often been impatient, or
even hostile to Thackeray. And I have been guided in my selection
also by the impression that too many readers today only know Thackeray as the author of *Vanity Fair* and *Henry Esmond*.

[11] "Hogarth, Smollett, and Fielding," in *English Humourists of the Eighteenth
Century*.

The Method of Allusive Irrelevancy

by G. K. Chesterton

There is no writer, certainly no writer of so high a rank, from
whom it is more difficult to make extracts than Thackeray. A book by
Dickens is like a sublime scrap-book; the pictures are separate, yet tell
their own tale like the pictures on a nursery screen or a child's toy
book. If nothing remained of *Pickwick* except the Sawyer supper
party, all the characters would be complete and clear, and it would
be impossible to guess that Jack Hopkins came in only for that scene
while Bob Sawyer ran through the whole book. Both would be comic
characters clearly depicted. By a sort of extravagant lucidity, by a
grotesque symbolism almost like that of heraldry, Dickens stamped
and branded on the brain in a few words all that it was essential to
say about anybody. But Thackeray worked entirely by diffuseness; by
a thousand touches scattered through a thousand pages. It is a method
admirably suited to his particular purpose; that of half-ironically
worming himself into the centre of a subject; politely insinuating
himself into the secrets of everybody before he begins to treat them
satirically. Brevity may be the soul of wit; but it would be quite as
true to say in such cases that lengthiness is the soul of satire. To batter
the worldly castle with the artillery of open derision, as Dickens did,
is a much swifter task than to blow it up from within with one carefully constructed bomb of irony. This was indeed one of the essentials
of Thackeray's power and position; he was attacking Vanity Fair from
the inside, and must have been at least sufficiently polite to get inside
it. Some might even have said that he was betraying his class; there is
no doubt at least that he was betraying himself. That noble title, *The
Book of Snobs*, would not have been so effective if he had not been
able to add "By one of Themselves." By the very nature of his satire
it had to be a slow satire. He could exhibit a stir of anger at the lux-

"The Method of Allusive Irrelevancy" (editor's title). From *Thackeray*, ed. G. K.
Chesterton (London: G. Bell & Sons, Ltd., 1909), pp. xix–xxi, xxii–xxv, xxxi–xxxii.
Copyright 1909 by G. Bell & Sons, Ltd. Reprinted by permission of the publisher.

ury of the rich. But he could not pretend to exhibit a start of surprise
at it, as Dickens could. He could not speak of ladies and gentlemen as
monsters whom he had just met on his travels; that was the great
speciality of Dickens. He has awakened to the evil of his world; but it
is essential to his method that he should have awakened slowly; therefore it is natural that the method of satiric revelation should be also
slow. Even the bodily description of his characters is scattered and dis-
seminated. The Dickens method is to say: "Lord Jones, a tall man
with a hook nose and a white pointed beard, entered the room."
Thackeray's method is to say, in Chapter I: "Lord Jones, being very
tall, had just knocked his head against the chandelier, and was in no
very agreeable temper"; in Chapter VII: "What jokes Jemima made
about Sir Henry's bald head, Lord Jones's hooked nose, and so on";
and in Chapter XXIII: "Little Mr. Frizzle, the hairdresser, had pursued Jones for years, advising his lordship to blacken artificially the
white pointed beard that he wore." This method of the million small
touches recurring at intervals is responsible in no small degree for the
entertaining quality of Thackeray taken as a whole; but it renders
almost impossible the task of separating portraits or landscapes or
other coherent pictures from the text. Thackeray has one ultimate
merit, or rather magic. Thackeray is *always* interesting; even in the
passages which are bad.

. . . No novelist ever carried to such perfection as Thackeray the
art of saying a thing without saying it. Human life is (so to speak) so
dense with delicacies, so thickly sown with things that are true and yet
may be misunderstood, that this is a very valuable faculty in a man
telling tales about men. It may be true to say that a man drinks too
much; yet it may be exactly false to say that he drinks. A man may
be hard or even exhausting to entertain; yet he may not be in any ordinary sense a fool or even a bore. It may be manifest that a woman
has too much to put up with in her married life; yet it may be quite
untrue to call it an unhappy marriage. A man may just fail to be
a gentleman; and yet be the very opposite of a cad. These gossamer
threads of truth, which are destroyed with the very touch of tracing
them, are very hard indeed to deal with in literature; and I think they
were never so well dealt with as by the Thackerayan method, the
method which may be defined as an allusive irrelevancy.
    When Thackeray wished to hint a truth which was just not true
enough to bear his whole weight, his way was to wander off into
similes and allegories which repeated and yet mocked the main story

like derisive and dying echoes. If Thackeray wished to say that Jones drank too much without calling Jones a drunkard, then he would go into a long dreamy parenthesis, quoting Horace, humorously invoking Bacchus, talking about Bohemia and vineyards, and so come back to Jones, without having insulted him, but having—shall we say—sobered him. If he wished to indicate that Mrs. Jones had more trouble in her married life than she had had on her honeymoon, he did not say brutally that she was a disappointed woman; which perhaps was not true. He merely touched on it and then trailed off into some epicurean song in prose about how youth must pass and roses fade, and by that avenue of universal autumn returns to Mrs. Jones, having humanely hinted at her melancholy without in the least suggesting (like a dirty modern) her despair.

I have described this style in the general, so that any Thackerayan must recognize my meaning; and not need many examples of the same thing in the particular. Such examples, however, could easily be given. Thus it was necessary to suggest that Clive Newcome had been, not a young blackguard, but something of a "young blood"; this Thackeray does by the use of a playful theatrical metaphor about having been behind the scenes. Thus again it was necessary to suggest that Dobbin did not get quite the reward of his own heroic simplicity in winning the silly little woman whom he loved; it is suggested by a fine stroke of airy philosophy, as of one changing the subject, in the final *"Vanitas vanitatum,* which of us has his wish in this world, or, having it, is satisfied?"* It was necessary to suggest that Arthur Pendennis (of whom it would have been grossly untrue to say that he was not a gentleman) was yet in a subtle manner less of a gentleman than his friend Warrington. This is indicated with just the right amount of airy emphasis by this fact, that while Warrington's unquestionable lineage is kept out of the picture altogether, the pages are full of fantastic excursions about the Prince of Fairoaks and the ancient escutcheon of Pendennis. The occasions are indeed very numerous in which Thackeray finds this knack of half-suggestion very convenient. How delicately he suggests the peculiar character of Helen Pendennis; a saint without a sense of honour. With how quiet a shade as of the coming on of twilight, does he convey the fact that Colonel Newcome's character was, after all, slightly spoilt in prosperity; suggests it less by any change in the old face with the gray moustaches than by a certain change in the faces of Clive or Laura or Ethel as they look at it. In this connection it is specially unjust to call Thackeray a cynic. He falls away into philosophizing not because his satire is merciless but because it is merciful; he wishes to soften the fall of his characters with a sense and suggestion of the weakness of all flesh. He often employs an universal cynicism because it is kinder than a personal sarcasm. He says that all men are liars, rather than say directly that Pendennis was lying. He says easily that all is vanity, so as not to say that Ethel Newcome was vain.

Of course he suffered in his later work, like most other great men, from a tendency to imitate himself. It is a remarkable fact in first-class authors that they not only write imitations of themselves; but they are generally bad imitations. They imitate their own externals and miss the point and the spirit exactly as if they were total strangers; I suppose they remember the way they had of saying things but forget what they were trying to say. Thus the parodists of Swinburne's exquisite early poetry started a stupid idea that his effects depended entirely on alliteration. It was not in the least true; but Swinburne believed it, and began to write merely alliterative poetry. In the same way, in some of his last books Thackeray did no doubt use this rambling style without its old subtle purpose of suggestion. He did not merely leave the subject, he lost it. He did not merely get into a parenthesis, but he never got out. I will give one comparison of his two uses of the irrelevant. When Ethel Newcome is about to be married to the great Lord Farintosh, Thackeray indulges in a long and amusing apologue about how women in the East are sold to dance in the temples and how natural it seems—in the East. In his later book, *Philip*, he seems to remember the success of this passage and introduces another long figurative chapter on the selling of Eastern maidens *apropos* of the decision of Agnes Twysden to marry Captain Woolcomb. But he does not notice that there is no need for this excursus in the second case; while there was a subtle psychological need for it in the first. A certain magnanimous mystery was deliberately kept up round the motives of Ethel Newcome. The reader was really not supposed to know, at least until he reviewed the book as a whole, how far that proud head had consciously stooped to the slavery of calculation, how far it had still the bewildered pride of a princess in captivity. It was, therefore, a strictly artistic touch to remind the reader, among other things, that there are societies where such sale does not feel degrading. But about Agnes Twysden there is no mystery at all; she is simply a cold-blooded minx. There is no sort of doubt whatever that she would have married for money in any society, Eastern or Western. Thackeray has put this character down in black and white—especially black. There is, therefore, no need for that hesitating and allusive style of allegory which was quite appropriate in the riddle of the Farintosh betrothal, when Thackeray had to fling a faint and fugitive shadow upon the shining face of the noblest of Victorian heroines. . . .

. . . In all things his great spirit had the grandeur and the weakness which belonged to the England of his time, an England splendidly secure and free, and yet (perhaps for that reason) provincial and innocent. He had nothing of the doctrinal quality of the French and Germans. He was not one who made up his mind, but one who let his mind make him up. He lay naturally open to all noble influences flowing around him; but he never bestirred himself to seek those that were not flowing or that flowed in opposite directions. Thus, for instance, he really loved liberty, as only a novelist can love it, a man mainly occupied with the variety and vivacity of men. But he could not see the cause of liberty except where the Victorian English saw it; he could not see it in the cause of Irish liberty (which was exactly like the cause of Polish or Italian liberty, except that it was led by much more religious and responsible men), and he made the Irish characters the object of much innocent and rather lumbering satire. But this was not his mistake, but the mistake of the atmosphere, and he was a sublime emotional Englishman, who lived by atmosphere. He was a great sensitive. The comparison between him and Dickens is commonly as clumsy and unreasonable as a comparison between Wilkie Collins and Charles Reade or Bulwer Lytton and Anthony Trollope. But the comparison really has this element of actuality: that Dickens was above all things creative; Thackeray was above all things receptive. There is no sense in talking about truth in the matter; both are modes of truth. If you like to put it so, the world imposed on Thackeray and Dickens imposed on the world. But it could be put more truly by saying that Thackeray represents, in that gigantic parody called genius, the spirit of the Englishman in repose. This spirit is the idle embodiment of all of us; by his weaknesses we shall fail and by his enormous sanities we shall endure.

The Panoramic Method

by Percy Lubbock

Thackeray saw [*Vanity Fair, Pendennis, The Newcomes, Esmond*] as broad expanses, stretches of territory, to be surveyed from edge to edge with a sweeping glance; he saw them as great general, typical impressions of life, populated by a swarm of people whose manners and adventures crowded into his memory. The landscape lay before him, his imagination wandered freely across it, backwards and forwards. The whole of it was in view at once, a single prospect, out of which the story of Becky or Pendennis emerged and grew distinct while he watched. He wrote his novel with a mind full of a surge and wash of memories, the tenor of which was somehow to be conveyed in the outward form of a narrative. And though his novel complies with that form more or less, and a number of events are marshalled in order, yet its constant tendency is to escape and evade the restrictions of a scenic method, and to present the story in a continuous flow of leisurely, contemplative reminiscence.

And that is evidently the right way for the kind of story that Thackeray means to create. For what is the point and purpose of *Vanity Fair,* where is the centre from which it grows? Can it be described as a "plot," a situation, an entanglement, something that raises a question of the issue? Of plots in this sense there are plenty in *Vanity Fair,* at least there are two; Becky dominates one, Amelia smiles and weeps in the other. They join hands occasionally, but really they have very little to exchange. Becky and her Crawleys, Becky and her meteoric career in Curzon Street, would have been all as they are if Amelia had never been heard of; and Bloomsbury, too, of the Osbornes and the Sedleys, might have had the whole book to itself, for all that Becky essentially matters to it. Side by side they exist, and for Thackeray's

"The Panoramic Method" (editor's title). From Chapter VII of *The Craft of Fiction*, by Percy Lubbock (London: Jonathan Cape, Ltd., 1921; New York: The Viking Press, 1957), pp. 93–109. All Rights Reserved. Reprinted by permission of The Viking Press, Jonathan Cape, Ltd., and The Executors of The Percy Lubbock Estate.

purpose neither is more important than the other, neither is in the middle of the book as it stands. Becky seems to be in the middle, certainly, as we think of her; but that is not where Thackeray placed her. He meant Amelia to be no less appealing than Becky is striking; and if Amelia fails and drops into the background, it is not because she plays a subordinate part, but only because she plays it with so much less than Becky's vivid conviction. They fill the book with incident between the two of them; something is always happening, from the moment when they drive out of Miss Pinkerton's gate at Chiswick till the last word that is told of either. But the book as a whole turns upon nothing that happens, not even upon the catastrophe of Curzon Street; that scene in Becky's drawing-room disposes of *her,* it leaves the rest of the book quite untouched.

Not in any complication of incident, therefore, nor in any single strife of will, is the subject of *Vanity Fair* to be discerned. It is not here but in the impression of a world, a society, a time—certain manners of life within a few square miles of London, a hundred years ago. Thackeray flings together a crowd of the people he knows so well, and it matters not at all if the tie that holds them to each other is of the slightest; it may easily chance that his good young girl and his young adventuress set out together upon their journey, their paths may even cross from time to time later on. The light link is enough for the unity of his tale, for that unity does not depend on an intricately woven intrigue. It depends in truth upon one fact only, the fact that all his throng of men and women are strongly, picturesquely typical of the world from which they are taken—that all in their different ways can add to the force of its effect. The book is not the story of any of them, it is the story which they unite to tell, a chapter in the notorious career of well-to-do London. Exactly how the various "plots" evolve is not the main matter; behind them is the presence and the pressure of a greater interest, the mass of life which Thackeray packs into his novel. And if that is the meaning of *Vanity Fair,* to give the succession of incident a hard, particular, dramatic relief would be to obscure it. Becky's valiant struggle in the world of her ambition might easily be isolated and turned into a play—no doubt it has been; but consider how her look, her value, would in that case be changed. Her story would become a mere personal affair of her own, the mischance of a certain woman's enterprise. Given in Thackeray's way, summarized in his masterly perspective, it is part of an impression of manners.

Such, I take it, is Thackeray's difference, his peculiar mark, the distinction of his genius. He is a painter of life, a novelist whose matter is all blended and harmonized together—people, action, background —in a long retrospective vision. Not for him, on the whole, is the detached action, the rounded figure, the scenic rendering of a story; as surely as Dickens tended towards the theatre, with its clear-cut isolation of events and episodes, its underlining of the personal and the individual in men and women, so Thackeray preferred the manner of musing expatiation, where scene melts into scene, impressions are foreshortened by distance, and the backward-ranging thought can linger and brood as it will. Every novel of his takes the general form of a discursive soliloquy, in which he gradually gathers up the long train of experience that he has in mind. The early chapters of *Esmond* or *Pendennis,* the whole fragment of *Denis Duval,* are perfect examples of Thackeray's way when he is most himself, and when he is least to be approached by any other writer of fiction. All that he has to describe, so it seems, is present to him in the hour of recollection; he hangs over it, and his eye is caught by a point here and there, a child-with a book in a window-seat, the Fotheringay cleaning her old shoe, the Major at his breakfast in Pall Mall; the associations broaden away from these glimpses and are followed hither and thither. But still, though the fullness of memory is directed into a consecutive tale, it is not the narrative, not its order and movement, that chiefly holds either Thackeray's attention or ours who read; the narrative is steeped in the suffusion of the general tone, the sensation of the place and the life that he is recalling, and it is out of this effect, insensibly changing and developing, that the novel is created.

For a nearer sight of it I go back to *Vanity Fair.* The chapters that are concerned with Becky's determined siege of London—"How to live well on nothing a year"—are exactly to the point; the wonderful things that Thackeray could do, the odd lapse of his power when he had to go beyond his particular province, both are here written large. Every one remembers the chapters and their place in the book. Becky, resolutely shaking off old difficulties for the moment, installs herself with her husband in the heart of the world she means to conquer; she all but succeeds, she just fails. Her campaign and its untimely end are to be pictured; it is an interlude to be filled with stir and glitter, with the sense of the passage of a certain time, above all with intimations of insecurity and precarious fortune; and it is to lead (this it must do) to a scene of final and decisive climax. Such is the effect to be drawn from the matter that Thackeray has stored up—the whole hierarchy of the Crawleys, Steyne, Gaunt House, always with Becky in the midst and to the fore. Up to a point it is precisely the kind of juncture in which Thackeray's art delights. There is abundance of vivid stuff, and the picture to be made of it is highly functional in the book. It is not merely a preparation for a story to follow; it is itself the story, a most important part of it. The chapters representing Becky's manner of life in Curzon Street make the hinge of her career; she approaches her turning point at the beginning of them, she is past it at the end. Functional, therefore, they are to the last degree; but up to the very climax, or the verge of it, there is no need for a set scene of dramatic particularity. An impression is to be created, growing and growing; and it can well be created in the loose panoramic style which is Thackeray's paramount arm. A general view, once more, a summary of Becky's course of action, a long look at her conditions, a participation in her gathering difficulties—that is the nature and the task of these chapters, that is what Thackeray proceeds to give us.

He sets about it with a beautiful ease of assurance. From his height he looks forth, takes in the effect with his sweeping vision, possesses himself of the gradation of its tone; then, stooping nearer he seizes the detail that renders it. But the sense of the broad survey is first in his thought. When he reflects upon Becky's life in London and all that came of her attempt to establish herself there, he is soon assailed by a score of definite recollections, tell-tale incidents, scraps of talk that show how things were going with her; but these, it would seem, arise by the way, they spring up in his mind as he reviews the past. They illustrate what he has to say, and he takes advantage of them. He brushes past them, however, without much delaying or particularizing; a hint, a moment, a glance suffices for the contribution that some event or colloquy is to make to the picture. Note, for example, how unceremoniously, again and again, and with how little thought of disposing a deliberate scene, he drifts into his account of something that Becky said or did; she begins to talk, you find there is some one else in the room, you find they are in a certain room at a certain hour; definition emerges unawares in a brooding memory. Briefly, to all appearance quite casually, the little incident shows itself and vanishes; there is a pause to watch and listen, and then the stream sets forward again, by so much enriched and reinforced. Or in a heightened mood, as in the picture of the midnight flurry and alarm of the great desolate house, when old Pitt Crawley is suddenly struck down, still it is as though Thackeray circled about the thought of the time and place, offering swift and piercing glimpses of it, giving no continuous and dramatic display of a constituted scene.

That foreshortening and generalizing, that fusion of detail, that subordination of the instance and the occasion to the broad effect, are the elements of the pictorial art in which Thackeray is so great a master. So long as it is a matter of sketching a train of life in broad free strokes, the poise and swing of his style are beyond praise. And its perfection is all the more notable that it stands in such contrast with the curious drop and uncertainty of his skill, so soon as there is something more, something different to be done. For Becky's dubious adventure has its climax, it tends towards a conclusion, and the final scene cannot be recalled and summarized in his indirect, reminiscential manner. It must be placed immediately before us, the collapse of Becky's plotting and scheming must be enacted in full view, if it is to have its proper emphasis and rightly round off her career. Hitherto we have been listening to Thackeray, on the whole, while he talked about Becky—talked with such extraordinary brilliance that he evoked her in all her ways and made us see her with his eyes; but now it is time to see her with our own, his lively interpretation of her will serve no longer. Does Becky fail in the end? After all that we have heard of her struggle it has become the great question, and the force of the answer will be impaired if it is not given with the best possible warrant. The best possible, better even than Thackeray's wonderful account of her, will be the plain and immediate *performance* of the answer, its embodiment in a scene that shall pass directly in front of us. The method that was not demanded by the preceding phases of the tale is here absolutely precribed. Becky, Rawdon, Steyne, must now take the matter into their own hands and show themselves without any other intervention. Hitherto, practically throughout, they have been the creatures of Thackeray's thought, they have been openly and confessedly the figures of *his* vision. Now they must come forward, declare themselves, and be seen for what they are.

And accordingly they do come forward and are seen in a famous passage. Rawdon makes his unexpected return home from prison, and Becky's unfortunate disaster overtakes her, so to say, in our very presence. Perhaps I may seem to exaggerate the change of method which I note at this point; but does it not appear to any one, glancing back at his recollection of the book, that this particular scene is defined and relieved and lighted differently, somehow, from the stream of impressions in which it is set? A space is cleared for it, the stage is swept. This is now no retrospective vision, shared with Thackeray; it is a piece of present action with which we are confronted. It is strictly dramatic, and I suppose it is good drama of its kind. But there is more to be said of it than this—more to be said, even when it has been admitted to be drama of rather a high-pitched, theatrical strain. The foot-lights, it is probably agreed, seem suddenly to flare before Becky and Rawdon, after the clear daylight that reigned in Thackeray's description of them; they appear upon the scene, as they should, but it must be owned that the scene has an artificial look, by comparison with the flowing spontaneity of all that has gone before. And this it is exactly that shows how and where Thackeray's skill betrays him. He is not (like Dickens) naturally inclined to the theatre, the melodramatic has no fatal attraction for him; so that if he is theatrical here, it is not because he inevitably would be, given his chance. It is rather because he must, at all costs, make this climax of his story conclusively *tell;* and in order to do so he is forced to use devices of some crudity—for him they are crude—because his climax, his *scène à faire,* has been insufficiently prepared for. Becky, Rawdon, Steyne, in all this matter that has been leading up to the scene, have scarcely before been rendered in these immediate terms; and now that they appear on their own account they can only make a sure and pronounced effect by perceptibly forcing their note. A little too much is expected of them, and they must make an unnatural effort to meet it.

My instance is a small one, no doubt, to be pressed so far; in lingering over these shades of treatment a critic, it may be thought, loses sight of the book itself. But I am not trying, of course, to criticize *Vanity Fair;* I am looking for certain details of method, and the small instance is surely illuminating. It shows how little Thackeray's fashion of handling a novel allowed for the big dramatic scene, when at length it had to be faced—how he neglected it in advance, how he refused it till the last possible moment. It is as though he never quite trusted his men and women when he had to place things entirely in their care, standing aside to let them act; he wanted to intervene continually, he hesitated to leave them alone save for a brief and belated half-hour. It was perverse of him, because the men and women would have acquitted themselves so strikingly with a better chance; he gave them life and vigour enough for much more independence than they ever enjoyed. The culmination of Becky's adventure offered a clear opening for full dramatic effect, if he had chosen to take advantage of it. He had steadily piled up his impression, carefully brought all the sense of the situation to converge upon a single point; everything was ready for the great scene of Becky's triumph in the face of the world, one memorable night of a party at Gaunt House. It is incredible that he should let the opportunity slip. There was a chance of a straight, unhampered view of the whole meaning of his matter; nothing was needed but to allow the scene to show itself, fairly and squarely. All its force would have been lent to the disaster that follows; the dismay, the disillusion, the snarl of anger and defiance, all would have been made beforehand. By so much would the effect of the impending scene, the scene of catastrophe, have been strengthened. There would have been no necessity for the sudden heightening of the pitch, the thickening of the colour, the incongruous and theatrical tone.

Yet the chance is missed, the triumphal evening passes in a confused haze that leaves the situation exactly where it was before. The episode is only a repetition of the kind of thing that has happened already. There are echoes of festive sound and a rumour of Becky's brilliance; but the significant look that the actual facts might have worn and must have betrayed, the look that by this time Thackeray has so fully instructed his reader to catch—this is not disclosed after all. There is still nothing here but Thackeray's amusing, irrepressible conversation *about* the scene; he cannot make up his mind to clear a space before it and give the situation the free field it cries out for. And if it is asked what kind of clarity I mean, I need only recall another page, close by, which shows it perfectly. Becky had made an earlier appearance at Gaunt House; she had dined there, near the beginning of her social career, and had found herself in a difficulty; there came a moment when she had to face the frigid hostility of the noble ladies of the party, alone with them in the drawing-room, and her assurance failed. In the little scene that ensues the charming veil of Thackeray's talk is suddenly raised; there is Becky seated at the piano, Lady Steyne listening in a dream of old memories, the other women chattering at a distance, when the jarring doors are thrown open and the men return. It is all over in half a page, but in that glimpse the story is lifted forward dramatically; ocular proof, as it were, is added to Thackeray's account of Becky's doubtful and delicate position. As a matter of curiosity I mention the one moment in the later episode, the evening of those strangely ineffective charades at Gaunt House, which appears to me to open the same kind of rift in the haze; it is a single glimpse of Steyne, applauding Becky's triumph. He is immediately there, an actor in the show, alive and expressive, but he is alone; none of the others so emerges, even Becky is only a luminous spot in the dimness. As for the relation of the three, Steyne, Becky, and her husband, which is on the point of becoming so important, there is nothing to be seen of it.

Right and left in the novels of Thackeray one may gather instances of the same kind—the piercing and momentary shaft of direct vision, the big scene approached and then refused. It is easy to find another in *Vanity Fair*. Who but Thackeray could have borne to use the famous matter of the Waterloo ball, a wonderful gift for a novelist to find in his path, only to waste it, to dissipate its effect, to get no real contribution from it after all? In the queer, haphazard, polyglot interlude that precedes it Thackeray is, of course, entirely at home; there it is a question of the picture-making he delights in, the large impression of things in general, the evocation of daily life; Brussels in its talkative suspense, waiting for the sound of the guns, feeding on rumour, comes crowding into the chapter. And then the great occasion that should have crowned it, into which the story naturally and logically passes—for again the scene is not a decorative patch, the story needs it—the Waterloo ball is nothing, leaves no image, constitutes no effect whatever; the reader, looking back on the book, might be quite uncertain whether he had been there or not. Nobody could forget the sight of Lady Bareacres, sitting under the *porte cochère* in her horseless carriage—of good Mrs. O'Dowd, rising in the dawn to equip her warrior for battle—of George Osborne, dead on the field; but these are Thackeray's flashes of revelation, straight and sure, and they are all the drama, strictly speaking, that he extorts from his material. The rest is picture, stirringly, vivaciously reflected in his unfailing memory—with the dramatic occasion to which it tends, the historic affair of the "revelry by night," neglected and lost.

There is scarcely need for more illustration of my point, but it is tempting to look further. In all these well-remembered books Thackeray, in an expansive mood, opens his mind and talks it out on the subject of some big, loosely knit company of men and women. He remembers, as we all remember, with a strong sense of the tone and air of an old experience, and a sharp recollection of moments that happened for some reason to be salient, significant, peculiarly keen or curious. Ethel Newcome, when she comes riding into the garden in the early morning, full of the news of her wonderul discovery, the letter shut in the old book; Blanche Amory, when she is caught out in her faithlessness, warbling to the new swain at the piano and whipping her handkerchief over his jewel-case as the old one enters;

Madam Esmond, on her balcony, defying the mob with "Britons, strike home"; old Sir Pitt, toasting his rasher in the company of the charwoman: I name them at random, they are all instances of the way in which the glance of memory falls on the particular moment, the aspect that hardens and crystallizes an impression. Thackeray has these flashes in profusion; they break out unforgettably as we think of his books. The most exquisite of all, perhaps, is in *Esmond,* that sight of the dusky choir of Winchester Cathedral, the shine of the candle-light, the clear faces of Rachel and her son as they appear to the re-turned wanderer. We no longer listen to a story, no longer see the past in a sympathetic imagination; this is a higher power of intensity, a fragment of the past made present and actual. But with Thackeray it is always a fragment, never to any real purpose a deliberate and continuous enactment.

For continuity he always recurs to his pictorial summary. *The New-comes* alone would give a dozen examples of this side of his genius—in the pages that recall the lean dignity of the refugees from revolu-tionary Paris, or the pious opulence of Clapham, or the rustle of fash-ion round the Mayfair chapel, or the chatter and scandal of Baden-Baden, or the squalid pretensions of English life at Boulogne. I need not lengthen the list; these evocations follow one upon another, and as quickly as Thackeray passes into a new circle he makes us feel and know what it was like to live there and belong to it. The typical look of the place is in his mind, the sense of its habitual life, the savour of the hours that lapse there. But *Esmond* again has the last word; the early chapters of the old days at Castlewood show a subtlety of effect that is peculiar and rare. It is more than a picture of a place and an impression of romance, it is more than the portrait of a child; besides all this it is the most masterly of "time-pictures," if that is a word that will serve. The effect I am thinking of is different from that of which I spoke in the matter of Tolstoy's great cycles of action;[1] there we saw the march of time recording itself, affirming its ceaseless move-ment, in the lives of certain people. This of Thackeray's is not like that; time, at Castlewood, is not movement, it is tranquillity—time that stands still, as we say, only deepening as the years go. It cannot therefore be shown as a sequence; and Thackeray roams to and fro in his narrative, caring little for the connected order of events if he can give the sensation of time, deep and soft and abundant, by de-laying and returning at ease over this tract of the past. It would be possible, I think, to say very precisely where and how the effect is

[1] [In ch. iv of *The Craft of Fiction*—ED.]

made—by what leisurely play with the chronology of the story, apparently careless and unmethodical, or by what shifting of the focus, so that the house of Castlewood is now a far-away memory and now a close, benevolent presence. Time, at any rate, is stored up in the description of the child's life there, quiet layers of time in which the recorded incidents sink deep.

Thackeray's Irony

by John W. Dodds

It is of great value, in attempting to understand Thackeray, to place over against his actual achievement his own theories of the art of his own work. He had definite views concerning the function of art. "The effect of the artist, as I take it," he writes, "ought to be to produce upon his hearer's mind, by his art, an effect something similar to that produced on his own by the sight of the natural object. Only music, and the best poetry, can do this." Nevertheless this is not a bad statement of what Thackeray himself tried to do in the novel. He laboured to keep his grip on reality, but reality as it turns up in *Vanity Fair,* for instance, is reality filtered through the cool mind and warm sensibilities of W.M.T., bearing the strong imprint of that personality. One takes with a grain of salt Thackeray's contention that his characters controlled him. He liked to stand off from them, praising them or blaming them, and pretending that they led independent lives. But in the selection of just the right, significant detail, the hand of the showman is always behind the puppet.

Thackeray thought of himself as a satirist but liked to think too that "under the mask satirical there walks about a sentimental gentleman who means not unkindly to any mortal person." [1] Many times he gives his creed as a craftsman: "To tell truth, hit no foul blow, give no servile puffery . . ." [2] Always he wanted to get as near the truth as he could.

> I cannot help telling the truth as I view it, and describing what I see.
> To describe it otherwise than it seems to me would be falsehood in that

"Thackeray's Irony" (editor's title). From *Thackeray: A Critical Portrait,* by John W. Dodds (New York: Oxford University Press, 1941), pp. 113–22. Copyright 1941 by Oxford University Press. Reprinted by permission of the author and the publisher.

[1] Letter to Dr. John Brown, 11 May 1848. See Brown's "Thackeray," *North British Review,* February 1864.

[2] "A Brother of the Press on . . . the Chances of the Literary Profession," *Fraser's,* March 1846.

calling in which it has pleased Heaven to place me; treason to that conscience which says that men are weak; that truth must be told; that faults must be owned; that pardon must be prayed for; and that love reigns supreme over all.[3]

In an important letter to Masson he holds that

> The Art of Novels *is* to represent Nature: to convey as strongly as possible the sentiment of reality—in a tragedy or a poem or a lofty drama you aim at producing different emotions; the figures moving, and their words sounding, heroically: but in a drawingroom drama a coat is a coat and a poker a poker; and must be nothing else according to my ethics, not an embroidered tunic, nor a great red-hot instrument like the Pantomime weapon.

Here he also took issue with Dickens who, he said, "has in many things quite a divine genius." But "I quarrel with his Art in many respects: which I don't think represents Nature duly; for instance Micawber appears to me an exaggeration of a man, as his name is of a name. It is delightful and makes me laugh: but it is no more a real man than my friend Punch is: and in so far I protest against him . . ."[4]

This, then, is his concept of realism. Some of his contemporaries, although impressed by the power of *Vanity Fair,* the "novel without a hero," had yet a restless feeling that Thackeray "hated excellence." Not a few reviewers carped at the absence of "noble" characters in the novel.[5] In spite of his reading of Victorian fiction in which pluperfect heroes walked through shoals of very decorous temptation and tribulation to reach a safe matrimonial harbour in the last chapter, Thackeray held stubbornly to the conviction that most men are not heroic and that it is the novelist's task to show men as they are. One of his critics has called him "the apostle of mediocrity," a charge to which Thackeray had humorously pleaded guilty as early as *The Paris Sketch Book*: "Let us thank Heaven, my dear sir, for according to us the power to taste and appreciate the pleasures of mediocrity. I have never heard that we were great geniuses. Earthy we are, and of the earth." Elsewhere he speaks angrily against "success-story fiction": "Why should we keep all our admiration for those who win in this world, as we do, sycophants that we are? When we write a novel, our great stupid imaginations can go no further than to marry the hero

[3] Lecture: *Charity and Humour.*
[4] *Cornhill Magazine,* June 1911, p. 797.
[5] The wheel has come full circle, and today the critics are as likely to be severe on Thackeray's "sentimentalism" as his contemporaries were on his "cynicism."

to a fortune at the end, and to find out that he is a lord by right. O blundering lick-spittle morality!" [6]

Thackeray, like all great humorists from Cervantes to Fielding, saw that most men are an inscrutable mixture of the heroic and the ridiculous, the noble and the ignoble; human nature is an infinitely complex thing, and its complexity needs to be underlined and accented rather than simplified for the sentimental reader. Possessing a strong vein of scepticism, Thackeray looked about him and saw that poetic justice, outside a popular novel, is a rare commodity. He felt keenly the affectations and hypocrisies of the world about him, and saw into the cosmic irony that injustice is as likely to be victorious as justice.

But Thackeray himself was as complex as any of his non-heroes. His scepticism, born of a native melancholy and a quivering sensitiveness which are basic in his personality, was crossed not merely by a love of the ludicrous but also by a strong vein of tenderness and humanity. This is seen in his expressed theories about humour. A sentimentalist who shrank from heavily larded sentiment, he was at the same time a satirist who, as he said, "hated Juvenal" and disapproved of Swift. His lecture on "Charity and Humour," delivered first in New York in 1853, is a revealing document. There he develops the idea that our humourous writers are "gay and kind week-day preachers" who have done much in the cause of the poor, the weak, and the unhappy, besides contributing to "our scorn for falsehood and pretension, to our righteous hatred of hypocrisy, to our education in the perception of truth, our love of honesty, our knowledge of life, and shrewd guidance through the world." "A literary man of a humoristic turn," he goes on to say, and he might almost be speaking of himself, "is pretty sure to be of a philanthropic nature, to have a great sensibility, to be easily moved to pain or pleasure, keenly to appreciate the varieties of temper of people round about him, and sympathize in their laughter, love, amusement, tears." Then comes the return upon himself which is so characteristically his: "I would arrogate no particular merit to literary men for the possession of this faculty of doing good which some of them enjoy. It costs a gentleman no sacrifice to be benevolent on paper; and the luxury of indulging in the most beautiful and brilliant sentiments never makes any man a penny the poorer . . ."

Humour, he concludes, is wit and love, and "the best humour is that which contains most humanity, that which is flavoured throughout with tenderness and kindness." Thackeray's comic spirit led him not infrequently into a wistful contemplation of the *lacrimæ rerum.* "The

---

[6] *Cornhill to Cairo.*

best of your poems," he wrote to Horace Smith, "instead of making me laugh, has had the other effect . . . Do you consider this an insult? All the best comic stuff so affects me—Sancho, Falstaff, even Fielding in 'Amelia.' " [7]

It is clear where a literary philosophy like this is likely to emerge. Join an antiseptic hatred for cruelty and insincerity to a corollary affection for gentleness and honesty; add to that a quality of subtle observation and a nice sense for just the right amount of artistic distortion, and you have the ironist of *Vanity Fair*. Some critics, misled by Thackeray's "I have no head above my eyes. I describe what I see," have brought heavy guns to bear on what they call his lack of a philosophy or even of an adequate equipment of ideas. It is true that Thackeray had small talent for abstract thinking; and his generalizations are not infrequently comfortably conventional. Nevertheless he did bring the scenes of the Fair within the framework of a conception of life which had point and penetration and which conveyed a moral concept of human nature, in its large sense. His thinking is fused thought, concrete, objectified in action and speech, but to the careful reader unmistakable. It is always expressed through character and exists, in the great novels, on several planes of realism, from near-caricature to the subtlest and most acute revelation of personality.

The clue to Thackeray's art in the novels, then, is not its occasional devastating satire, or its wit, or its amiable moralizing digressions, or its occasional bursts of sentiment controlled and tempered by a quizzical humour (and nothing is more distinctive in Thackeray than his checking himself in the midst of sentiment, turning its edge back against himself). The clue to his art is the complete and covering irony through which his view of life is filtered. It is an irony softened by a sad and wistful humanity, sharpened at times by an indignation against cant and affectation, but warmed also by the gentle melancholy that comes with the ironist's perception of the gap between man's aspiration and achievement.

Of the irony which lies in the twist of a phrase Thackeray makes judicious use in *Vanity Fair*. Thus Figs, in the Swishtail Seminary, writes a letter to his mother, "who was fond of him, although she was a grocer's wife." Pitt Crawley, at college, "failed somehow, in spite of a mediocrity which ought to have insured any man a success." After Becky, already secretly married to Rawdon Crawley, has listened to the offers of Sir Pitt Crawley, Thackeray asks, "What well-bred young

[7] Centenary Biographical Edition of the *Works*, ed. Lady Ritchie, 26 vols., London, 1910–11, ix, xxviii.

person is there in all Vanity Fair, who will not feel for a hard-working, ingenious, meritorious girl, who gets such an honorable, advantageous, provoking offer, just at the very moment when it is out of her power to accept it? I am sure our friend Becky's disappointment deserves and will command every sympathy." And one final passage of extended ironic comment in Thackeray's best manner:

> I protest it is quite shameful in the world to abuse a simple creature, as people of her time abuse Becky, and I warn the public against believing one-tenth of the stories against her. If every person is to be banished from society who runs into debt and cannot pay—if we are to be peering into everybody's private life, speculating upon their income, and cutting them if we don't approve of their expenditure—why, what a howling wilderness and intolerable dwelling Vanity Fair would be! Every man's hand would be against his neighbour in this case, my dear sir, and the benefits of civilisation would be done away with. We should be quarrelling, abusing, avoiding one another. Our houses would become caverns: and we should go in rags because we cared for nobody. Rents would go down. Parties wouldn't be given any more. All the tradesmen of the town would be bankrupt. Wine, wax-lights, comestibles, rouge, crinoline-petticoats, diamonds, wigs, Louis-Quatorze gimcracks, and old china, park hacks, and splendid high-stepping carriage horses—all the delights of life, I say— would go to the deuce, if people did but act upon their silly principles, and avoid those whom they dislike and abuse. Whereas, by a little charity and mutual forbearance, things are made to go on pleasantly enough; we may abuse a man as much as we like, and call him the greatest rascal unhanged—but do we wish to hang him therefore? No. We shake hands when we meet. If his cook is good we forgive him, and go and dine with him; and we expect he will do the same by us. Thus trade flourishes— civilisation advances: peace is kept; new dresses are wanted for new assemblies every week; and the last year's vintage of Lafitte will remunerate the honest proprietor who reared it.

With this sort of thing *Vanity Fair* is liberally and saltily sprinkled. It does not, however, bite as deeply as the less tangible but more pervasive ironic tone which marks Thackeray's whole view of the Fair and its inhabitants—a philosophic irony, a sense of the irony of things, of the contrast between the real and the apparent: that the best love is often expended upon unworthy objects; that rascals flourish while innocence suffers; that virtue is frequently dull and rascality lively; that old age and disappointment are as likely to sour character as to sweeten it. All this is explored relentlessly—never sneeringly but with consummate skill.

It is worth noting that Thackeray never expands a comic scene just for the sake of the comedy, as Dickens does. His laughter is seldom gusty and free. Comedy is refracted through the lenses of his critical spectacles and becomes a humorous commentary on life. Perhaps this was one reason that Thackeray was never as popular as Dickens. Satire the Victorians knew and liked; humorous exaggeration they delighted in; tears were a benediction to them. But irony left them uneasy. The reader never knew when his superior laughter might be stifled by a sudden sense of self-recognition. Give us blacks and whites; confound these greys! The only hope for the reader is that in the puzzling blend of light and shadow which makes up his world Thackeray may make us recognize—not ourselves, of course—but our neighbours!

Connected with this large ironic treatment is the point of view from which Thackeray tells the story. It is not as easy to identify and fix here as it is in the later novels. Sometimes he seems to be the omniscient novelist, sharing the inmost thoughts and feelings of his characters; sometimes the spectator *ab extra,* pretending to be unable to know the minds of his people, even going out of his way to validate their independent existence. These inconsistencies, however, distress the critic more than the reader. For all practical purposes, with one exception to be noted later, we know sufficiently well at any given point in the story where Thackeray stands. Moreover, he seized upon the one method which could give coherence to his sprawling, panoramic materials, and which at the same time would allow him to stand in very close personal relation to the story.

This method is of course the seemingly casual, chatty soliloquizing of a man sitting in his arm-chair by the fireside and telling a story. It is of all narrative manners the most flexible, but also the one most likely to lead into windy digression. Thackeray keeps the digressions under reasonably good control in *Vanity Fair,* although his approach allows for a variety of moods and comments. Typically it permits him to pluck the reader by the sleeve and draw him off into a corner, there to comment familiarly upon the passing scene. Thus the reader "will please to remember that this history has 'Vanity Fair' for a title, and that Vanity Fair is a very vain, wicked, foolish place, full of all sorts of humbugs and falsenesses and pretensions. And while the moralist, who is holding forth on the cover (an accurate portrait of your humble servant), professes to wear neither gown nor bands, but only the very same long-eared livery in which his congregation is arrayed: yet, look you, one is bound to speak the truth as far as one knows it, whether one mounts a cap and bells or a shovel-hat; and a deal of disagreeable matter must come out in the course of such an undertaking." He makes clear, too, that he reserves the right, as master of the puppet-show, to come down into the crowd to look at his own creations.

> And, as we bring our characters forward, I will ask leave, as a man and a brother, not only to introduce them, but occasionally to step down from the platform, and talk about them: if they are good and kindly, to love them and shake them by the hand: if they are silly, to laugh at them confidentially in the reader's sleeve: if they are wicked and heartless, to abuse them in the strongest terms which politeness admits of. . . . Some there are, and very successful too, mere quacks and fools: and it was to combat and expose such as those, no doubt, that Laughter was made.

Thackeray's comments usually take the form of an amused, whimsical aside, often with an ironic twist. For instance, he tells about the griefs of those in high station:

> And let us, my brethren, who have not our names in the Red Book, console ourselves by thinking comfortably how miserable our betters may be, and that Damocles, who sits on satin cushions, and is served on gold plate, has an awful sword hanging over his head in the shape of a bailiff, or an hereditary disease, or a family secret, which peeps out every now and then from the embroidered arras in a ghastly manner, and will be sure to drop one day or the other in the right place.

Thackeray has come in for a good deal of abuse because of this habit. The test ought to be: does it help the story or get in the way? Does it make it seem more or less real? Does it add to or detract from our enjoyment? Thackeray's literary affinities were with the eighteenth century, and it was Fielding who introduced him to such a personal embroidery of the text. Fielding, however, usually held his comments to specific sections and Thackeray sticks them into the interstices of his story.

It seems to me that Thackeray's interpolations add, in the long run, to the illusion of reality, certainly to our enjoyment of the story. In the dramatic novel they would be quite out of place, but in the discursive novel of manners they indicate the mood of the story and intensify the mellow, introspective manner which is the very tissue of a Thackeray novel. The answer to the question hinges largely upon the quality of the mind which makes the comments. When it is Thackeray, we can usually afford to pause with him briefly. One distinction needs to be made, however. When he is adding an ironic or a whimsical note to the margin of the action he can be completely felicitous.

Yet occasionally the moralist defeats the artist and upon the characters are poured the vials of Thackeray's ethical indignation. Still worse are the places where, in a fervour of sentimental adoration, Thackeray releases a flood of sensibility about some character who, on his own showing, is not worth the emotion.

Usually his comments are only parenthetical observations on the passing show, often ruefully humorous, in a vein of tempered melancholy. Thus in describing Miss Crawley's illness he admits that

> Sick-bed homilies and pious reflections are, to be sure, out of place in mere story-books, and we are not going (after the fashion of some novelists of the present day) to cajole the public into a sermon, when it is only a comedy that the reader pays his money to witness. But, without preaching, the truth may surely be borne in mind, that the bustle, and triumph, and laughter, and gaiety which Vanity Fair exhibits in public, do not always pursue the performer into private life, and that the most dreary depression of spirits and dismal repentances sometimes overcome him . . . O brother wearers of motley! Are there not moments when one grows sick of grinning and tumbling, and the jingling of cap and bells? This, dear friends and companions, is my amiable object—to walk with you through the Fair, to examine the shops and the shows there; and that we should all come home after the flare, and the noise, and the gaiety, and be perfectly miserable in private.

There is much of Thackeray in that passage, not merely the self-inclusion in the parade of vanities, but also the wistful recognition of the gulf that stretches between man's outward mirth and the lonely places of his soul.

The Social Critic

by J. Y. T. Greig

No doubt a man may be an earl of eleven descents, and yet be
a pitifully mean creature. All the same for that, I am of opinion that it takes three generations to make a gentleman.
(Thackeray in conversation, as reported by Jeaffreson, i. 250.)

I

It sounds like Thackeray, though Cordy Jeaffreson is not to be
wholly trusted in these matters. Thackeray would never have doubted
his own right to the title of "gentleman"; nor, it would seem, did
anybody else in his time challenge him on the point. The Victorians
recognized a gentleman when they saw one—or at least thought they
did. They perfectly understood Thackeray when, in describing poor
half-imbecile Plantagenet Gaunt Gaunt, he remarked: "And yet you
see somehow that he is a gentleman." [1] They also understood when
Thackeray commented on Bloundell, the card-sharper, that he had
been a gentleman once, and still retained "some faint odours of that
time of bloom." [2]
None the less, there are signs in Thackeray's works that he is not
quite so sure about the "gentleman" as he sounds.

II

"The Snobs of England," afterwards republished as *The Book of
Snobs,* appeared weekly in *Punch* from 28 February 1846 to 27 Febru-

"The Social Critic." From *Thackeray: A Reconsideration,* by J. Y. T. Greig
(London: Oxford University Press, 1950), pp. 90–101. Copyright 1950 by Mrs.
M. T. Greig. Reprinted by permission of Mrs. M. T. Greig. Some abbreviations in
the notes have been expanded.

[1] "Dr. Birch and his Young Friends," *Christmas Books,* 96. Unless otherwise
stated page references in the notes are to the Biographical Edition of Thackeray's
Works, ed. Anne Ritchie, 13 vols. (London: Smith, Elder & Co., 1900).

[2] "Kickleburys on the Rhine," *ibid.* 199.

ary 1847. Considered as a piece of literature, the book is rather tiresome. Though sometimes entertaining, it is much too long, too full of repetitions; its humour is often forced, and its wit flat. Considered as a fact in the life of Thackeray, however, it is most important. For one thing, the astonishing success of the weekly papers gave him confidence in himself, which he had previously lacked. He now knew that, at last, he "had taken the great stupid public by the ears";[3] among the *Punch* men, he had now taken his place alongside, and perhaps a little ahead of, Douglas Jerrold. He had still an immense distance to travel before he could catch up with Charles Dickens. That, he would have admitted readily enough. Nevertheless, he was now moving steadily in the right direction.

The "Snob" papers may also be regarded as a sort of catchment-area in the development of Thackeray as a writer. Turbulent streams from a great many of his earlier works flow into them, settle, then pour out again, purified, less turbulent, and less turbid, into later novels. After this series in *Punch* it is always the mature Thackeray that we encounter in print. For better, for worse, he is what he is. Though he may still develop and improve his technical skills, yet the substance of his work, his prevailing interests, themes, types of character, and opinions on life—these will change very little in the seventeen years still remaining to him. His mind and habits of thinking were formed by the time he completed "The Snobs of England."

How casual, accidental, and imprecise his mind and habits of thinking were may be shown by the use he made of the very word *snob*. It was a Cambridge word; and he had been familiar with it since his days as an undergradate. Originally meaning only "townsman," as opposed to "gownsman," it had soon been turned by members of the University into a term of abuse roughly equivalent to "low fellow, cad, or bounder." Thackeray now and then makes use of it in this sense in his earlier writings, and even continues to do so after *The Book of Snobs* has established it in general slang with the more restricted meaning, "person with an exaggerated respect for wealth or social position." The truth is that although Thackeray himself must be held chiefly responsible for giving the world this special twist of meaning, he did not set out with this intention; nor did he realize at any stage of composition exactly what he had done. He had no clear notion what the word meant to him or to anybody else. His

---

[3] The exasperated Thackeray, in a letter to the man who had just seen *The Second Funeral of Napoleon* (1841) through the press for him, asks rhetorically how he is to do this.

chief need was for a short explosive term which he could fling like a hand grenade at the people he disliked. The term *snob* seemed to him as good a projectile as any other. It exploded prettily—though it often missed the target.

His famous definition of a snob as one "who meanly admires mean things," [4] though it may sound excogitated, was in fact casual, irrelevant, and at once forgotten by Thackeray himself. In any event, it was far too comprehensive. A little later, while blundering round a meaning, he equated snobbishness, first with worldliness, then with humbug, then with "an unhappy passion for peacock's feathers." [5] Then he admitted nonchalantly: "We can't say what it is, any more than we can define wit, humour, or humbug; but we *know* what it is"—[6] a statement to which his own "Snob" papers give the lie.

No student of Victorian England in the forties will dispute that snobbishness (in the modern, restricted sense of "exaggerated respect for wealth or social position") needed scourging. The comparatively stable society of the previous century had been thrown off balance. The Industrial Revolution had produced, and the Reform Bill of 1832 had enfranchised, a vast body of manufacturers, tradesmen, merchants large and small, apothecaries, surgeons, physicians, lawyers, and speculators who were elbowing their way up the crowded steps of the social pyramid, aping the manners of the older landed gentry, but without knowing very clearly what they wanted. It is always in these conditions, when the climbers feel uncertain of their footing, that the attitude of mind which we call snobbishness, and the actions which we call snobbery, prevail; and we do not need Thackeray's exposures to convince us that the people we call snobs were ubiquitous in the England of which he was writing. But the trouble with him was that he had no relatively firm social theory to control his pen. He had no standards, except the vague ones of a "gentleman," by which he could measure social aberrations. Like many another social physician, he could only name the disease, and attack its symptoms. To get down to ultimate causes would have needed more systematic thinking than his untrained and inconstant mind was capable of undertaking.

No doubt he made many of his victims uneasily conscious of their symptoms. Berdmore believes that during the vogue of the "Snob" papers many hosts stopped dribbling their sherry, and many hostesses

---

[4] "Snobs," *Contributions to "Punch," etc.* 311.

[5] *Ibid.* 344, 368, 373.

[6] *Ibid.* 461.

stopped boasting of their titled relatives.[7] London clubmen, too, grew a little nervous of Thackeray when he dined at the same table with them, or stationed himself in his lordly manner with his back to the fire-place in the same smoking-room. To the bulk of them, perhaps, this *Punch* was a ribald rag; but they read it; and this Thackeray was a dangerous Radical; but they thought it safer to admire his wit. So the sales of the rag and the fame of the Radical increased.

Beyond this, he did little to reform those he pilloried. He had no effective cure for the "sickness of an acquisitive society." He delivered his blows so impulsively and indiscriminately that they fell almost as often on the innocent as on the guilty. His values were confused and variable; and the final impression after a reading of *The Book of Snobs* is one of exasperation. If everybody is a snob (including Mr. Snob, the author), and if nearly every human action is an example of snobbery, both terms are meaningless.

III

Perhaps the nearest that Thackeray ever got to a general principle of social conduct was the maxim, "We must live according to our degree."[8] This meant, not only that no one must act as if he were wealthier or better born than the facts warranted, but also that no one must act as if he were poorer or worse born. When the amiable but sententious Mr. Brown, whose "Letters to his Nephew" ran in *Punch* from March to August 1849, and who may be taken for a much cooler and less vituperative critic of society than the earlier Mr. Snob, rebukes his nephew for becoming rather too familiar with "an uncommonly good-looking parlourmaid," we assume him to be speaking with the voice of Thackeray: "The butcher-boy who brings the leg of mutton to Molly, may converse with her over the area railings; or the youthful grocer may exchange a few jocular remarks with Betty at the door as he hands in to her the tea and sugar; but not you."[9] This is also the burden of the *Roundabout* (April 1861) in which Thackeray discourses lightly on domestic servants.

> Between me and those fellow-creatures of mine who are sitting in the room below, how strange and wonderful is the partition! . . . If I met

[7] Septimus Berdmore, "Thackeray," *Westminster Review*, N.S., XXVI, July 1864, 173.

[8] "Brown's Letters," *Contributions to "Punch*," etc. 617.

[9] *Loc. cit.*

Hannah in the street with a bonnet on, I doubt whether I should know her. And all these good people with whom I may live for years and years, have cares, interests, dear friends and relatives, mayhap schemes, passions, longing hopes, tragedies of their own, from which a carpet and a few planks and beams utterly separate me.[10]

This is the "gentleman" speaking; kindly, of course, as a gentleman should be; but perfectly sure of his own superiority. The gentleman has always been privileged; for his rank cuts diagonally across others, as Broadway cuts across the avenues of Manhattan. A gentleman can associate on equal terms will all other gentlemen, whether they are peers or commoners, rich or poor, merchants or professional men. It does not hurt him in the least to be "utterly separated" from the people who are not gentlemen—the butcher-boy, the youthful grocer, John and Molly in the servants' hall, his tailor, and all members of what used to be called "the labouring classes" or "the lower orders." The rank of Gentleman, in fact, is a typically English institution, ill defined, far from rigid, mitigating the rigours of social stratification, and enabling individuals in a lower group, in special circumstances, and as it were inadvertently, to escape into a higher without seriously disordering the social scheme.

Unfortunately there is apt to be disagreement as to who is, or is not, a gentleman. Thackeray himself would pass, no doubt, but some of those he rejected would be passed by others. For the chastiser of snobs, so indeterminate a principle as "We must live according to our degree" seemed scarcely adequate: it laid him open to the charge of snobbishness himself. And the case against him was strengthened by his own Mr. Brown, who also laid it down as a maxim that "It is good for a man to live where he can meet his betters, intellectual and social." [11] This is possible, no doubt, for the gentleman. Even he, however, if he gratifies the ambition too freely, may be called a "tuft-hunter."

Thackeray had a bitter tongue for the tuft-hunter. When Harrison Ainsworth bought the *New Monthly Magazine,* and advertised that he had secured for it "writers eminent not only for talent but for high rank," Thackeray pounced on him.

> A literary gentleman who respects his calling doesn't surely mean to propitiate the public by saying, "I am going to write for you, and—and Lord Fitzdiddle is going to write too." Hang it, man, *let* him write—

[10] "On a Chalk Mark on a Door," *Lovel, Roundabout Papers, etc.* 285.
[11] "Brown's Letters," *Contributions to "Punch," etc.* 624.

write and be—successful, or write and be—unsuccessful, according to his merits. But don't let us talk about high rank in the republic of letters— let us keep *that* place clear.[12]

This is excellent—or it would have been, if Thackeray had not at the same time been engaged in a private quarrel with Ainsworth on another matter. The previous owner of the *New Monthly Magazine* had been guilty of a piece of sharp practice towards Thackeray; Thackeray had protested sharply to Ainsworth, and had received no reply; and had there and then written "Immense Opportunity" (from which the quotation above is taken) for *Punch*. Ainsworth's apology arrived after the article had gone to press, and there is something a little disturbing in Thackeray's hasty counter-apology. Although, he says, he would always think this advertisement of Ainsworth's "very objectionable," yet he would not have raised his hand to smite his friend if the explanation, not of the advertisement, but of the sharp practice, had arrived in time.[13]

IV

Far too many of Thackeray's salvos against snobs leave us with the uncomfortable feeling that he is not quite disinterested. Whibley does not exaggerate when he says that the author of *The Book of Snobs* "seems to be haunted by a species of self-consciousness; he is surprised that he is where he is; he knows that somebody is above or below him; but he cannot take his place in the world (or anybody else's place) for granted." [14]

Once again it is a case of egocentricity and wavering. In a conversation in America, as reported by Thomas W. Parsons, Thackeray admitted this wavering, but assigned the blame for it to England.

There is one thing in this country [i.e. America] which astonishes me [he is reported as saying]. You have a capacity for culture which contradicts all my experience. There are —— (mentioning two or three names well known in New York) who I know have risen from nothing, yet they are fit for any society in the world. . . . Now, in England, a man who has made his way up, as they have, doesn't seem to feel his

---

[12] "Immense Opportunity," *Punch*, 5 July 1845.
[13] M. H. Spielmann, *The Hitherto Unidentified Contributions of W. M. Thackeray to "Punch"* (London) , 1899, p. 133.
[14] Charles Whibley, *William Makepeace Thackeray*, Modern English Writers Series (London, 1903), p. 84.

social dignity. A little bit of the flunkey sticks in him somewhere. I am, perhaps, as independent in this respect as anyone I know, yet I'm not entirely sure of myself.[15]

The last sentence does not ring true, and for my own part I doubt if Thackeray ever uttered it in the form reported. He always considered himself a gentleman by birth and breeding, and it is highly improbable that he would speak of himself as one who had "made his way up" socially. The rest of the alleged statement, however, is extremely Thackerayan.

He may have been right about England. A century has passed since "The Snobs of England" appeared in *Punch,* and the country has undergone enormous changes; but no impartial observer of the English will deny that flunkeydom and snobbishness still flourish among them. It is probable enough, also, that Thackeray casually admitted "a little bit of the flunkey" in himself, though without suggesting that he had brought it up with him from a lower position in society. To be honest, he had more than a little bit.

After *Vanity Fair* took the public's fancy, Thackeray became an eminent novelist; he was "courted by dukes and duchesses, and wits of both sexes." At least, so his friend Fitzgerald said.[16] And Thackeray's letters confirm it. One evening he is to dine with the Dowager Duchess of Bedford, and to go on afterwards to two parties, one at Mrs. Procter's and the other at Lady Granville's;[17] then he has to attend "a grand dinner in Jewry";[18] and in the spring of 1850 he has "an awful week of festivities":

> To day Shakespeare's birthday at the Garrick Club, dinner and speech —lunch Madame Lionel Rothschild   ball Lady Waldegrave   She gives the finest balls in London & I've never seen one yet—tomorrow of 5 invitations to dinner the first is Mr. Marshall—the D of Devonshire's Hevening party Lady Emily Dundas's ditto—Thursday Sir Anthony Rothschild—Friday the domestic affections, Saturday Sir Robert Peel, Sunday Lord Lansdowne—

And so on it went, for years, in both London and Paris.

Thackeray liked being lionized by dukes and countesses, Presidents of France and of the United States, princes of banking and their

---

[15] J. G. Wilson, *Thackeray in the United States,* 2 vols. (London, 1904), ii, 36f.
[16] Edward Fitzgerald, *Letters and Literary Remains,* ed. W. A. Wright, 3 vols. (London, 1889), i, 193.
[17] *The Letters and Private Papers of William Makepeace Thackeray,* ed. Gordon N. Ray, 4 vols. (Cambridge: Harvard University Press, 1945-46), ii, 683.
[18] *Ibid.* 644.

ladies. It is beyond question that he liked it, because he continued to accept invitations long after he knew that grand dinners and lunches were ruining his health. Nor is it difficult to forgive him for letting his head be turned at first. After some ten years of struggle and comparative poverty in Grub Street, it was pleasant to be taken up by peers and prime ministers. And when he wrote, to Jane Brookfield or some other kind female correspondentess, about the grand dinners and balls to which he had been invited, it was always jokingly, as if he knew how little it all amounted to. For example, in continuation of the passage just quoted, he remarks to Mrs. Brookfield:

> Isn't it curious to think (it was striking my great mind yesterday as Anny was sorting the cards in the chimney glass) that there are people who would give their ears or half their income to go to these fine places. I was riding with an old Bailey Barrister yesterday in the park and his pretty wife (On les aime jolies Madame)—he apologized for knowing people who lived in Brunswick Square, and thought to prove his gentility by calling it "that demmed place." [19]

But all this was precisely what we should expect from the equivocal Thackeray. He has an eye for a snob because he is himself "Mr. Snob"; he knows how to reveal the flunkey because there is something of the flunkey in his own character.

Later, he thought up an excellent excuse for his alleged tuft-hunting. "If," he said, "I don't go out and mingle in society, I can't write." [20] Later still, he revised this statement in a review of John Leech's *Pictures of Life and Character:* "A social painter," he said, "must be of the world he depicts, and native to the manners he portrays." [21]

Perhaps it is the final phrase that is most significant. After all, although Thackeray might profess republican and anti-aristocratical views, might abuse Society for its "lordolatry" and "mammoniacal superstitions," and might often, immediately after some grand dinner or ball in Mayfair, be found in Evan's Supper Rooms in the company of true Bohemians, he could not, even if he would, cancel the effects of his own birth and breeding. He had been born a gentleman, and brought up by one whom he thought and spoke of as one

[19] *Ibid.* 665.
[20] Herman Merivale and Frank T. Marzials, *Life of W. M. Thackeray* (London, 1891), p. 147.
[21] "Leech," *Ballads, etc.* 488.

of the finest ladies in the land. He was "native to the manners he portrayed."

At the same time, as I have tried to show again and again, he never felt secure. All snobbery has its origin in a feeling of insecurity. It is little wonder, then, that this historian and satirist of snobs should have suffered from the very ailment that he diagnosed in others. It would seem that you cannot have a "gentleman" of the Thackeray sort, without some traces of the "gentleman's gentleman."

V

Thackeray "appealed to the middle classes." [22] Most of the Victorian novelists did, but only Thackeray affirmed it quite so openly. One result of this is to-day so obvious that it needs no elaboration: the calculated omission from Victorian novels of such vast and capital experiences as religion, speculation on Man's place in Nature and his relation to the supernatural, and the passionate loyalties and destructive infamies of sex. These may be hinted at in Thackeray, but all too discreetly.

It is more important to underline the courage than the timidity of the greater Victorians—a point made with force by Mr. G. M. Young:

> The world desired to be instructed: it was given Grote and Thirlwall, Milman and Macaulay, Lyell's *Principles of Geology*, Mill's *Logic*, Mill's *Political Economy*; to be elevated: it had *Past and Present, Modern Painters,* and *In Memoriam*; it asked for theology and got Newman, for education and got Arnold. Out of the Minerva Press came Disraeli, out of the horseplay of sentimental Cockneys, Dickens.[23]

One is tempted to add that it asked for frank comments on its social system and got *Vanity Fair, Pendennis,* and *The Newcomes.*

But this addition would be hardly legitimate. Few Victorians of the forties and fifties seem to have asked at all persistently for a frank comment on their social system. Those who might have done so, having most to gain, were of "the lower orders" and, as yet, mainly inarticulate. "The higher orders" took the social system very much for granted. For this reason we may say that *Yellowplush, Jeames's Diary, The Book of Snobs,* and *Vanity Fair* were not so much supplying a demand as creating one. They were forcing some of the more

---

[22] *Vanity Fair*, 79.
[23] G. M. Young, *Victorian England: Portrait of an Age* (Oxford University Press, 1936), p. 15.

obvious imperfections of society upon their readers' notice; and there-fore, and to this extent only, we may class the author with the early Socialists. A dangerous Radical he was not—whatever London club-men may have thought. But he was so far Radical, that he helped to undermine what had once seemed firm and unshakable.

He was dimly aware of this himself. Writing to his mother on 26 March 1851 he said:

> The present politics are behind the world: and not fit for the intel-ligence of the nation. The great revolution's a coming a coming: and the man not here who's to head it.—I wonder whether he's born and where he lives?—The present writers are all employed as by instinct in unscrew-ing the old framework of society, and get it ready for the Smash. I take a sort of pleasure in my little part in the business and in saying destruc-tive things in a good humoured jolly way.[24]

Nearly all Victorians were individualists to a degree now possible only in Americans. At a time when the family and the churches—per-haps the only social institutions that were well enough organized to count—pressed more heavily upon the individual than at any time for two centuries, men continued to pretend that the individual had the fullest liberty to go to hell or heaven in the way that seemed good to him; they remained curiously unconscious of the influence that society was exerting on them, in their offices, their drawing-rooms, their clubs, even in their double beds; and they felt not a little shocked when a member of their community began telling them about it in his sub-acid way. This, to be sure, proved more irritating and less effectual than the frontal attacks launched by Dickens on the private schools, Bumbledom, debtors' prisons, the Circumlocution Office, and the Court of Chancery. Dickens was, in their view, an honest fellow, bluff and hearty, coming himself from "the lower or-ders." He was privileged; he could make them laugh abundantly; he could also make them cry. But this Thackeray! He was a gentleman. He was an ironist. Instead of attacking this or that abuse, he was undermining the entire Code from within. It made them uncomfort-able. They decided that he sneered.

And of course he did. He sneered and withdrew. Lacking a co-herent, integrated social theory, he grew timid and unsure, like a sniper who decamps when the battle grows warm. His avowed doc-trine, "Fun is good, truth better, love best of all," though it sounded well, did not seem to bear directly on his practice as novelist or critic.

He lacked the jaunty optimism of Dickens, which most of the other Victorians both understood and approved, being jaunty optimists themselves. Dickens's work was buoyed up by his genuine belief in the goodness of man, and in the power of charity to reform the world. That was excellent; it was individualism moralized and justified. Thackeray, on the contrary, presented human society as Vanity Fair —"not a moral place certainly; nor a merry one, though very noisy." [25] He informed his readers that his "amiable object" was to walk with them through the Fair; and he advised them that after their walk they "should all come home . . . and be perfectly miserable in private." [26] Nor could he find any more comfortable words with which to end his first full-length novel than: "Ah! *Vanitas Vanitatum!* which of us is happy in this world? Which of us has his desire? or, having it, is satisfied?—Come, children let us shut up the box and the puppets, for our play is played out."

To appeal to the Victorian middle classes in a tone so *morne* was extraordinary, irritating, and in the end ineffectual. Had they taken it for the genuine expression of a whole man—whole though splenetic and probably mistaken, like the Sage of Chelsea—they would probably have listened, even when they disagreed. For the Victorians on the whole were not petty: they recognized and respected conviction. But the Sage of Chelsea spoke for the majority of his contemporaries when he called Thackeray "very uncertain and chaotic." Dickens with his gusto, and despite much cheap jollity and still cheaper pathos, did more to shake the Victorians' complacency than his saturnine, disjointed rival. Dickens hung together. Thackeray did not.

[25] "Before the Curtain," *Vanity Fair*, xliii.
[26] *Vanity Fair*, 174.

Thackeray as Preacher

by Mario Praz

Thackeray is indeed bitter and harsh, but he remains always a gentleman, he remains, that is, within the framework of Victorian society; he is a cynic in yellow gloves, respectful, when all is said and done, of the conventions. He does not truly see life as it is, but with a caricature-like distortion which is conditioned by the exigencies of morality, and it is thanks to this moralizing tendency that his criticism is acceptable to an extremely moral society; he does not depict vice either under alluring forms, as the French did, or under forms so totally repugnant that they shock the moral sense, but rather as it is depicted by a preacher,[1] so that it remains always in the world of logic and argument and never descends to the point of direct, emotional contact. The thrill of intuitive, electrical contact is lacking in Thackeray: his appeal is to the mind of his reader rather than to his emotional experience.

This is the bourgeois, the Biedermeier aspect of this so-called cynic: he is a moralist, he carries on, in a less agreeable, less artistic form, the work of correcting manners that had been begun by Addison—Addison whom he finds to be synonymous with perfection. Thackeray is, as we shall see, essentially anti-heroic; yet he presents the figure of Addison (in *The English Humourists*) as that of a being without faults, natural, good, noble, smiling, courteous, calm: a humorist who never loses the urbanity of a gentleman, a gentleman not only in manner, but—which is more important—in character, for he has perfect self-control and serenity of spirit. Addison, for Thackeray,

"Thackeray as Preacher" (editor's title). From *The Hero in Eclipse in Victorian Fiction*, by Mario Praz, trans. Angus Davidson (London: Oxford University Press, 1956), pp. 207–13. Copyright 1952 by G. C. Sansoni. Reprinted by permission of G. C. Sansoni. This selection is part of a long chapter on Thackeray.

[1] With regard to an attack in *The Times* reproving *The Newcomes* as a book damaging to morals and religion, Thackeray remarked to Whitwell Elwin: "With regard to religion, I think, please God, my books are written by a God-loving man; and the morality—the vanity of success, etc., of all but love and goodness—is not that the teaching *Domini nostri?*"

is almost the only proof of the possibility of perfection in man, he is—as far as Thackeray's conception could reach—a superman, almost as Goethe is nowadays represented by some modern writers: "It is in the nature of such lords of intellect to be solitary—they are in the world, but not of it; and our minor struggles, brawls, successes, pass under them. . . . He must have stooped to put himself on a level with most men." And it is noteworthy that Macaulay, too, bowed down before Addison as before a model: which confirms, on the one hand, the description of "Victorian *ante litteram*" given to Addison by Professor Bonamy Dobrée, and, on the other, signifies a community of ideals in Thackeray and Macaulay—both of them Victorians, though of different types.

Thackeray's method, too, of taking the reader aside and commenting in a familiar fashion upon the spectacle of the world, recalls Addison's and Fielding's benevolent, confidential tone; except that in Thackeray this kind of urbane conversation acquires an even more bourgeois tinge: the writer, in his slippers, delivers his comments from the fireside. It is a method that accentuates the rhythm of passing time, the sense of slow corrosion brought about by the years and by human passions and weaknesses, but it prevents the story from taking a dramatic course: plot is forgotten in the moral analysis of character.

Instead of *The Spectator* club, it is, with Thackeray, the snobs' club: but life is always analysed according to plan, never directly: Addison's sketches carry on the tradition of Ben Jonson's "humours," and Thackeray's *Snobs of England*, too, are "characters," samples, generalizations. Descended from a family which (as already mentioned) could count among its numbers at least nineteen clergymen, Thackeray was born with the vocation of a lay preacher; and Taine observed that it would be possible to dig out of his novels a volume or two of essays in the manner of La Bruyère or Addison. In any case Thackeray himself does not hesitate to reveal that his mission is that of lay preacher; he said this in conversations with friends, he wrote it in various pages of his novels. In one chapter (the thirty-eighth) of *The Newcomes*, for example, we read:

> This book is all about the world and a respectable family dwelling in it. It is not a sermon, except where it cannot help itself, and the speaker pursuing the destiny of his narrative finds such a homily before him. O friend, in your life and mine, don't we light upon such sermons daily? don't we see at home as well as amongst our neighbours that battle betwixt Evil and Good? Here on one side is Self and Ambition and Ad-

vancement, and Right and Love on the other. Which shall we let to triumph for ourselves, which for our children?

His preaching vocation is evident even in the most vivid episodes of his best novels. See, for instance, chapter vi of Book III of *Esmond,* where Esmond gives Beatrix the news of Hamilton's death—Hamilton who had represented the crowning of all her worldly ambitions. Beatrix wants to make Esmond admire the great gold salver with the Hamilton arms upon it ("a pretty piece of vanity," says Esmond); at the first hint of the fatal news, she drops the salver on the floor (its fall, it is hardly necessary to point out, is a symbol of the ruin of Beatrix's splendid ambitions), and believes that Hamilton has left her from unfaithfulness. The speech in which Esmond tells her how matters stand has all the tone of a sermon: "Vain and cruel woman! kneel and thank the awful Heaven which awards life and death, and chastises pride," &c. And, when he alludes to the tradesmen who have brought their sumptuous wares to the house in connexion with Beatrix's approaching marriage: "The army of Vanity Fair, waiting without, gathered up all their fripperies and fled aghast." For Thackeray's "homily" manner see also passage in *Pendennis* on the subject of Fanny Bolton's condemnation by all honest women, and the novelist's warning to the latter, or his other warning to "the Clarissas of this life." "O you poor little ignorant vain foolish maidens!" &c. And his observations on the chain of universal love intended by the Creator, in the *Journey from Cornhill to Grand Cairo.* This preaching vocation becomes more and more accentuated in Thackeray's career, so that the last works, such as *The Adventures of Philip,* are practically sermons pure and simple. There is no mistaking the pulpit tone in phrases such as: "Oh blessed they on whose pillow no remorse sits! Happy those who have escaped temptation!" or again: "Honour your father and mother. Amen. May his days be long who fulfils the command." In *The Roundabout Papers* the account of a recent infamous crime (*On two Roundabout Papers which I intended to write*), or of the singularity of certain gifts which place people above the common run of humanity (*A Mississippi Bubble*), or of the ignominious end of a dishonest public figure (*On a Pear-tree*) suggest the perorations of real sermons; and in the essay *On a Medal of George IV* the argument is transported on to the moral plane in this way: "Ah, friend, may our coin, battered, and clipped, and defaced though it be, be proved to be Sterling Silver on the day of the Great Assay!"

But it is, in point of fact, from the depths of disillusioned meditations upon mortality and the impermanence of all human things (ancient themes of the preacher) that a breath of poetry most often arises, in Thackeray's pages. As early as 1839 (in *Catherine*), in front of a copy of the *Daily Post* of a hundred and ten years before, in which there was an account of the murder of Hayes and the execution of the culprits, he had exclaimed:

> Think of it! it has been read by Belinda at her toilet, scanned at "Button's" and "Will's," sneered at by wits, talked of in palaces and cottages, by a busy race in wigs, red heels, hoops, patches, and rags of all variety— a busy race that hath long since plunged and vanished in the unfathomable gulf towards which we march so briskly. Where are they? "Afflavit Deus"—and they are gone! Hark! is not the same wind roaring still that shall sweep us down? and yonder stands the compositor at his types who shall put up a pretty paragraph some day to say how, "*Yesterday*, at his house in Grosvenor Square," or "At Botany Bay, universally regretted," died So-and-So.

And in the sixth chapter of the third book of *Esmond*, Esmond, returning from Kensington, where he has announced Hamilton's death to Beatrix, meets the streetcriers shouting the news and sees the town coming to life in the sunny, early, November morning:

> The world was going to its business again, although dukes lay dead and ladies mourned for them . . . So night and day pass away, and tomorrow comes, and our place knows us not.[2] Esmond thought of the courier now galloping on the North road, to inform him who was Earl of Arran yesterday that he was Duke of Hamilton to-day; and of a thousand great schemes, hopes, ambitions, that were alive in the gallant heart, beating a few hours since, and now in a little dust quiescent.

So also in *Pendennis* (chap. xxxvi):

> At this time of his life Mr. Pen beheld all sorts of places and men; and very likely did not know how much he enjoyed himself until long after, when balls gave him no pleasure, neither did farces make him laugh; nor did the tavern joke produce the least excitement in him; nor did the loveliest dancer that ever showed her ancles cause him to stir from his chair after dinner. At his present mature age all these pleasures are over: and the times have passed away too. It is but a very very few years since—but the time is gone, and most of the men. Bludyer will no more bully authors or cheat landlords of their score. Shandon, the learned and thriftless, the witty and unwise, sleeps his last sleep. They buried honest Doolan the other day: never will he cringe or flatter, never pull long-bow or empty whiskey-noggin any more.

[2] *Job*, vii. 10.

A little farther on Thackeray reflects upon intimate details of the private life of certain old dandies or bucks who study to appear youthful, and imagines how, "if any parson in Pimlico or St. James's were to order the beadles to bring [such a one] into the middle aisle, and there set him in an armchair, and make a text of him, and preach about him to the congregation, [he] could be turned to a wholesome use for once in his life, and might be surprised to find that some good thoughts came out of him." Such a sermon, one supposes, might have sounded like some of Donne's: "Thou hast a desire to please some *eyes*, when thou hast much to doe, not to displease every *Nose;* and thou wilt solicit an adulterous entrance into their beds who, if they should but see thee goe into thine own bed, would need no other mortification, nor answer to thy solicitation" (Sermon XX).

And again in *Pendennis* (chap. xli):

> The bloom disappears off the face of poetry after you begin to shave. You can't get up that naturalness and artless rosy tint in after days. Your cheeks are pale, and have got faded by exposure to evening parties, and you are obliged to take curling-irons, and macassar, and the deuce-knows-what to your whiskers; they curl ambrosially, and you are very grand and genteel, and so forth; but, ah! Pen, the spring time was the best.

Or the passage on Congreve in *The English Humourists:*

> I have read two or three of Congreve's plays over before speaking of him; and my feelings were rather like those, which I daresay most of us here have had, at Pompeii, looking at the Poet's house and the relics of an orgy: a dried wine jar or two, a charred supper-table, the breast of a dancing-girl pressed against the ashes, the laughing skull of a joker, a perfect stillness round about, as the cicerone twangs the moral, and the blue sky shines calmly over the ruin. The Congreve muse is dead, and her song choked in Time's ashes. We gaze at the skeleton, and wonder at the life which once revelled in its mad veins. We take the skull up, and muse over the frolic and daring, the wit, scorn, passion, hope, desire, with which that empty bowl once fermented. We think of the glances that allured, the tears that melted, of the bright eyes that shone in those vacant sockets; and of lips whispering love, and cheeks dimpling with smiles, that once covered yon ghastly yellow framework. They used to call those teeth pearls once. See! there's the cup she drank from, the gold chain she wore on her neck, the vase which held the rouge for her cheeks, her looking-glass, and the harp she used to dance to. Instead of a feast we find a gravestone, and in place of a mistress, a few bones.

Thackeray's repressed romanticism—we shall have occasion to return to this point later—"took vent," as one critic (Emerson Grant Sutcliffe) has remarked, "in the sentiment and didacticism which so oddly colour his satire." Hence his continually taking his reader aside, his turning to him with a perpetually implied "de te fabula," his alteration of the "dear brethren" of the pulpit into the layman's "my friend." M. Las Vergnas, taking up a remark by Charles Whibley ("He acts like the sheep-dog to his characters"), goes so far as to write:

> Il est indéniable que Thackeray a considéré ses personnages comme autant de brebis égarées, et si, de la métaphore du troupeau, il fallait retenir quelque trait, ce serait, non pas l'image brutale du chien, mais celle, au double sens heureux des termes, du pasteur grave et doux.

And M. Las Vergnas asks himself, what else is *Pendennis* but a series of reflections upon man, a kind of animated psychological treatise, a philosophy in action? And is not *Vanity Fair* a sermon on a text from Ecclesiastes? Thackeray might be consulted for moral advice by the chance opening of the page—*sortes thackerayanae*. Yet is this accessory quality in the novel, which M. Las Vergnas considers much more noteworthy than the plot itself, really so rich in shades and subtleties of meaning as the French critic supposes? Thackeray's reflections stand out prominently against the narrative plot, they are pointers placed continually in the margin of the page, and—which is worse—they are usually trite and pedestrian in character. For Thackeray had no original, revolutionary view of the world; his morality is "correct," like his gentlemanly suit of clothes. A gentleman is a man who has nothing showy either in his clothes or in his manners. The quality of a gentleman is a golden mean, an avoidance of all excess, an admirable mediocrity.

This, then, was why Thackeray, in spite of his bitterness, found favor with the Victorians: because he was a preacher, and because he was a non-revolutionary preacher. He was like the boatswain who beat time for the oarsmen in a galley; he whipped the lazy ones, but did not seek to impose upon them a different "time" from the one they already had. The Victorian age had several writers who took upon themselves this boatswain's function: but a Carlyle, an Arnold, wished to alter the rhythm of the rowers, to quicken it up. Thackeray alone was the boatswain elect, the one who did not claim to work miracles, who kept to the old rhythm.

Thackeray's Mothers-in-Law

by Juliet Sutton

"You are always attacking mothers-in-law!" [1] Laura indignantly accuses Pendennis in *Philip*, and with justice. It is certaily impossible to read far in Thackeray's novels without coming across one of these appalling women who tyrannizes over her daughter, abuses and cheats her son-in-law, and antagonizes the servants and tradesmen. There is, of course, a biographical explanation for the recurrence of this figure in the novels. Thackeray interrupted his reading of one of the tirades of the Campaigner in *The Newcomes* to comment, "that's my she-devil of a mother-in-law, you know"; [2] and, as most of the critical biographies of Thackeray point out, his wife's mother, Mrs. Shawe, is the original of all such she-devils in his novels. Professor G. N. Ray, [3] the major authority on the parallels between Thackeray's fiction and his life, demonstrates, for instance, the resemblance between Mrs. Shawe and Mrs. Gam of "Denis Haggarty's Wife," and Mrs. Baynes of *Philip*. Lambert Ennis, [4] who finds in Thackeray's novels a "contrast between his mother as a principle of good and Mrs. Shawe as a spirit of evil," speaks of how Thackeray seems to have found it necessary to work off his antagonism to his wife's mother every so often "by adding another figure to the terrible row of mothers-in-law that stalks through his books like the dumb show in *Macbeth*." The list starts with Mrs. Shum in *The Yellowplush Papers*, and includes Mrs. Gam, Mrs. Gashleigh, Mrs. Cuff, Mrs.

"Thackeray's Mothers-in-Law" by Juliet Sutton. From *Literature and Psychology*, XV (1965), 171–79. Copyright © 1965 by Leonard F. Manheim and Morton Kaplan. Reprinted by permission of the author and the editors. Slightly revised by the author.

[1] *Philip*, p. 234. *The Oxford Thackeray*, ed. George Saintsbury, 17 vols. (London, 1908). Referred to by title of novel, or as *Works*, with volume and page number in the text.

[2] See Gordon N. Ray, ed. *The Letters and Private Papers of William Makepeace Thackeray* (London, 1945–6), III, 465.

[3] *Thackeray. The Uses of Adversity, 1811–1846* (London, 1955), p. 337; and *Letters*, I, clxiv.

[4] *Thackeray: The Sentimental Cynic* (Evanston, Ill., 1950), p. 73.

Crum, Lady Kicklebury and her later incarnation as Lady Baker in *Lovel the Widower,* as well as Mrs. Mackenzie and Mrs. Baynes. J. Y. T. Greig,[5] sharing Laura's exasperation at this repetitive abuse, says that "the mother-in-law, always selfish, grasping, interfering, snobbish, domineering, ruining the peace of her daughter's household, is a stereotype in Thackeray, an obsession in his mind."

However, there is more to be said about the mothers-in-law in Thackeray's novels than that they are simply recurring hostile portraits of his own mother-in-law. It is worth examining them as they appear in the fiction and considering them as independent literary creations before we dismiss them as "stereotypes."

It is noticeable that each mother-in-law does not appear as a full-fledged dragon; she often begins by being quite harmless and even amiable. She becomes a dragon by a process of psychological evolution which the writer is careful to indicate. In his most fully developed examples of the species he has taken the trouble to depict, unobtrusively but still quite clearly, the psychological drives to which they are reacting. Their motivation is complex; Mrs. Mackenzie and Mrs. Baynes would both be excellent subjects for a psychoanalyst.

The evolution of the dragon mother-in-law is dependent on a relationship which Thackeray found particularly interesting, that of mother and daughter. The bond between these two he frequently envisages as so strong that it almost amounts to identification. His imagery repeatedly presents mother and daughter as though they were a single composite being. Rachel and Beatrix Esmond are recurrently seen in relation to each other as *mater pulcra, filia pulcrior* (*Esmond,* 176); the have their shoes made from the same last and look "like a pair of sisters" (*Esmond,* 337). Mother and daughter are always entwined in mutual embraces which are often described in floral imagery. In the early stages of our acquaintance with Mrs. Mackenzie and Rosey we see them thus devoted: "More caresses follow. Mamma is in a rapture. How pretty they look—the mother and daughter—two lilies twining together" (*Newcomes,* 287). Helen Pendennis and her foster-daughter Laura are also to some extent identified, and it is when Pen sees Laura giving his mother Helen a rose that "the image of the two women remained for ever after in his mind" (*Pendennis,* 299). Similarly, when we hear that Charlotte Baynes is "blooming like a rose, . . . the very image of her mother," the narrator comments drily, "in this case poor Charlotte must have

[5] *Thackeray: A Reconsideration* (London, 1950), p. 69.

looked like a yellow rose, for Mrs. Baynes was of a bilious temperament and complexion" (*Philip*, 290).

An early instance of this kind of identification of mother and daughter occurs in "The Ravenswing," where Mrs. and Morgiana Crump meet the handsome Mr. Walker at the hairdresser's:

> Humouring the mistake which Mrs. Crump had just made, Mr. Walker thrust the curling-irons into the fire in a minute, and looked round at the ladies with such a fascinating grace, that both . . . blushed and giggled, and were quite pleased. Mamma looked at 'Gina, and 'Gina looked at mamma; and then mamma gave 'Gina a little blow in the region of her little waist, and then both burst out laughing, . . . and both fixed their large shining black eyes repeatedly on Mr. Walker . . .
>
> "He can't stay," said Mrs Crump, all of a sudden, blushing red as a peony.
>
> "I shall have on my peignoir, mamma," said miss, looking at the gentleman, and then dropping down her eyes and blushing too (*Works*, IV, 355).

Here mother and daughter (peonies this time), with the same black eyes, and the same gestures and reactions, both blush for the same man, whom they both find attractive. Mrs. Crump is good-humoured, even if Mr. Walker pays more attention to Morgiana, for when Morgiana lets down her beautiful black hair, her main sexual attraction, and he is rapt in admiration, she is able to "make her daughter's triumph her own":

> "Heigho! when I acted at the Wells in 1820, before that dear girl was born, *I* had such a head of hair as that, to a shade, sir, to a shade. They called me Ravenswing on account of it [the name which Morgiana later inherits]. I lost my head of hair when that dear child was born, and I often say to her, 'Morgiana, you came into the world to rob your mother of her 'air' " (*Works*, IV, 356).

If we take into account the sexual symbolism of this passage, the deep sexual rivalry that is implicit in the identification of mother and daughter becomes apparent. The mother can for a while live through her daughter, and this is why, we gather from Thackeray's novels, mothers are such ardent match-makers; they themselves are in some sense carrying on a vicarious love affair with their daughters' suitors. General Lambert may well ask in bewilderment, "what is this burning desire all you women have for selling and marrying your daughters?" (*Virginians*, 219). The answer is in the same novel:

No woman was ever averse to the idea of her daughter getting a husband, however fathers revolt against the invasion of the son-in-law. As for mothers and grandmothers, those good folks are married over again in the marriage of their young ones; and their souls attire themselves in the laces and muslins of twenty—forty years ago (*Virginians,* 339).

No wonder Mrs. Mackenzie can say cheerfully, "I live for my darling girls now" (*Newcomes,* 286), as she spreads her net to catch Clive Newcome as a husband for Rosey.

The sexual motive in the development of Thackeray's termagant mothers-in-law is often suggested and even asserted in the novels. Nor is it a one-way attraction; the son-in-law is shown as finding some attraction in both the mother and the daughter, whom he so often sees as closely identified. We tend to think of Mrs. Mackenzie as the dreadful Campaigner of the last part of *The Newcomes,* but we should also remember that she was not always such a dragon. When Clive is considering Rosey as a wife, we hear that "he laughed and joked and waltzed alternately with Rosey and her mamma. The latter was the briskest partner of the two" (*Newcomes,* 284). And once he even admits half-jocularly of Mrs. Mackenzie, "I thought her delightful for three days, I declare I was in love with her" (315). George Warrington in *The Virginians* describes a stage in his relations with the Lambert family when Mrs. Lambert, during her promotion of his match with her daughter Theo, preens herself on her attractions, dislikes being reminded of her age, and pays George all sorts of sentimental attentions which he enjoys and reciprocates. He later recollects this with surprise: "Strange infatuation of passion—singular perversity of reason! At some period before his marriage, it not infrequently happens that a man actually is fond of his mother-in-law!" (*Virginians,* 705–6). Even Philip in his relation with Mrs. Baynes—who, being old and of bilious complexion, is the least physically attractive of these mothers-in-law—was not always as hostile as he becomes in later life, when "he fumes, shouts and rages against them, as if all were like his" (*Philip,* 618). There was a time when his allegiance was to her and against his friend Pendennis, and when he listened respectfully to her endless anecdotes about military life in India (236–39). Similarly, we remember there was also a time when she considered him the family's gallant deliverer, and was eager to promote his match with Charlotte. Her initial motivation is exposed in a revealing dialogue between her and her sister Mrs. MacWhirter, who becomes Philip's defender after Mrs. Baynes has turned against him:

"Of course, as a feeling mother, I feel that poor Charlotte is unhappy, my dear."

"But what makes her so, my dear?" cries Mrs. MacWhirter, who presently showed that she was mistress of the whole controversy. "No wonder Charlotte is unhappy, dear love! Can a girl be engaged to a young man, a most interesting young man, a clever, accomplished, highly educated young man—"

"*What?*" cries Mrs. Baynes.

"Haven't I your letters? . . . Didn't you tell me so over and over again; and rave about him, till I thought you were in love with him yourself almost?" cries Mrs. Mac.

"A most indecent observation!" cries out Eliza Baynes, in her deep, awful voice (*Philip*, 399).

Inevitably there comes a time when the mother ceases to be able to live a vicarious love affair through her daughter, a time when she finds that her daughter has the young man's whole allegiance and that he has forgotten his sentimental attachment to her and may even actively dislike her. Her reaction, when she finds herself thus excluded, is a violent change from her tenderness to hostility. So there is in fact a carefully conceived psychological basis for the metamorphosis of the charming Mrs. Mackenzie into the terrible Campaigner of the *The Newcomes,* and for that of Mrs. Baynes from match-maker to match-breaker in *Philip.*

Thackeray usually offers a social motive as well for this change in the daughter's mother. Mrs. Baynes says she wants a better financial match for Charlotte than the out-at-elbow Philip, and Mrs. Mackenzie is at her worst when Colonel Newcome has lost her money. But the sexual motive of thwarted tenderness for the son-in-law is undoubtedly present too, and is perhaps the more genuine.

Freud describes just this process in the relationship of mother, daughter, and son-in-law when he is discussing the impulse towards incest and its suppression:

A mother, as she grows older, saves herself from the uneventfulness of her emotional life by putting herself in her children's place, by identifying herself with them; and this she does by making their emotional experiences her own. . . . A mother's sympathetic identification with her daughter can easily go so far that she herself falls in love with the man her daughter loves; and in glaring instances this may lead to severe forms of neurotic illness as a result of her violent mental struggles against this emotional situation. In any case, it very frequently happens that a mother-in-law is subject to an *impulse* to fall in love in this way, and this impulse itself or an opposing trend are added to the tumult of conflicting forces in her mind. And very often the unkind, sadistic components of her love are directed on to her son-in-law in order that the forbidden, affectionate ones may be the more severely suppressed.[6]

It is clear that Thackeray does have such a situation in mind, and that he regards a woman like Mrs. Baynes as neurotic. "Ah fond mother of fair daughters!" Mr. Batchelor moralizes in *Lovel the Widower*, "how strange thy passion is to add to thy titles that of mother-in-law! I am told, when you have got the title, it is often but a bitterness and a disappointment" (*Works*, XVII, 90).

To notice the sexual motivation which Thackeray clearly attributed to mothers-in-law, and the sexual rivalry that is always implicit in the mother-daughter relationship, is to find an added tension in certain key relationships in the novels.

Many critics have noticed that Thackeray anticipates modern psychoanalytical discoveries when he says of Helen Pendennis's supervision of her son's loves, "I have no doubt there is a sexual jealousy on the mother's part, and a secret pang" (*Pendennis*, 298). And indeed there is much here which suggests an Oedipal relationship between mother and son like that between Hamlet and Gertrude, with whom Thackeray repeatedly compares them. In the history of Pen's loves, his mother Helen is always the jealous rival; the only woman she is willing to see Pen marry is Laura. As Ennis points out,[7] this does not represent a conquest of her jealousy; "rather it was an effort to hold on to her son by lashing him to a bride whom she had reared as a virtual extension of her own personality." Laura, we remember, is Helen's ward and the daughter of the man she had loved. Helen's matchmaking between Pen and Laura is so eager that in Chapter XXVII, when she wakes Pen up early, pushes him out into the garden to propose, and watches the scene from behind the window, it becomes definitely repellent. It is no accident that the only woman she wants Pen to marry is virtually her own daughter; for, after the usual pattern of Thackeray's mothers-in-law elect, she is vicariously wooing her daughter's lover herself; in this case, however, the lover is her own son. There is even a hint that she too would have become a hostile and thwarted "mother-in-law" had her match-making been successful;

---

[6] *Totem and Taboo*, in *The Standard Edition of the Complete Psychological Works of Sigmund Freud*, ed. James Strachey *et al.* (London, 1955–), XIII, 15.
[7] *Op. cit.*, p. 159.

much later in the book Laura shrewdly observes, "If Pen had loved me as you wished, I should have gained him, but I should have lost you, mamma, I know I should" (716).

There is a clear depiction of the sexual attraction between the daughter's lover and her mother in *Esmond*, where Henry, after trying for ten years to make Rachel his mother-in-law, finally makes her his wife instead.[8] There is an interesting repetition of the symbolism of "The Ravenswing" in the fact that Rachel, like Mrs. Crump, loses her hair. It is when she catches the smallpox, and Beatrix escapes with her father; and the event marks a turning-point in Rachel's life, after which her daughter begins to monopolize the love of both her husband and her young admirer, Henry. The main psychological tension in the novel is the triangle situation in which mother and daughter are rivals for the lover; it is this that gives a deeply ironic significance to such scenes as that in which Henry kisses Beatrix's foot while Rachel looks on:

> Mamma's feet began to pat on the floor during this operation, and Beatrix, whose bright eyes nothing escaped, saw that little mark of impatience. She ran up and embraced her mother, with her usual cry of, "Oh, you silly little mamma: your feet are quite as pretty as mine," says she: "they are, cousin, though she hides 'em; but the shoemaker will tell you that he makes for both off the same last."
>
> "You are taller than I am, dearest," says her mother, blushing over her whole sweet face—"and—and it is your hand, my dear, and not your foot he wants you to give him," and she said it with a hysteric laugh, that had more of tears than laughter in it; laying her head on her daughter's fair shoulder, and hiding it there. They made a very pretty picture together, and looked like a pair of sisters (*Esmond*, 336).

We remember that even when her beautiful rival Beatrix is out of the way, and she is safely married to Henry, Rachel is jealous of her second daughter, the child of her old age (9).

Incidentally, Thackeray's continuing interest in this triangle relationship is attested by his choice of a poem by Monkton Milnes for inclusion in *The Cornhill Magazine* in 1860. The poem, called "Unspoken Dialogue," depicts just such a situation.

The relationship between Rosey and Mrs. Mackenzie, with the

---

[8] See William H. Marshall, "Dramatic Irony in *Henry Esmond*," *Revue des langues vivantes*, 35–42, citing Howard O. Brogan, "Rachel Esmond and the Dilemma of the Victorian Ideal of Womanhood," *Eng. Lit. Hist.*, XIII (1946), 226n.

mother's strange alternation between effusive tenderness and spiteful enmity, is carefully evoked. We know that Mrs. Mackenzie, besides her brief flirtation with Clive, had at one time set her cap at his father. "Should you like a stepmother, Mr. Clive, or should you prefer a wife?" a friend asks him, during her husband-hunting campaign (*Newcomes*, 285). Thus, when she finds that Rosey has monopolized Colonel Newcome's affection as well as Clive's, she is doubly thwarted, and correspondingly savage to the men. But she maintains her stranglehold on her daughter. Jung describes the mother-complex of a daughter, which consists in identification with the mother, in these terms: "The mother lives out for her beforehand all that the girl might have lived for herself. . . . The daughter leads a shadow existence, often visibly sucked dry by her mother, and she prolongs her mother's life by a sort of continuous blood transfusion." [9] The image recalls Mrs. Shum of *The Yellowplush Papers*, "who stuck by [her daughter's] side as close as a wampire, and made her retchider and retchider" (*Works*, I, 182); and the general description is vividly incarnated in Mrs. Mackenzie's relation with Rosey. Pendennis finds Clive and his family in reduced circumstances in Boulogne. Rosey, dominated by her mother, is already sickening:

> The young woman being in the habit of letting mamma judge for her, continued it in this instance; and whether her husband stayed or went, seemed to be equally content or apathetic. "And is it not most kind and generous of dear Mr. and Mrs. Pendennis to propose to receive Mr. Newcome and the colonel?" This opportunity for gratitude being pointed out to Rosey, she acquiesced in it straightway—it was very kind of me, Rosey was sure. "And don't you ask after dear Mrs. Pendennis and the dear children—you poor, suffering, darling child?" Rosey, who had neglected this inquiry, immediately hoped Mrs. Pendennis and the children were well. The overpowering mother had taken utter possession of this poor little thing. Rosey's eyes followed the Campaigner about, and appealed to her at all moments. She sat under Mrs. Mackenzie as a bird before a boa-constrictor, doomed—fluttering—fascinated (*Newcomes*, 935).

For all the sentimental imagery of mother and daughter as "two lilies twining together" and the like, there is also the complementary imagery of mother and daughter as boa-constrictor and bird, vampire and victim. In Thackeray's last novel, the fragment *Denis Duval*, the

---

[9] "Psychological Aspects of the Mother Archetype," *The Collected Works of C. G. Jung*, ed. Sir Herbert Read *et al.* (London, 1954–), 9, pt. ii.

heroine's mother in a fit of madness actually tries to kill her baby daughter. The very closeness of the bond between mother and daughter makes their enmity the more savage when they become rivals.

Such is the relationship which Thackeray described in the novels. It is tempting to find parallels in the development of his own relationship with Mrs. Shawe. We know she is depicted in the savage Campaigner and the hostile Mrs. Baynes; it seems likely that she is also the original of the attractive Mrs. Mackenzie and the tender Mrs. Baynes.

Like Mrs. Baynes, Mrs. Shawe was apparently not always averse to Thackeray as a suitor for Isabella. In his letters to his fiancée there are certainly hints of a definite tenderness towards her mother. "Give my love to yr. Mother" (*Letters*, I, 302) is stereotyped enough; but "ask your dear Mother to bestow 10000000 kisses on you and place them to the account of your obedient Servant" (307) certainly does suggest the kind of triangle relationship that exists in *Esmond*. It is possible, in fact, that it was not his relation with his mother or with Jane Brookfield alone that he had in mind when he created the Henry-Rachel situation, but his relation with Mrs. Shawe as well.

One of Thackeray's letters to Isabella in particular seems to have turned Mrs. Shawe against him. He wrote: "Are you ready and willing to give up your home, & your bedfellow, and your kind mother, to share the fate of a sulky grey headed old fellow with a small income, & a broken nose?" (303). Isabella's answering letter, evidently written under the influence of her mother, has not survived, but its contents are suggested in Thackeray's reply:

> What in God's name have I been saying to hurt you (for I see you are hurt) and your Mother?—What a scoundrel should I be were I to endeavour to weaken such a tie as exists between you two—The separation to wh. I alluded did not go farther than the bedroom—If I recollect rightly this was the chief object of my thoughts at the moment, and I opined that you would be unwilling to quit your bedfellow, and your present comfortable home for another with me. If you are my wife you must sleep in my bed and live in my house—voilà tout—I have no latent plans—no desire for excluding you from those whom I shd. think very meanly of you, were you to neglect (*Letters*, I, 309).

"*Voilà tout*"!—this would hardly placate Mrs. Shawe if, as seems possible, the reason for her anger was her full realization at last that it was Isabella and not herself who was to share Thackeray's bed. Possibly it was not disapproval of Thackeray's ardour as a lover that

Vanity Fair

by Kathleen Tillotson

I

Thackeray's first full-length novel began to appear when he was thirty-five; it represents a fresh start in his literary career, and the emergence of such a novel as a "first" novel has something of the miraculous. Behind him lay ten or twelve years of miscellaneous journalism—writing verses, sketches, reviews, and tales, works most of which seemed in comparison "jokes, and schoolboy exercises as it were." [1] He had written under many disguises—Charles Yellowplush, Ikey Solomons, Fitz-Boodle, Our Fat Contributor, Michael Angelo Titmarsh, and over a dozen more; the multiplicity suggests an unwillingness to commit himself, an awareness that he had not yet found his medium. "Pen and Pencil Sketches of English Society," the original title, and later sub-title, of *Vanity Fair,* well describes the main mass of his earlier writing, but is ludicrously inadequate to the novel. There is common material, a common preoccupation with snobs and humbugs; but there is in these writings little preparation for a work so large in scale, so complex in organization or so mature in outlook, as *Vanity Fair.* Some preparation for its deeper tone may be found in Thackeray's private life; in the new stability of his *ménage,*[2] his change from Bohemianism to domesticity, and the greater assurance of his view of life and of the writer's function.[3] It is possible by such means to account for one change that is manifest in *Vanity Fair:* the enfold-

"Vanity Fair." From *Novels of the Eighteen-Forties,* by Kathleen Tillotson (London: Oxford University Press, 1954), pp. 224–56. Copyright 1954 by Oxford University Press. Reprinted by permission of the author and the publisher. The chapter reprinted here is only part of Prof. Tillotson's discussion of *Vanity Fair.* Cross references in the notes have been modified or dropped.

[1] *The Letters and Private Papers of . . . Thackeray,* ed. Gordon N. Ray, 4 vols. (Cambridge, Mass., 1945–46) , ii. 316; letter to A. Hayward, 5 September 1847.

[2] In June 1846 he took a house in Kensington and in the autumn brought his young daughters to live with him.

[3] Cf. *Letters,* ii. 234, 255–6, 282–3.

ing of the satirist within the moralist. For the first time, Thackeray is openly the preacher.

And while the moralist, who is holding forth on the cover (an accurate portrait of your humble servant), professes to wear neither gown nor bands, but only the very same longeared livery in which his congregation is arrayed: yet, look you, one is bound to speak the truth as far as one knows it, whether one mounts a cap and bells or a shovel-hat; and a deal of disagreeable matter must come out in the course of such an undertaking.[4]

The firm planning and complex unity of the novel must be partly explained by long preliminary reflection; such an interval for premeditation, unlikely for any earlier work, being here allowed by the early false start and the publishers' rejections. *Vanity Fair,* more than any later novel save *Esmond,* bears the marks of what Trollope called "forethought . . . the elbowgrease of the novelist"; and more than any, it has at the same time the buoyant improvisation in detail arising from the practised skill of the journalist.[5]

But the earlier writings contribute one important connecting thread to the "figure in the carpet" of Thackeray the novelist. That is, Thackeray's constant *criticism* of novel-conventions, seen especially in his many reviews and his burlesques. For many years before the publication of *Vanity Fair* he had been clearing the ground for himself and his readers by indicating the kinds of novel he would never write. He had taken his full share in *Fraser's* campaign against Bulwer;[6] in 1844–5 he was reviewing novels by Mrs. Trollope, Lever, and Disraeli; his *Catherine,* as we have seen, was directed against the "Newgate novels" of the thirties, especially Bulwer's *Eugene Aram* and Ainsworth's *Jack Sheppard.* There is a more affectionate teasing of historical romances in *A Legend of the Rhine* (1845) and *Rebecca and Rowena, A Romance upon Romance;*[7] and in the same year as *Vanity Fair* he produced his most specific and exuberant burlesques, in *Punch's Prize Novelists,* where the unmistakable targets are Bulwer

[4] Ch. viii, which opens No. III. What are now chs. i–ix were originally written early in 1845. See Gordon N. Ray, "Vanity Fair," in *Essays by Divers Hands,* Royal Society of Literature, N.S. XXV (1950), 92–93.

[5] The buoyancy is also that of good health (which Charlotte Brontë regarded as indispensable equipment for a serial-writer), and contrasts with the intermittent lassitude of the later novels. Thackeray was never really well after the serious illness of 1849, which interrupted the publication of *Pendennis.*

[6] E.g. *Yellowplush Papers,* viii. (*The Oxford Thackeray,* ed. George Saintsbury, 17 vols. [Oxford, 1908], i. 315–33. Hereafter referred to as *Works.*)

[7] This was first planned in 1841; the first version appeared in *Fraser's* in 1846, the revised version as a "Christmas Book" in 1849.

Lytton, Disraeli, Lever, G. P. R. James, Mrs. Gore, and Fenimore Cooper.[8] Here he proclaims his rejection especially of pretentiousness of style,[9] of sham romance, of the pseudo-heroic, and all the stereotypes through which the novelist evades his responsibility for giving both an impression and an interpretation of life. These burlesques bear the same serious relation to Thackeray's own creative work as do Chaucer's *Sir Thopas* and Jane Austen's *Volume the First* and *Love and Freindship* to theirs; there is the same half-delighted familiarity with the original to weight and yet soften the attack, the same steady discrimination between the fake and the genuine. And like Chaucer and Jane Austen, Thackeray continues this criticism obliquely in his own narratives. In *Vanity Fair* even the method of burlesque survives in an early chapter.

We might have treated this subject in the genteel, or in the romantic, or in the facetious manner. Suppose we had laid the scene in Grosvenor-square, with the very same adventures—would not some people have listened? Suppose we had shown how Lord Joseph Sedley fell in love, and the Marquis of Osborne became attached to Lady Amelia, with the full consent of the Duke, her noble father: or instead of the supremely genteel, suppose we had resorted to the entirely low, and described what was going on in Mr. Sedley's kitchen;—how black Sambo was in love with the cook, (as indeed he was), and how he fought a battle with the coachman in her behalf; how the knife-boy was caught stealing a cold shoulder of mutton, and Miss Sedley's new *femme de chambre* refused to go to bed without a wax candle; such incidents might be made to provoke much delightful laughter, and be supposed to represent scenes of "life." Or if, on the contrary, we had taken a fancy for the terrible, and made the lover of the new *femme de chambre* a professional burglar, who bursts into the house with his band, slaughters black Sambo at the feet of his master, and carries off Amelia

[8] They were collected, with some omissions, in *Miscellanies*, ii (1856) under the title *Novels by Eminent Hands*. The separate titles are *George de Barnwell*, by Sir E. L. B. L., Bart.; *Codlingsby*, by D. Shrewsberry, Esq.; *Phil Fogarty a tale of the Fighting Onety-oneth*, by Harry Rollicker; *Barbazure*, by G. P. R. Jeames, Esq., &c.; *Lords and Liveries*, by the authoress of *Dukes and Déjeuners, Hearts and Diamonds, Marchionesses and Milliners*, &c., &c.; *The Stars and Stripes*, by the author of *The Last of the Mulligans*. See also *Crinoline*, by Jeames de la Pluche; and "A Plan for a Prize Novel" (1851), in which the "novel with a purpose" is mocked. It was Thackeray's intention to include Dickens, but he was dissuaded by Bradbury and Evans. Lever and Disraeli were the authors most offended, and both retaliated with satirical portraits of Thackeray (in *Roland Cashel* and *Endymion*).

[9] Cf. letter to Lady Blessington, 1848 (*Letters*, ii. 485): "there are [in Lytton's novels] big words which make me furious, and a pretentious fine writing against which I can't help rebelling."

in her nightdress, not to be let loose again till the third volume, we
should easily have constructed a tale of thrilling interest, through the
fiery chapters of which the reader should hurry, panting.[10]

This is perhaps overweighted; more effective is a passing side glance
at the conventions, as in the opening of the Waterloo number:

> We do not claim to rank among the military novelists. Our place
> is with the non-combatants. When the decks are cleared for action
> we go below and wait meekly. We should only be in the way of the
> manœuvres that the gallant fellows are performing overhead.[11]

So much for the authors of *Phil Fogarty* and *The Last of the Mulligans.*

But such parenthetic comments are merely incidental to the pervasive and positive criticism offered by *Vanity Fair.* One of Thackeray's
most perceptive critics writes of it that

> Coming as it did into the world of fiction occupied by the writers
> burlesqued in the "Novels by Eminent Hands," its substitution of
> truth for convention had something almost fierce in it.[12]

Its difference from popular novels—a difference concealed under intermittent and teasing similarities—and the author's seeming contempt for popular taste struck Thackeray's early readers more than we
realize. He takes cunning advantage of the serial-writer's confiding
relation with his public, but his attitude is not as friendly as Dickens's.
Deliberately he defeats conventional expectation; he is at pains to
warn his readers in the opening chapter that "Amelia is not a heroine," and often employs her as a medium for mockery at the sweet
insipid contemporary novel-heroine. It is indeed part of his object to
exclude heroism:

> holding that the Art of Novels is . . . to convey as strongly as possible
> the sentiment of reality as opposed to a tragedy or poem, which may
> be heroical.[13]

This exclusion is again proclaimed in the sub-title given to the novel
when it appeared in volume form: "A Novel without a Hero." [14] His
intention was not, as some have thought, to substitute for a hero a

[10] Ch. vi. The burlesque is much fuller in the first edition, where Thackeray
went on to give actual samples of the rejected modes. See *Works,* xi, Appendix,
pp. 882–4.
[11] Ch. xxx.
[12] W. C. Brownell, *Victorian Prose Masters* (1902), p. 33.
[13] Letter of May 1851 (*Letters,* ii. 772–3).
[14] The phrase appears in the letters as early as March 1846: *Letters,* ii. 233.

heroine with masculine resourcefulness; nor yet to strip the semblance of novel-hero from George Osborne in order to reveal unsuspected heroism in the uncouth Dobbin. He refuses the role to Dobbin too. This history has been written to very little purpose if the reader has not perceived that the Major was a spooney.[15] He rejects heroism in the name of morality as well as of "reality."

> My object . . . is to indicate, in cheerful terms, that we are for the most part an abominably foolish and selfish people . . . all eager after vanities. Everybody is you see in that book,—for instance if I had made Amelia a higher order of woman there would have been no vanity in Dobbins falling in love with her, whereas the impression at present is that he is a fool for his pains[,] that he has married a silly little thing, and in fact has found out his error . . . I want to leave everybody dissatisfied and unhappy at the end of the story—we ought all to be with our own and all other stories.[16]

This rejection of heroism, this conveyance of the "sentiment of reality," was recognized as a novelty by contemporary readers. Their response might be approving or otherwise. Mrs. Procter found it a relief that the "characters [were] neither devils nor angels . . . neither appear through a trapdoor, nor change their father and mother in the third volume";[17] *Fraser's* reviewer was repelled by "a loathsome truth, like that of Hogarth in *Gin Lane*." [18] The revulsion of some readers of Thackeray lent itself to images of nausea; Ruskin said that he "settled like a meat fly on whatever one had got for dinner and made one sick of it";[19] Whately was more elaborate:

> If you were to serve up a dinner with top dish a roasted fox, stuffed with tobacco and basted with train oil, and at bottom an old ram goat, dressed with the hair on, and seasoned with assafoetida, the side dishes being plain boiled rice, this would give an idea of what his fictions are to my taste.[20]

By these admittedly extreme examples we may gauge the general level of defeated expectation in Thackeray's readers. They found "the

---

[15] Ch. lxvi.

[16] Letter to Robert Bell, September 1848 (*Letters*, ii. 423).

[17] Letter to Abraham Hayward, 23 July 1847 (*Letters*, ii. 312–13).

[18] Compare the *Times* reviewer who remarked on a story illustrated by the author that he preferred the sketches, because "he cannot *draw* his men and women with their skins off."

[19] *Fors Clavigera*, ii, letter xxxi.

[20] Letter to Nassau Senior, 12 January 1853; E. Whately, *Life and Correspondence of Richard Whately* (1866), ii. 263–4. *Vanity Fair* was the only one of the novels that Whately had "been able to get through."

established usages of novels . . . entirely set aside";[21] they were cheated even of a neat ending. The curtain does not fall either on a death-bed or wedding bells, both of which had in the past been the objects of Thackeray's mockery:

> It is much better to look at the end of a novel; and when I read "There is a fresh green mound in Brentford Churchyard, and a humble stone, on which is inscribed the name of 'Anna Maria' " . . . I shut the book at once declining to agitate my feelings needlessly.[22]

> You, dear young ladies, who get your knowledge of life from the circulating library, may be led to imagine that when the marriage business is done, and Emilia is whisked off in the new travelling carriage, by the side of the enraptured Earl; or Belinda, breaking away from the tearful embraces of her excellent mother, dries her own lovely eyes upon the throbbing waistcoat of her bridegroom—you may be apt, I say, to suppose that all is over then, that Emilia and the Earl are going to be happy for the rest of their lives in his Lordship's romantic castle in the north, and Belinda and her young clergyman to enjoy uninterrupted bliss in their rose-trellised parsonage in the west of England . . .[23]

The early arrival of Amelia's marriage (in the eighth number) must in itself have made readers suspicious; and Thackeray's comment draws attention to his divergence:

> As his hero and heroine pass the matrimonial barrier, the novelist generally drops the curtain, as if the drama were over then: the doubts and struggles of life ended: as if, once landed in the marriage country, all were green and pleasant there: and wife and husband had nothing to do but to link each other's arms together, and wander gently downwards towards old age in happy and perfect fruition.[24]

When the return of Dobbin brings the situation within sight of conventional sentiment, a dramatized comment is ready to hand.

> "There they are," said Miss Polly. . . . She was a confidante at once of the whole business. She knew the story as well as if she had read it in one of her favourite novel-books—"Fatherless Fanny," or the "Scottish Chiefs." [25]

But Dobbin does not win his Amelia (nor Laura her Pendennis) until

[21] *Fraser's* (September 1848), p. 332.
[22] "Jérôme Paturot. With considerations on novels in general"; *Fraser's* (September 1843; *Works*, vi. 321) .
[23] *Rebecca and Rowena*, ch. i (*Works*, x. 499–500) .
[24] *Vanity Fair*, ch. xxvi.
[25] Ch. lviii.

some illusions have been lost on both sides. Within sight of the end of *Vanity Fair* Thackeray produces his "fake" conclusion, puncturing its sentiment by a single word:

> This is what he pined after. Here it is—the summit, the end—the last page of the third volume. Good-bye, Colonel—God bless you, honest William!—Farewell, dear Amelia—Grow green again, tender little parasite, round the rugged old oak to which you cling!

to be followed on the actual last page by the true conclusion:

> the Colonel seizing up his little Janey, of whom he is fonder than of anything in the world—fonder even than of his "History of the Punjaub."
>
> "Fonder than he is of me," Emmy thinks, with a sigh. But he never said a word to Amelia that was not kind and gentle; or thought of a want of hers that he did not try to gratify.
>
> Ah! *Vanitas Vanitatum!* . . .

So too does Thackeray evade obvious "poetic justice," the slick "nemesis" on which Charley Tudor's editor insisted;[26] Carker may be cut to pieces by an express train, but our last sight of Becky is as a wealthy and charitable lady hanging about Bath and Cheltenham and arranging stalls at Fancy fairs. (Though this is perhaps the most fitting retribution for her—to be driven to "religion," the social climber's last resource.)

In *Vanity Fair*, though not always in his later novels, Thackeray also avoids, as Mrs. Procter points out, startling and sensational turns of plot: what he was later to call "the professional parts of novels," choosing an instance with rueful self-mockery:

> Ask *me*, indeed, to pop a robber under a bed, to hide a will which will be forthcoming in due season! [27]

The most nearly "professional" situation in *Vanity Fair* is Rawdon's discovery of Becky and Lord Steyne, which approaches the stock scene of the penny theatres:

> There is always a wicked lord kicked out of the window. . . . Enter sturdy Blacksmith.—Scuffle between Blacksmith and Aristocratic minion: exit wicked Lord out of the window.[28]

[26] See ch. xix of Trollope's *Three Clerks* (1858).
[27] *Roundabout Papers*, "On a Peal of Bells." This paper appeared in the *Cornhill* in September 1862, and *Philip*, in which a hidden will is finally discovered, had been concluded in August. Compare the mystery about Blanche's parentage in *Pendennis*.
[28] "Charity and Humour," 1852 (*Works*, x. 624). In "Before the Curtain" Lord Steyne is referred to as the "Wicked Nobleman."

But the divergence of Becky from the penny theatre's innocent victim is decisive. The ironic use of stereotyped novel-material would also be evident to contemporaries in the opening situation and its development through the novel. The varying fortunes and contrasted characters of two closely associated young women was a stock pattern in novels, and indeed traditional in romance. Good girl and bad (often also blonde and brunette) were paired in numerous novels, as sisters, twins, half-sisters (preferably unaware of their kinship), cousins or friends.[29] But never, surely, with such subtleties and surprises as in *Vanity Fair*.

II

Thackeray turns away, then, from heroes and heroines, from the conventional ending, from the "professional parts of novels." And he evades the contemporary categories: *Vanity Fair* is not a novel of low life (its lowest level is the apartments at Fulham, or—unexpectedly—the elder Sir Pitt's *ménage* in Great Gaunt Street), nor of high life (the highest level is the ball at Gaunt House, which would contain some surprises for the devotees of Mrs. Gore);[30] it is not a military novel, despite Waterloo, nor a domestic novel, despite the number of family scenes. It is not historical, although it is a novel about the past; the period in which it is set is robbed of its usual glamour, and the past is strangely interpenetrated by the present. Thackeray's preface, "Before the Curtain," illustrates his almost malicious way of teasing expectation:

> There are scenes of all sorts; some dreadful combats, some grand and lofty horse-riding, some scenes of high life, some of very middling indeed: some love-making for the sentimental, and some light comic business; the whole accompanied by appropriate scenery, and brilliantly illuminated by the Author's own candles.

[29] A few closely contemporary instances are Miss Jewsbury's *The Half-Sisters* (1848), Lady Georgiana Fullerton's *Grantley Manor* (1847), Mrs. Gore's *The Diamond and the Pearl* (1849). Hannah Maria Jones in *The Curate's Daughter, or the Twin Roses of Arundale* (n.d.; 1830's?) had made great play with the sensational if implausible situation of identical twins, indistinguishable in appearance but as different in character as wolf and lamb. *Sense and Sensibility* makes its original use of the contrasted-sister pattern; and there is even something like the Amelia-Becky contrast in *Mansfield Park*.

[30] Mrs. Proctor said, "He has avoided the two extremes in which so many of our popular writers delight" (*Letters*, ii. 313).

He promises variety; but he also gives unity, and not only by the continuous presence of the "author's own candles." The principles of organization in *Vanity Fair* must next be considered: the positive truth which Thackeray substitutes for the conventions of fiction.

By choosing as his field "the debatable land between the middle classes and the aristocracy" [31] he takes a social area which, though less extensive than Dickens's, gives him considerable vertical range. All the characters are seen in relation to "society," living in it or on it; for each character he defines the rung on the ladder, the place on the slippery slope, the rocky ledge where they hang by finger-tips. None are unplaced; which means that the "other nation" is excluded —it was not beyond his ken, but he chose to ignore it here.

There is less scope for oddity than in Dickens's world, for Vanity Fair is a world in which it is important to conform. Those who give up the pretence of conforming, like Sir Pitt Crawley or Lord Steyne, show that Thackeray can provide his own grotesques, with only the monstrosity which actual life provides. Specific comparison with Dickens illustrates Thackeray's different attitude to reality: the observed reality is often the same, but Thackeray mines into it, where Dickens makes it a springboard into fantasy. Even in his names Thackeray wishes "to convey the sentiment of reality." Dickens's may be actual, but they are chosen for their oddity and comic appropriateness, while Thackeray masks his satire in plausibility, preferring a subtle suggestiveness; as in "Steyne," with its pun and its relation to Regency Brighton; or the contrast, rich in association, of the liquid and romantic "Amelia Sedley" with the hinted racial astuteness of "Rebecca Sharp."

Thackeray's characters exist in a denser context than perhaps any characters in fiction. They are aware of past time; they draw on childhood memories.

> "Am I much better to do now in the world than I was when I was the poor painter's daughter, and wheedled the grocer round the corner for sugar and tea? Suppose I had married Francis who was so fond of me. . . ." [32]

It is the only time we ever hear of "Francis." In the shadow, just beyond every character, but ready to catch the spotlight for a single in-

---

[31] Review-article by W. C. Roscoe in *National Review* (January 1856); collected in *Poems and Essays* (2 vols., 1860).

[32] Ch. xli.

stant when needed, seem to be all the people the character has ever met. Here is the sole appearance of Edward Dale:

> the junior of the house, who purchased the spoons for the firm, was, in fact, very sweet upon Amelia, and offered for her in spite of all. He married Miss Louisa Cutts (daughter of Higham and Cutts, the eminent corn-factors) with a handsome fortune in 1820; and is now living in splendour, and with a numerous family, at his elegant villa, Muswell Hill.[33]

Odd corners of their houses, or possessions, may similarly light up at a touch. Their ancestries and family histories may be given; the baptismal names of the Crawley ancestors, according well with their surname, epitomize the political vanities of two centuries. And no single paragraph about Lord Steyne tells us more about him and his society, or about vanity in high places, than that list of titles and honours in his "obituary":

> the Most Honourable George Gustavus, Marquis of Steyne, Earl of Gaunt and of Gaunt Castle, in the Peerage of Ireland, Viscount Hellborough, Baron Pitchley and Grillsby, a Knight of the Most Noble Order of the Garter, of the Golden Fleece of Spain, of the Russian Order of Saint Nicholas of the First Class, of the Turkish Order of the Crescent, First Lord of the Powder Closet and Groom of the Back Stairs, Colonel of the Gaunt or Regent's Own Regiment of Militia, a Trustee of the British Museum, an Elder Brother of the Trinity House, a Governor of the White Friars, and D.C.L. . . .[34]

Such fullness of documentation, never introduced heavily, but ready to be drawn on where it is needed, is significant of Thackeray's emphasis on character in its social relations. This has been noted by all his critics, and best defined by Brownell:

> Thackeray's personages are never portrayed in isolation. They are a part of the *milieu* in which they exist, and which has itself therefore much more distinction and relief than an environment which is merely a framework. How they regard each other, how they feel toward and what they think of each other, the mutuality of their very numerous and vital relations, furnishes an important strand in the texture of the story in which they figure. Their activities are modified by the air they breathe in common. Their conduct is controlled, their ideas affected, even their desires and ambitions dictated, by the general ideas of the society that includes them.[35]

[33] Ch. xvii.
[34] Ch. lxiv.
[35] W. C. Brownell, op. cit., p. 29.

But it would be wrong to see Thackeray as a fatalist about character. That Becky believes she might have been a good woman on five thousand a year is itself part of her character ("Becky consoled herself . . .");[36] some virtues may be accidental, but "circumstance only brings out the latent defect or quality, and does not create it." [37] Thackeray is not optimistic enough about human nature (less so, for example, than George Eliot) to have much belief in the power of people to change themselves:

> We alter very little. . . . Our mental changes are like our grey hairs and our wrinkles—but the fulfilment of the plan of mortal growth and decay.[38]

His characters are so mixed, so often on a moral borderland, so subject to time, and also so gradually unfolded—often with unpredictable detail—that they do not give the impression of being static. But they are not shown as evolving, nor do they undergo much inward conflict; and so the unity given to a novel by dominating or developing characters is not found. Only one of Thackeray's novels—*Pendennis* —is even formally built upon the fortunes of a single character; and Arthur Pendennis is less an interesting individual than a nineteenth-century variant of Everyman.

III

Without recourse to obvious devices, without a hero or heroine or any single central figure, without any "inward" study of development in character, Thackeray nevertheless makes us feel *Vanity Fair* a unity. This has sometimes been underestimated, and the novel apologized for as loose, rambling, and casual, though admitted to be rich and comprehensive: the apology may even lay the blame on the serial form. But the serial novel, serially written, is, as I have already suggested, really the less likely to be loose and rambling; only some degree of forethought makes such writing even possible; and the reader's interest, spread over a year and a half, will not be held unless there is a genuine continuity and a firm centre of interest. It is a contention of this whole study that both novelists and critics of this time were interested in "unity"; we may recall that Lytton claimed that

---

[36] Ch. xli.
[37] *Pendennis*, ch. lix; and cf. *Esmond*, Book II, ch. i.
[38] *Pendennis*, ch. lix.

"composition" should be recognized in novels as in paintings, and *Fraser's* critic of 1851 says firmly:

> One of the great achievements . . . in the art of the novelist is unity. If we cannot get that, the next best thing is progress.[39]

A more reputable critical view, one indeed that is insidiously tempting, is that Thackeray's formal purpose is a "picture" of society. This view, so persuasively set forth in Lubbock's *Craft of Fiction,* does admit of composition, even if "picture" is extended to "panorama"; but it accounts only for a part of *Vanity Fair.* For it allows too little for our fascinated sense of progression; too little also for Thackeray the moralist.

The clear and obvious line of progression in the novel is surely also, when closely considered, the chief of its unities: that is, the converging and diverging, parallel and contrasting fortunes of the two girls, Rebecca Sharp and Amelia Sedley.[40] In narrative terms, the basis of the contrast is simple (the moral contrast, on the other hand, is ironic and complex); it is that Rebecca attempts actively to shape her own fortunes, while Amelia passively accepts hers. They begin with "the world before them," on their last day at Minerva House Academy in Chiswick Mall. Their manner of leaving Miss Pinkerton's differentiates them at the outset in character as well as social status. Rebecca is nineteen and Amelia sixteen, but Rebecca has never been a child (Thackeray refers early to her "dismal precocity") and Amelia is never to grow up. But throughout the first number (chapters i to iv) their similarity as well as difference is emphasized; both are occupied with the "vanity" of husband-hunting (the title of chapter ii is "In which Miss Sharp and Miss Sedley prepare to open the campaign"); Rebecca is laying her snares for Jos Sedley, Amelia sighing and smiling at George Osborne. In the closing number, after seventeen years, Amelia at last consents to forget George, and Rebecca at last has Jos inescapably in her toils. Throughout the narrative a balance of interest between Amelia and Rebecca is steadily maintained; in every number there is something of both, and when they are apart the juxtaposition of chapters defining the progress in their histories still forms a pattern. In Number V (chapters xv to xviii) Rebecca is thrown out of favour with the Crawleys when her marriage to Rawdon is revealed;

---

[39] *Fraser's* (October 1851), p. 382.

[40] The point has of course been made by several critics, from *Fraser's* (September 1848, p. 347) to our own day, but I think with insufficient sense of the subtlety of Thackeray's intentions.

Mr. Sedley has failed in business and George Osborne's defection is threatened, but there is a hopeful turn at the end to bring Amelia's marriage into sight and match the close of Number IV. In Number XIV (chapters xlvii to l) there is a simple contrast between the zenith of Becky's fortunes (presented at Court, dining at Gaunt House) and the nadir of Amelia's (in poverty, and parted from her son). In Number XVI comes Becky's "fall," set beside the first hint of Amelia's "rise," the number closing with Dobbin's return from India (chapter lvi). There are also the subtler running contrasts of Becky's treatment of her son Rawdon, Amelia's of George: subtle, because Thackeray is critical both of heartless neglect and passionate possessiveness. Or the likeness within difference of Amelia's stupid fidelity to her husband's memory, and Becky's stupid infidelity to Rawdon. Each is an egoist; Thackeray's comment when Dobbin leaves Amelia is pointed:

> She didn't wish to marry him, but she wished to keep him. She wished to give him nothing, but that he should give her all. It is a bargain not unfrequently levied in love.[41]

Outside its context, the second of these sentences would be taken as describing Becky.

But the structural ironies are clearest when the two histories converge and entangle:

> [Becky] was thinking in her heart, "It was George Osborne who prevented my marriage."—And she loved George Osborne accordingly.[42]

Her small revenge of malicious teasing in chapter xiv (where these words are echoed) is the prelude to her triumph at Brussels:

> [George] was carrying on a desperate flirtation with Mrs. Crawley. He . . . passed his evenings in the Crawleys' company; losing money to the husband and flattering himself that the wife was dying in love for him. It is very likely that this worthy couple never absolutely conspired, and agreed together in so many words: the one to cajole the young gentleman, whilst the other won his money at cards: but they understood each other perfectly well. . . .[43]

At the ball on the night before Waterloo she receives his note "coiled like a snake among the flowers"—a note whose substance is not divulged until the closing number. The next day she visits the half-suspecting Amelia:

---

[41] Ch. lxvi.
[42] Ch. vi.
[43] Ch. xxix.

Amelia . . . drew back her hand, and trembled all over. "Why are
you here, Rebecca?" she said, still looking at her solemnly, with her
large eyes. These glances troubled her visitor.

"She must have seen him give me the letter at the ball," Rebecca
thought.

But Amelia's accusations are in general terms, and are so answered:

"Amelia, I protest before God, I have done my husband no wrong,"
Rebecca said, turning from her.

"Have you done *me* no wrong, Rebecca? You did not succeed, but
you tried. Ask your heart if you did not?"

She knows nothing, Rebecca thought.[44]

The number ends with George Osborne's death on the battlefield;
from this mid-point in the novel proceed Amelia's simple subsequent
fortunes—ten years of widowhood sentimentally faithful to a mythical
memory, and resistance to Dobbin's suit. The two converge again
when Amelia, abroad with Jos and Dobbin, meets Rebecca, now dis-
graced and outside the social pale, but resilient as ever. She renews her
designs on Jos, and when Dobbin, at last despairing of Amelia, returns to England, finds Amelia in her way. She reproaches her for
refusing Dobbin:

"I tried—I tried my best, indeed I did, Rebecca," said Amelia dep-
recatingly, "but I couldn't forget—"; and she finished her sentence
by looking up at the portrait.

"Couldn't forget *him!*" cried out Becky, "that selfish humbug, that
low-bred cockney dandy, that padded booby, who had neither wit, nor
manners, nor heart. . . . He never cared for you. He used to sneer
about you to me, time after time; and made love to me the week after
he married you."

"It's false! it's false! Rebecca," cried out Amelia, starting up.

"Look there, you fool," Becky said, still with provoking good-humour,
and taking a little paper out of her belt, she opened it and flung it
into Emmy's lap. "You know his handwriting. He wrote that to me—
wanted me to run away with him—gave it me under your nose, the
day before he was shot—and served him right!" Becky repeated.[45]

Apparently then the wheel comes full circle: Becky ending as she began, as Amelia's friend. But Thackeray has one more surprise in store:
the revelation is not decisive, for Amelia has already relented and
written to recall Dobbin. The inner necessity of the scene is rather to

[44] Ch. xxxi.
[45] Ch. lxvii.

leave no sham unexposed, and to keep our moral attitude to the two "heroines" complicated to the last. For Becky's is the true view of the case, and her action righteous, though from mixed motives. But Amelia's actions, although muddle-headed, are to the last motivated by love.

"Anyone who mistakes [Amelia] for a simple character has missed *Vanity Fair*." [46] The mistake has been common, and has in modern times taken the particularly silly form of regarding Amelia as the straight representation of an ideal now outmoded. But even apart from Thackeray's own view, writ large in phrase after phrase, his contemporaries did not unanimously applaud Amelia. Some went even too far in the other direction: "No woman resents Rebecca . . . but every woman resents his selfish and inane Amelia." [47] (It was perhaps more gratifying to the woman of the eighteen-forties, and certainly rarer, to see herself presented in fiction as a clever rogue than as an amiable fool.) If Thackeray has an ideal in mind, then Amelia and Becky are both far (though not equally far) removed from it; of the disproportion between heart and brain possible to the feminine character they provide extreme instances. Some readers may be more legitimately misled by the necessary difference in treatment. The active Becky can be displayed, where the suffering, yielding Amelia must be described. The tone of the description is deliberately ambiguous, seeming often sentimentally protective, but with enough impatience breaking through to show that the author wishes to confuse and make fun of the sentimental reader. It is not necessary to attribute confusion to Thackeray himself; there is room with such a character for genuine indulgence as well as impatience. Besides, he has an ulterior, "literary" motive in Amelia: Becky is a wholly new kind of heroine, Amelia the old kind ironically exposed. It is possible that Amelia may sometimes be imperfectly disengaged from "the unwritten part" of his novels, not quite free from her moorings in his own emotional life;[48] whereas Becky swims free in the pure element of

[46] Brownell, op. cit., p. 31.

[47] Mrs. Jameson, as quoted by J. W. Dodds, *Thackeray* (1941), p. 130; Mrs. Brookfield, and Thackeray's mother made similar comments.

[48] He told Mrs. Brookfield that she was "a piece of Amelia—My Mother is another half: my poor little wife *y est pour beaucoup*" (30 June 1848; *Letters*, ii. 394). But it is difficult to take this seriously; the three women can have had little in common with each other or with Amelia except charm and obstinacy. Perhaps there is something of Jane Brookfield's faithfulness to a husband Thackeray was coming to think unworthy of her. But J. Y. T. Greig, who has pressed this interpretation furthest (in *Thackeray: A Reconsideration, 1950*) seems to make his bricks of very little straw.

art.[49] Becky is one of those characters—like Chaucer's Pardoner—who can fully engage our aesthetic sympathies while defying most of our moral ones; Thackeray is not less a moralist for allowing us to enjoy her as a spectacle, for his judgement of her is firm. Her attraction is partly that of the triumphant knave in a world of knaves and fools; enjoyment is not complicated by pity for the less successful knaves, like the younger Sir Pitt, nor yet for the fools, like Jos Sedley or even Briggs; these belong to the world of satirical comedy, where we have the freedom of feeling that "fools are responsible for their folly." The comic inventiveness of these triumphs provides some of the most brilliant flashes of the book:

> She listened with the tenderest kindly interest, sitting by him, and hemming a shirt for her dear little boy. Whenever Mrs. Rawdon wished to be particularly humble and virtuous, this little shirt used to come out of her work-box. It had got to be too small for Rawdon long before it was finished, though.[50]
>
> "How I have been waiting for you! Stop! not yet—in one minute you shall come in." In that instant she put a rouge-pot, a brandy-bottle, and a plate of broken meat into her bed. . . .
> . . . "I had but one child, one darling, one hope, one joy . . . and they tore it from me;" and she put her hand to her heart with a passionate gesture of despair, burying her face for a moment on the bed.
>
> The brandy-bottle inside clinked up against the plate which held the cold sausage.[51]

But Thackeray does not go too far in enlisting the reader's pleasure on the side of wickedness. For this he had criticized Bulwer and Ainsworth:

> Don't let us have any juggling and thimble-rigging with virtue and vice, so that, at the end of three volumes, the bewildered reader shall not know which is which.[52]

For this he was even, unjustly, criticized himself:

> Sin is fire; and Mr. Thackeray makes fireworks of it.[53]

But his judgement of Becky never falters, and it is made plain to the reader through one character in particular: Rawdon Crawley. The

[49] There are two possible "originals" for Becky, Sydney Morgan and Theresa Reviss; but they can have provided no more than the "germ of the real."
[50] Ch. xliv.
[51] Ch. lxv.
[52] *Catherine*, ch. i (*Works*, iii. 31).
[53] Roscoe, loc. cit.

words in the "discovery" scene are pointed: "I am innocent," says
Becky. "Was she guilty or not?" asks Thackeray, and apparently leaves
it an open question. But the technical question is not the most relevant
one: her essential guilt rests in Rawdon's simple accusation: "You
might have spared me £100, Becky; I have always shared with you."
The words take us back to the night before Waterloo, with Rawdon
making his last dispositions—"my duelling pistols in rosewood case
(same which I shot Captain Marker)"; and Becky stands condemned
of cold-hearted treachery.

The relation of these two is one of the main sources of "progression" in the novel, and is worth tracing. "Rawdon's marriage," says
Thackeray, "was one of the honestest actions which we shall have to
record in any portion of that gentleman's biography." Unlike George
Osborne (the contrast is firmly indicated) he married for love; which
puts him at an initial disadvantage with Becky, who married him in
hopes of his aunt's money.

> Is his case a rare one? and don't we see every day in the world many
> an honest Hercules at the apron-strings of Omphale, and great whis-
> kered Samsons prostrate in Dalilah's lap?" [54]

Becky's contempt is masked at first:

> "If he had but a little more brains," she thought to herself, "I
> might make something of him;" but she never let him perceive the
> opinion she had of him. . . .[55]

But not masked for long; not when Miss Crawley's favour seems again
within reach:

> "You fool! you ought to have gone in, and never come out again,"
> Rebecca said.
> "Don't call me names," said the big guardsman, sulkily, "Perhaps I
> *was* a fool, Becky, but you shouldn't say so." [56]

Their relation is fully and picturesquely defined in the farewell scene
before Waterloo; but its deterioration is also hinted, in the narrative
that so lightly sketches the "three or four years" [57] which follow. At
first, Rawdon's illusions are still intact; "He believed in his wife as
much as the French soldiers in Napoleon"; and with as little grounds.
We are left to infer that, his aunt having died and left him only

[54] Ch. xvi.
[55] Ch. xvii.
[56] Ch. xxv.
[57] Chs. xxxiv, xxxvi, and xxxvii.

£100, Rawdon is no longer an investment worth nursing. Becky is flying at higher game. The scene that marks the change is of the kind that lights up far more than itself: the evening scene in Curzon Street, Becky in the centre of a party of gentlemen including Lord Steyne. (It is our first introduction to Lord Steyne; Thackeray's method is to make us feel that he has been there a long time.) Rawdon is "sitting silent without the circle," engaged in "shearing a Southdown." The closing words mark the grouping as typical:

> "How is Mrs. Crawley's husband," Lord Steyne used to say by way of a good day when they met; and indeed that was now his avocation in life. He was Colonel Crawley no more. He was Mrs. Crawley's husband. . . .
>
> "Hang it, I ain't clever enough for her—I know it. She won't miss me," he used to say: and he was right: his wife did not miss him.
>
> Rebecca was fond of her husband. She was always perfectly good-humoured and kind to him. She did not even show her scorn much for him; perhaps she liked him the better for being a fool. He was her upper servant and *maître d'hôtel.*

Two years later he is "more and more isolated every day . . . beat and cowed into laziness and submission. Dalilah had imprisoned him and cut his hair off, too." [58]

The "discovery" scene is led up to with great skill; Rawdon's arrest is sprung on the reader as on Rawdon himself, and only then does Thackeray wind back over past events to show how Lord Steyne with Becky's connivance had previously got rid of young Rawdon and the "sheepdog" Briggs—"And so two of Rawdon's out-sentinels were in the hands of the enemy." [59] It is as near as he comes to saying that the arrest was framed.

There is a moral comment in the fact that Becky's downfall comes through the relations that she most despised; it is the innocent and stupid who confound her. She calculates brilliantly, but, like Iago, not quite brilliantly enough. Her neglect of her son disturbed Rawdon. When she kissed the child at Queen's Crawley she had not thought that he might say, "You never kiss me at home, mother." Lady Jane "never felt quite the same to Becky after that remark." And Lady Jane's simple kindness defeats Becky's calculation, when she releases Rawdon from the spunging-house in time for him to find Lord Steyne

---

[58] Ch. xlv.

[59] Ch. lii. Greig, missing the subtlety of method, remarks that this chapter "is chronologically misplaced, and was probably an afterthought" (op. cit., p. 116).

at Curzon Street. This is Becky's true nemesis. Contempt for other people is necessary to successful villainy; but within it lie the seeds of its own defeat. The walls of egoism rise, in the end, too high. By suggesting all this, Thackeray does more than condemn Becky; he gives a less pessimistic moral direction to his story. Goodness is not wholly ineffectual.

IV

These, then, are some of the ways in which Thackeray gives shape and purpose to his great pictorial mass; but the most important way has been often undervalued by later readers, because misunderstood. The whole is "brilliantly illuminated by the author's own candles"; Thackeray is constantly present, commenting on the action. Only in this novel is it undisguised. Elsewhere he partly identifies himself with a character—Pendennis, or Esmond; or uses a character as narrator— Pendennis in *The Newcomes* and *Philip*, with Clive and Philip as further "projections" within the story. (The latter device, caught, he admitted, from the despised Lytton, was purposeful: "I shall be able to talk more at ease than in my own person.")[60] In *Vanity Fair* there is no disguise; the author is present, with a varying range of visibility. He talks to us, about the story and characters, or about something it reminds him of;[61] he is frankly the manufacturer of the narrative ("there are some terrific chapters coming presently"); he is the "producer" of particular characters (especially of Amelia, who can do so little for herself); he is by turns the responsible, omniscient narrator ("for novelists have the privilege of knowing everything"),[62] the irresponsible, baffled spectator ("Was she guilty or not?"), even the mere reporter (himself meeting the characters at Pumpernickel in 1830). Above all he is the moral commentator, the "preacher in cap and bells," amused, melancholy, hortatory—and constantly barbing his shafts with a *de te fabula*. The atmosphere of his personality—not his private, but his artistic personality—envelops the story.

Nowadays, apparently, this practice requires defence; and several

---

[60] Letter of August 1853 (*Letters*, iii. 298). There is a hint of it in the use of Tom Eaves in *Vanity Fair*, ch. xlvii.

[61] Sometimes with a journalist's sense for the immediately topical, as in ch. lv: "Fifine went off in a cab, as we have known more exalted persons of her nation to do under similar circumstances." This number appeared in April 1848.

[62] Ch. iii.

lines of defence are valid. There is the historical defence. This method was not new or peculiar to Thackeray, save in extent and subtlety. Behind it lies the tradition of Fielding's role of epic poet, with such modifications as the "comic epic in prose" requires; it is as comedy that Thackeray sees his own novels, and comedy always allows more room for the author. There is also the seeming casualness of Sterne, taking us behind the scenes, showing us the raw material of a novel in process of being worked up. There is also as we have seen the peculiar audience-relation of the serial-writer, reassembling his listeners, responding to their comments with his own. All this helped to make Thackeray's technique easily acceptable in his own time.[63] The average modern reader starts with a prejudice in favour of "dramatic" presentment; the novel having, since Thackeray's time, foregone many of its advantages in favour of a fancied "objectivity," and the novelist having dwindled into invisibility. But to press the historical defence might be to admit a limited appeal: or to suggest that he adopted this method unthinkingly. The true justification lies in its appropriateness to his kind of novel.

Thackeray has often been called the novelist of memory; all his stories are seen restrospectively. "Let us have middle-aged novels," he said in *Rebecca and Rowena*; it is what he gives us, with the light of irony or pathos playing on past fashions and the morning ideals of youth. His commentary is in part a bridge between past and present, suggesting what time changes, what it leaves unchanged; putting past and present alike in a longer perspective. And it is a moral perspective. Thackeray gives us what seems a whole world, densely peopled, varied in scene, with the miscellaneousness and wastage and loose threads of the actual world; but through his comments he makes it plain that he sees the "tower on the toft" above the "field full of folk." The title itself is a comment, the title that came to him in the night "as if a voice had whispered";[64] it suggests both the observer, and the preacher who "cries his sermon." Without Thackeray's own voice, the melancholy and the compassion of his attitude to Vanity Fair might escape us. It is needed merely as relief, from a spectacle that might otherwise be unbearably painful. And not only morally painful, but mentally impoverished. The characters, the best as well as the worst, are almost without ideas; the intellectual atmosphere of the novel is provided by the commentary.

[63] Contemporary objectors were rare; one was G. H. Lewes, in *The Leader* (21 December 1850), p. 929.
[64] *Letters*, i. p. cxxvi.

Can the reader do all this for himself? If he can, and can do it as
well as Thackeray does it for him, he may consider it surplusage.[65]

Thackeray does not escape into commentary from any weakness in
presentation; *Vanity Fair* is particularly rich in single scenes which
reveal his power of presenting characters and action without comment, through dialogue, grouping, and gesture. Nor is he impulsively
allowing his stored reflections to overflow; the effect of casualness in the
commentary is as calculated as in Sterne. The commentary is itself art,
selective and economical. Thackeray never tells everything; he leaves
much to be read between the lines; the tone of intimate confidence
often masks a real reserve. He knows when not to comment directly at
all. Much could have been said on the death of George Osborne; this
is all that is said:

> No more fighting was heard at Brussels—the pursuit rolled miles
> away. The darkness came down on the field and city, and Amelia
> was praying for George, who was lying on his face, dead, with a
> bullet through his heart.[66]

It is no simple statement; not only is the immediate reference mag-
nified by the drawing together of Brussels and the battlefield, but its
very brevity and the silence surrounding it mark its subject—not the
death of one George Osborne, sufficiently shown as odious and contemptible, but Death, sudden, august, and mysterious. But all this is
implicit. Yet equally impressive in its own way, and equally enlarged
beyond the particular circumstance, is the leisurely commentary on
the death of Mr. Sedley;[67] appropriate to a death that is not sudden,
but long prepared for, domestic and not dramatic, enmeshed in practical circumstance, and apparently presented as a mere change in
habitation. The one method is as essentially part of the novel's texture
as the other.

The commentary springs also from Thackeray's wish to "convey the
sentiment of reality." Through it he openly admits, as no modern
novelist dare, *all* the relations of the novelist to his story. The novelist
does write what he knows to be "terrific chapters," he does construct
and manipulate his characters, and he is also carried beyond his conscious self ("I have no idea where it all comes from").[68] He remembers,
and observes; he is affected, as he writes, by what is happening around

[65] Brownell, op. cit., p. 7; and cf. pp. 9–10.
[66] Ch. xxxii, at the close of the ninth number.
[67] Ch. lxi.
[68] *Letters*, iii. 468 n.

him—the "unwritten parts" of novels. Thackeray's candour about all this is part of his love of truth. Believing in truth, he can afford to admit that what he writes is fiction. And the illusion is not thereby broken. When he calls his characters puppets, it is not their smallness, but their separateness from him, that strikes us; and perhaps his own largeness. "Thackeray is a Titan . . . [his words] as solemn as an oracle." [69]

> Ah! *Vanitas Vanitatum!* Which of us is happy in this world? which of us has his desire? or, having it, is satisfied?—Come children, let us shut up the box and the puppets, for our play is played out.

The great picture is not the less great from our final awareness that we and the author stand outside its frame. The words are a recall to life and individual responsibility as the preacher lays his cap and bells aside.

[69] Charlotte Brontë, in a letter of 1848; *The Brontës, their Lives, Friendships, and Correspondence,* 4 vols. (Shakespeare Head Brontë, Oxford, 1932), ii, 201.

On the Style of *Vanity Fair*

by G. Armour Craig

> . . . there is still a very material difference of opinion as to the real nature and character of the Measure of Value in this country. My first question, therefore, is, what constitutes this Measure of Value? What is the signification of that word "a Pound"?
>
> Speech of Sir Robert Peel on the Bank Charter Acts
> (6 May 1844)

> Perhaps I might be a heroine still, but I shall never be a good woman, I know.
>
> Mrs. Gaskell, *Wives and Daughters* (1866)

"Among all our novelists his style is the purest, as to my ears it is also the most harmonious. Sometimes it is disfigured by a slight touch of affectation, by little conceits which smell of the oil;—but the language is always lucid." The judgment is Anthony Trollope's and the lucidity he praises is Thackeray's: "The reader, without labour, knows what he means, and knows all that he means." [1] The judgment has been shared by many, perhaps even by Thackeray himself, for he was vigilant in detecting "fine writing" or "claptraps" in the work of others,[2] and for himself he insisted that "this person writing strives to tell the truth. If there is not that, there is nothing." [3] Yet some reconciling is necessary, for the truth is not always lucid and lucidity may not always be quite true.

"On the Style of *Vanity Fair*" by G. Armour Craig. From *Style in Prose Fiction*, ed. Harold C. Martin, English Institute Essays (New York: Columbia University Press, 1959; London: Oxford University Press, 1959). Copyright © 1959 by Columbia University Press. Reprinted by permission of the author and the publishers.

[1] *An Autobiography*, ed. by Frederick Page (London, 1950), p. 244.

[2] See, e.g., his review of "A New Spirit Of The Age," *Works—The Oxford Thackeray*, ed. by George Saintsbury (17 vols.; London 1908), VI, 424; or some advice on "fine writing" in *The Letters and Private Papers of William Makepeace Thackeray*, ed. by Gordon N. Ray (4 vols.; Cambridge, Mass., 1945), II, 192.

[3] Preface to *Pendennis*.

There is at any rate a passage in chapter 42 of *Vanity Fair*[4] for Trollope's judgment of which the modern reader—at least this reader —would give a good deal. It describes the life of Jane Osborne keeping house for her father: her sister is now the fashionable Mrs. Frederick Bullock, her brother, disowned by their father for his marriage to Amelia Sedley, has been killed at Waterloo, and Jane now lives in idle spinsterhood in the great glum house in Russell Square.

It was an awful existence. She had to get up of black winter's mornings to make breakfast for her scowling old father, who would have turned the whole house out of doors if his tea had not been ready at half-past eight. She remained silent opposite to him, listening to the urn hissing, and sitting in tremor while the parent read his paper, and consumed his accustomed portion of muffins and tea. At half-past nine he rose and went to the City, and she was almost free till dinner-time, to make visitations in the kitchen and to scold the servants: to drive abroad and descend upon the tradesmen, who were prodigiously respectful: to leave her cards and her papa's at the great glum respectable houses of their City friends; or to sit alone in the large drawing-room, expecting visitors; and working at a huge piece of worsted by the fire, on the sopha, hard by the great Iphigenia clock, which ticked and tolled with mournful loudness in the dreary room. The great glass over the mantle-piece, faced by the other great console glass at the opposite end of the room, increased and multiplied between them the brown holland bag in which the chandelier hung; until you saw these brown holland bags fading away in endless perspectives, and this apartment of Miss Osborne's seemed the centre of a system of drawing-rooms. When she removed the cordovan leather from the grand piano, and ventured to play a few notes on it, it sounded with a mournful sadness, startling the dismal echoes of the house. (pp. 441–42)

Thackeray's prose is seldom better than this. The passage comes from a paragraph that comments on the difference between Jane Osborne's life and that of her sister: "One can fancy the pangs" with which Jane regularly read about Mrs. Frederick Bullock in the "Morning Post," particularly the account of her presentation at the Drawing-room. The reader, characteristically, is invited to supply from his own observation the sort of vulgar envy that feeds upon accounts of "Fashionable Reunions" in the newspaper and to look down on Jane Osborne's suffering as no more than the deprivation of the snobbish pleasures of elegant society. The passage begins, then, easily enough: "It was an awful existence." And "awful" is at first simply a colloquial affectation. It

[4] References are to the Modern Library College Editions reprint (New York, 1950), which is based on the edition of 1864.

becomes something more, however, as we move into the account of Jane's routine and ascend from the tremors of the breakfast table to the solitude of the drawing room with its covered chandelier "fading away in endless perspectives": the conversational pitch turns momentarily solemn with the vision of "this apartment of Miss Osborne's" as "the centre of a system of drawing-rooms"—including perhaps even that most august of all such apartments where her sister has been received. It would be hard to find this an example of the "little conceits which smell of the oil," for even here Thackeray does not lose his customary confidential hold upon the reader. The vision is kept close to us by his usual resource: the opposing mirrors "increased and multiplied between them the brown holland bag in which the chandelier hung; until *you* saw these brown holland bags fading away in endless perspectives." The "you" is no doubt as unobtrusive as an idiom. But it is not inconsistent with Thackeray's constant and fluent address to his reader, an address at its best as easy as idiom. In this very short passage Thackeray has moved from an example of the snobbery he loved to detect to a memorable symbol of the society in which snobbery flourishes. It is a society of endless perspectives, a system of drawing rooms whose center is everywhere, whose circumference is nowhere.

But is this what Thackeray meant? And is it the "all" that he meant? Certainly the symbol is not characteristic—it is indeed unique in *Vanity Fair.* Usually, or at any rate perhaps too often, Thackeray renders the barren routines of high life in mock genealogies or in the kind of mildly allegorical guest list that follows this passage. We are told that twice a month the solitary dinners of Mr. and Miss Osborne are shared with "Old Dr. Gulp and his lady from Bloomsbury Square, . . . old Mr. Frowser the attorney, . . . old Colonel Livermore, . . . old Serjeant Toffy, . . . sometimes old Sir Thomas Coffin." *Vanity Fair,* we recall, began as "Pen and Pencil Sketches of English Society," as an extension of *The Book of Snobs.* Yet Thackeray seems to have felt the need of some larger, more inclusive presiding idea. In the early stages of writing the first few numbers he "ransacked" his brain for another title, and "Vanity Fair," he said, came to him suddenly in the middle of the night.[5] It seems to have summed up for him a position from which he could confidently go on with his "Novel without a Hero," but a position of course very different from John Bunyan's. The original Vanity Fair as described by Evangelist is the dwelling place of abominations. But it is after all only one more obstacle on

[5] Gordon N. Ray, *Thackeray: The Uses of Adversity: 1811–1846* (New York, 1955), pp. 384–85.

the road to the Celestial City, and all such obstacles are rewards in disguise. "He that shall die there," says Evangelist, "although his death will be unnatural, and his pain perhaps great, he will yet have the better of his fellow." While there are some unnatural and painful deaths in Thackeray's Fair, there seems to be no act of resistance or sacrifice by which anyone can get the better of anyone else, and the irony of the title has no doubt been lively in the minds of many readers. But Evangelist lays down a more poignantly ironical prescription: "he that will go to the [Celestial] City, and yet not go through this Town [where Vanity Fair is kept], *must* needs *go out of the World.*" [6] If there is no Celestial City beyond Thackeray's Fair, and if there is no hero determined to fight on to a heavenly peak, it is even more certain that none of Thackeray's characters shall go out of this world. On every page of *Vanity Fair* we find description, exposure, comment, from a position much less elevated and secure than that of an evangelist, yet one from which we do see into an "all" as large as a whole society.

Certainly the style of all this commenting and exposing is this-worldly to a degree that would have puzzled Bunyan as much as it has troubled some of his descendants. In the preface to *Pendennis* Thackeray speaks of his work as "a sort of confidential talk between reader and writer," and it was the excess of this conception of himself—"the little earmark by which he is most conspicuous"—that Trollope found "his most besetting sin in style." The "sin" is "a certain affected familiarity": Thackeray "indulges too frequently in little confidences with individual readers, in which pretended allusions to himself are frequent. 'What would you do? what would you say now, if you were in such a position?' he asks." [7] Yet for Trollope, although this familiarity might breed occasional contempt, it did not finally compromise the great virtue of Thackeray's lucidity. "As I have said before, the reader always understands his words without an effort, and receives all that the author has to give." [8] But to know what, and to know all, a writer means is to be in his confidence indeed, and it would be a serious lapse of style that this confidence should break down in affectation or something worse.

In "Before the Curtain," the preface he wrote in 1848 for the completed novel, Thackeray promises his reader "no other moral than

[6] *The Pilgrim's Progress* . . . , ed. by Edmund Venables, rev. by Mabel Peacock (Oxford, 1925), pp. 82 ff.

[7] Anthony Trollope, *Thackeray* (London, 1879), pp. 197–98.

[8] *Ibid.*, p. 198.

this tag to the present story," that after wandering with him through the Fair, "When you come home, you sit down, in a sober, contemplative, not uncharitable frame of mind, and apply yourself to your books or your business." He raises no literary expectations, he promises no carefully graduated feast of human nature, he does not even excuse himself to those who find all Fairs "immoral" and hence refuse to enter this one. The stern moralists may be quite right in withholding their custom, but those "of a lazy, or a benevolent, or a sarcastic mood, may perhaps like to step in for half an hour and look at the performance." This casualness, the queer juxtaposition of "lazy," "benevolent," and "sarcastic," may seem like the very height of good breeding. It does sum up the uncomfortable collocation of responses that any reader must make to some stretches of the novel. But it also promises that this writer will keep us free from violent emotions as we read. It is the guarantee of a special detachment.

Such detachment is often suggested by a coy version of one of Fielding's comic devices. When we witness the departure of Becky and Amelia from Chiswick Mall, the last flurry of farewells is recounted thus: "Then came the struggle and the parting below. Words refused to tell it. . . ." The congregation of servants and pupils, the hugging and kissing and crying are such "as no pen can depict, and as the tender heart would fain pass over" (chap. 1, p. 6). Or, on the morning after the fatal excursion to Vauxhall, Joseph Sedley lies "groaning in agonies which the pen refuses to describe" (chap. 6, p. 55) while he suffers the aftermath cf rack punch. Becky, disappointed in her attempt to capture Joseph, goes away from the Sedley house to her duties as governess: "Finally came the parting with Amelia, over which I intend to throw a veil" (chap. 6, p. 61). Such mild affectations as these amuse a good deal less than their frequency suggests they should, however obliquely they may glance at sentimental explorations of young female affection or the tract-writer's interest in the heavy repentance of the drunkard. But they are the simplest and the least interesting form of a larger kind of detachment.

About other episodes the narrator is more artfully silent. Perhaps the most interesting is the courtship of Rawdon Crawley, which extends over several chapters and is concealed in the narrative of Becky's ministrations to old Miss Crawley. It will be recalled that the success of Becky's attentions to this lady, the old aunt whose wealth is the object of all the Crawleys' envy and scheming, alarm Mrs. Bute Crawley— whose portrait, incidentally, as well as that of her family and of her husband the Rector, make one wonder that Thackeray could have

quarreled with Jerrold's anticlericalism.[9] Mrs. Bute's scheming to secure
Miss Crawley's money for her own leads her to warn Rawdon that
when his stepmother dies, old Sir Pitt will marry Becky. Rawdon's
response sets the level of intrigue exactly:

> "By Jove, it's too bad," thought Rawdon, "too bad, by Jove! I do
> believe the woman wants the poor girl to be ruined, in order that
> she shouldn't come into the family as Lady Crawley." (chap. 14, p. 133)

He proceeds to the recommended seduction, but is outguessed by the
frank and outraged role that Becky adopts when he "rallie[s] her in
his graceful way about his father's attachment." The game goes on,
Miss Crawley recovers from her surfeit under Becky's assiduous care,
and shortly news comes that the meek Lady Crawley is dead. Rawdon
and his aunt discuss the matter while Becky stands by.

> Rebecca said nothing. She seemed by far the gravest and most im-
> pressed of the family. She left the room before Rawdon went away
> that day; but they met by chance below, as he was going away after
> taking leave, and had a parley together. (chap. 14, p. 143)

And the next thing we know, old Sir Pitt has come to town and is
down on his knees to ask for the hand of Becky. The narrator comments:

> In the course of this history we have never seen her lose her presence
> of mind; but she did now, and wept some of the most genuine tears
> that ever fell from her eyes. (chap. 14, p. 144)

But what does "genuine" mean here? Or "they met by chance" in the
passage above? Are we to infer that during their "parley" Becky uses
the threat of a proposal from the father to make sure of the son? Are
we to infer that the tears are genuine because she has planned too well
—the threat she has used to get one husband has turned out to be
prophetic, and she might have had the father? Are they tears of rage?
of regret? As we move on to the next chapter we certainly find no
circumstantial report of when and how Becky and Rawdon are married; instead there is a good deal of indirect veiling of the scene and
refusing of the pen. "How they were married is not of the slightest
consequence to anybody." Perhaps, it is conjectured, they went off one
afternoon when Becky was presumed to be visiting Amelia. But the
matter is left in uncertainty. On the one hand, "Who needs to be told,
that if a woman has a will, she will assuredly find a way?" And on the

---

[9] See Ray, *Uses of Adversity*, pp. 370–71.

other: "who on earth, after the daily experience we have, can question the probability of a gentleman marrying anybody?" (chap. 16, p. 153).

The concealment of the circumstances of the marriage may appeal to the lazy, may satisfy the benevolent, and it may give the sarcastic something to work on too. But its most important effect is that the narration here, clustered about with confidential comments and dismissive questions, sets before us a way of knowing the world. It is a way so inferential, so dependent upon unfinished implications, that it comes close to the character of gossip. And a good gossip, while its unfinished sentences and its discreet and indiscreet omissions may keep us from the exhilaration of indignation or rhapsody, can suggest values and insights superior to the vocabulary of the purveyor or the listener. Here, whatever the meaning of that "by chance" that modifies the meeting of Becky and Rawdon, or whatever the meaning of that "genuine" that modifies her tears, we can only infer that the marriage is the result neither of grand passion nor of mean seduction. The veiling of the secret here means that we can only accept Becky's marriage as a convenience. Even the grossness of Mrs. Bute's plotting is lost in the shadows.

The questions with which Thackeray disposes of this affair—"Who needs to be told . . . who can question the probability . . ."—are of course the most conspicuous earmark of his detachment in *Vanity Fair*. There is the issue of who made the first move in Becky's first romance, with the young Reverend Mr. Crisp who came infatuated to tea at Chiswick Mall: after a parenthetical cloud of hints and counter-hints the narrator concludes, "But who can tell you the real truth of the matter?" (chap. 2, p. 14). Just as when the pen refuses to tell, the implication here is only coy. But a good many hundred pages later, in what is called "A Vagabond Chapter" (chap 64), this kind of coyness can exasperate. It comes in a passage summarizing Becky's career after her fall from polite society in London: "When she got her money she gambled; when she had gambled it she was put to shifts to live; who knows how or by what means she succeeded? . . . The present historian can give no certain details regarding the event" (p. 681). The detachment inculcated here is vast and affluent indeed; it is perhaps matched only by the elaborate veiling of the circumstances of Joseph Sedley's death. But the most puzzling questions in the book are those that comment upon its crucial passage.

Every reader of *Vanity Fair* remembers the "discovery scene" of chapter 53—the scene in which Becky suffers exposure and isolation after her husband and Lord Steyne violently clash. And every student of the novel knows that this scene is a battleground upon which the judgments of a number of Thackeray's critics have collided. Rawdon, having been freed from the spunging house, hurries "across the streets and the great squares of Vanity Fair," and bursts in upon his wife and Lord Steyne in something less than *flagrante delicto* though ready for embarrassment.

Steyne was hanging over the sofa on which Becky sate. The wretched woman was in a brilliant full toilette, her arms and all her fingers sparkling with bracelets and rings; and the brilliants on her breast which Steyne had given her. He had her hand in his, and was bowing over it to kiss it, when Becky started up with a faint scream as she caught sight of Rawdon's white face. At the next instant she tried a smile, a horrid smile, as if to welcome her husband; and Steyne rose up, grinding his teeth, pale, and with fury in his looks.

He, too, attempted a laugh—and came forward holding out his hand. "What, come back! How d'ye do, Crawley?" he said, the nerves of his mouth twitching as he tried to grin at the intruder.

There was that in Rawdon's face which caused Becky to fling herself before him. "I am innocent, Rawdon," she said; "before God, I am innocent." She clung hold of his coat, of his hands; her own were all covered with serpents, and rings, and baubles.

"I am innocent.—Say I am innocent," she said to Lord Steyne.

He thought a trap had been laid for him, and was as furious with the wife as with the husband. "You innocent! Damn you!" he screamed out. "You innocent! Why, every trinket you have on your body is paid for by me. I have given you thousands of pounds which this fellow has spent, and for which he has sold you. Innocent, by—! You're as innocent as your mother, the ballet-girl, and your husband the bully. Don't think to frighten me as you have done others. Make way, sir, and let me pass"; and Lord Steyne seized up his hat, and, with flame in his eyes, and looking his enemy fiercely in the face, marched upon him, never for a moment doubting that the other would give way.

But Rawdon Crawley springing out, seized him by the neckcloth, until Steyne, almost strangled, writhed, and bent under his arm. "You lie, you dog"! said Rawdon. "You lie, you coward and villain!" And he struck the Peer twice over the face with his open hand, and flung him bleeding to the ground. It was all done before Rebecca could interpose. She stood there trembling before him. She admired her husband, strong, brave, and victorious.

"Come here," he said.—She came up at once.

"Take off those things."—She began, trembling, pulling the jewels from her arms, and the rings from her shaking fingers, and held them all in a heap, quivering, and looking up at him. "Throw them down," he said, and she dropped them. He tore the diamond ornament out of her breast, and flung it at Lord Steyne. It cut him on his bald fore-head. Steyne wore the scar to his dying day. (pp. 554-55)

The theatricality of the passage—Becky's clinging and quivering, the serpents and baubles on her hands, Rawdon's springing out and his terse manifesto, the flame in the eyes of the wicked nobleman and the lifelong scar on his head—all such features suggest that the creator of Punch's Prize novelists is once again engaged in something like parody.[10] On the other hand it has been asserted that far from a joke, the scene "is the chief ganglion of the tale; and the discharge of energy from Rawdon's fist [*sic*] is the reward and consolation of the reader." [11] The most extensive criticism of the scene finds it unprepared for and conveyed by a dramatic technique foreign to Thackeray's genius,[12] but this judgment has in turn been disposed of by another critic who finds Thackeray's usual stamp upon it and some other felicities as well. He suggests that one of these is the way in which "Steyne wore the scar" echoes "Steyne wore the star." [13] By the same sort of reasoning we might infer from "He tore the diamond ornament out of her breast" that Becky's heart is surpassing hard; and certainly Thackeray tells us that the battle takes the heart out of her. But the one touch upon which Thackeray himself is known to have commented is Becky's response to the sudden burst of energy from Rawdon: "She stood there trembling before him. She admired her husband, strong, brave, and victorious." Of this observation Thackeray is reported to have said that it was a touch of genius,[14] and it does consort well with his special genius in the rest of the book.

For although the battle seems to be the expression of outraged honor, it is a collision that misses its main issue and prize. As the resistless masses meet, Becky stands off to one side, and although her admiration is unacceptable or even unknown to Rawdon, and although we are told that her life seems so "miserable, lonely, and profitless" after Rawdon has silently departed that she even thinks of suicide,

---

[10] As has been suggested by Kathleen Tillotson, *Novels of the Eighteen-Forties* (Oxford, 1954), pp. 233-34 [pp. 71-72 above].

[11] Robert Louis Stevenson, "A Gossip on Romance," *Memories and Portraits* (New York, 1910), p. 239 (Vol. 17 of the Biographical Edition of the Works). Stevenson's judgment is endorsed by Professor Ray in *Uses of Adversity*, p. 410.

[12] Percy Lubbock, *The Craft of Fiction* (London, 1954), pp. 101 ff. [pp. 24 ff. above]. Lubbock's argument has been criticized by Professor Ray (*Uses of Adversity*, pp. 409-10) and by Geoffrey Tilloston, *Thackeray the Novelist* (Cambridge, 1954), pp. 82 ff.

[13] G. Tillotson, *Thackeray the Novelist*, p. 84.

[14] See Ray, *Uses of Adversity*, p. 500, n. 19; and *Letters and Private Papers*, II, 352*n*.

there is still a profound irrelevance in this violent scene. Becky's maid comes upon her in her dejection and asks the question that is in every reader's mind: *"Mon Dieu,* madame, what has happened?" And the "person writing" concludes this crucial chapter with an enlargement of the same question:

> What *had* happened? Was she guilty or not? She said not; but who could tell what was truth which came from those lips; or if that corrupt heart was in this case pure? All her lies and her schemes, all her selfishness and her wiles, all her wit and her genius had come to this bankruptcy. (p. 556)

Becky lies down, the maid goes to the drawing room to gather up the pile of trinkets, and the chapter ends. If Thackeray has not risen to a cruel joke on those readers who find consolation and reward in the discharge of energy from Rawdon, he has at least interrupted their satisfaction.

Lord Steyne's meaning of "guilty"—"He thought a trap had been laid for him" by Becky and Rawdon—is of course quite false, though it corroborates the characterization of Steyne as one experienced in double-dealing. "Guilty" from Rawdon's point of view of course means, as he tells Pitt next day, that "it was a regular plan between that scoundrel and her" to get him out of the way (chap. 54, p. 559). And Thackeray goes to as great lengths to make it impossible for us to know that this interpretation is true as he does to conceal the timing and motives of Becky's marriage. To see the entangling and displacing of any clear answer, we need only ask "guilty of what?" The usual answer is of course "guilty of adultery" (or guilty of getting ready for it),[15] and Thackeray's silence is commonly attributed to his awareness of the "squeamishness" of his public. Indeed he himself lends real authority to this account of the matter. In 1840, writing on Fielding, he complains that the world no longer tolerates real satire. "The same vice exists now, only we don't speak about it; the same things are done, but we don't call them by their names." [16] And in *Vanity Fair* he complains that he must be silent about some events in Becky's later career because he must satisfy "the moral world, that has, perhaps, no particular objection to vice, but an insuperable repugnance to hearing vice called by its proper name" (chap. 64, p. 671). There may well be evidence in Thackeray's personal history to suggest in addition that he was, perhaps

---

[15] See, e.g., Ray, *Uses of Adversity,* p. 502, n. 14.
[16] *Works,* III, 385.

even before the separation from his mad wife, evasive and unclear on the subject of sexual behavior. But however complicated the tensions of Thackeray's own emotional experience, and however rigid the scruples of his audience, the answer to the questions with which he comments on this most important episode cannot be a single "name" or possess any "proper name." For he has led us here, however uneasily, with mingled attitudes of parody and outrage, to a startling though incomplete vision of a new social world, a vision exactly proportioned to the irrelevance of the violence we have witnessed.

The words of the passage that command our moral response are precisely those that most nearly approach parody: Becky responds to a nameless "that" in Rawdon's face by exclaiming "I am innocent." If the reader trained in melodrama scoffs at the response and turns Becky into a consummate villain, he will have some trouble getting through the rest of the novel, and it is likely that he will long since have become exasperated with Thackeray's tone, his silences and implications. The same is true, moreover, of the sentimental reader who throws down the volume and declares that Becky has been monstrously wronged and victimized by wicked men in a bad world. But the reader who says, in effect, "it is impossible to tell whether or of what she is guilty" is exactly in the difficult position of one who accepts Thackeray's narrative as it is given. And what such a reader sees from this position must fill him with wonder if not dismay. For he sees that while he wants to answer these questions, he cannot do so, and he can only conclude that he is looking at a situation before which his moral vocabulary is irrelevant. Becky in her isolation has finally gone out of this world, and it will take a new casuistry to bring her back. Thackeray uses some strong moral words in his comment, it is true: "who could tell what was truth which came from those lips; or if that corrupt heart was in this case pure?" But while we know that Becky has lied heartily to Steyne, and to his hearty admiration, we cannot know that she is lying to Rawdon when she insists on her innocence. Whatever corruption we may have seen, the question this time is in earnest. The qualities named in the final statement, and especially by its last word, tell us where we are: "All her lies and her schemes, all her selfishness and her wiles, all her wit and her genius had come to this bankruptcy." For these are the terms not so much of moral as of financial enterprise, and "this bankruptcy" is the real touch of genius in the passage. Thackeray's questions and his comment express neither indignation nor sympathy. Rather, they bring before us the terrible irresolution of a society in which market values and moral values are discontinuous and separate. And Thackeray will not—he can not—support us as we revolt from such a spectacle.

The ghostly paradigm upon which human nature plays in *Vanity Fair* is the credit economy that in Thackeray's own lifetime finally developed from a money economy. Even the constant gambling in Thackeray's Fair, historically appropriate as it may be to his Regency setting (and much of his own early experience as it may reflect), suggests the unpredictability of the system. Distant though the gambler may be from respectability, his luck is only a little less mysterious than the power his winnings confer upon him. However it may be in the most famous conversation recorded in modern literary history, it is all too true in *Vanity Fair* that rich people are different because they have more money. Thackeray exposed himself to some high-minded criticism from George Henry Lewes when he published the number containing Becky's famous reflection, "I think I could be a good woman if I had five thousand a year." For he had commented, "And who knows but Rebecca was right in her speculations—and that it was only a question of money and fortune which made the difference between her and an honest woman?" (chap. 41, p. 436). In its interrogative form the comment is much more precise than the declaration Thackeray wrote to Lewes. The latter called it "detestable" to say that "honesty is only the virtue of abundance." Thackeray replied that he meant "only that he in the possession of luxuries . . . should be very chary of despising poor Lazarus on foot, and look very humbly and leniently upon the faults of his less fortunate brethren." This is of course no answer; or if it is, it asks for a curious forbearance towards Becky Sharp. But Thackeray qualifies at once: "I am quite aware of the dismal roguery . . . [which] goes all through the Vanity Fair story—and God forbid that the world should be like it altogether: though I fear it is more like it than we like to own." [17] The likeness to "the world" is in the belief that money is magic and in the frightening awareness, no doubt recently reinforced by the financial crisis of 1847, that no theory had yet been devised to control it. Walter Bagehot, in the *Economic Studies* he was composing in the 1870's, confessed to "a haze" in the language in which he described the growth of capital, and he remarked too with admiration that "a very great many of the strongest heads in England spend their minds on little else than on thinking whether other people will pay their debts." [18] For him that system was "marvellous" by which

---

[17] *Letters and Private Papers*, II, 353–54.

[18] *The Works and Life of Walter Bagehot*, ed. by Mrs. Russell Barrington (10 vols.; London, 1915), VII, 248, 131.

"an endless succession of slips of written promises should be turned into money as readily as if they were precious stones"—so marvelous indeed that it "would have seemed incredible in commerce till very recent times." [19] Thackeray's attitude, doubtless shaped by the short period he spent as a bill broker in 1833—an episode he apparently tried hard to forget[20]—was not so admiring. His Fair, at any rate, is a market the movements of which are perplexing in the extreme.

The first mention of the "guilt" or "innocence" of Becky's relations to Lord Steyne comes in a passage about the "awful kitchen inquisition" of the servants of Vanity Fair. We are told that Raggles, the retired butler of Miss Crawley, who owns the house in Curzon Street where Becky and Rawdon live well on nothing a year, is ruined by his extension of credit to them. But he is the victim of something more than the simple excess of liabilities over assets. The *"Vehmgericht* of the servants'-hall" early pronounces Becky guilty:

> And I shame to say, she would not have got credit had they not believed her to be guilty. It was the sight of the Marquis of Steyne's carriage-lamps at her door, contemplated by Raggles, burning in the blackness of midnight, "that kep him up," as he afterwards said; that, even more than Rebecca's arts and coaxings. (chap. 44, pp. 461–62)

The question of guilt here is quite subordinate to the question of credit, and Raggles is ruined not because he is right about Becky's guilt but because he believes in a strict correlation between Becky's moral and financial status. The last of Raggles is seen at the drunken party of the servants on the morning after the battle; our last glimpse of him is not as he suffers in ruin but as he looks at his fellows "with a wild surprise" upon hearing from Becky that Rawdon "has got a good appointment" (chap. 55, p. 565). It is no wonder that Thackeray should have said in a letter to his mother written during the very month when the "discovery scene" appeared,

> I cant find the end of the question between property and labour. We want something almost equal to a Divine Person to settle it. I mean if there is ever to be an elucidation of the mystery it is to be solved by a preacher of such novelty and authority, as will awaken and convince mankind—but O how and when? [21]

Whatever the fate of the larger question, Thackeray does do some

[19] *Ibid.,* p. 251.
[20] See *Uses of Adversity,* pp. 159–60.
[21] *Letters and Private Papers,* II, 356.

novel preaching upon bankruptcy in one section of *Vanity Fair*. John
Sedley, we recall, is ruined in the uncertainties following Napoleon's
escape from Elba (chap. 18, pp. 170 ff.), and Thackeray's extended
portrait of the "business and bustle and mystery of a ruined man"
(chap. 20, p. 195) seems at first sight disproportionate. Of course the
bankruptcy accounts for the career of Amelia, but not for all of it.
For old Osborne, who also emerges from the background just here, is
described as behaving towards his former friend Sedley "with savage-
ness and scorn." Our attitude is shaped precisely by Osborne's insisting
that as a bankrupt Sedley must be wicked—that he is both out of
business and out of the circle of decency. "From a mere sense of con-
sistency, a persecutor is bound to show that the fallen man is a villain
—otherwise he, the persecutor, is a wretch himself" (chap. 18, p. 173).
And Osborne is characterized more grossly still by his opposition to
Amelia for his son, by his insistence that George marry the rich mulatto
Miss Schwarz, and by his vast self-righteousness. Osborne is perhaps an
inept caricature of the City man who has succumbed completely to the
superstitions of money, but he is a new kind of portrait, and one not
less complicated than Dickens's portrait of another hard businessman
whose adventures were being issued in installments at the same time.

While Thackeray's Mr. Osborne is a crude warning to those who
identify bankruptcy and corruption, Dickens's Mr. Dombey is an
astonishing testimonial to the degree of violence that must be exerted
to link the experience of bankruptcy with moral reform. In the same
month, March of 1848,[22] in which they read of the collision between
Rawdon and Lord Steyne, readers who followed both authors were
shaken by a passage of dreadful violence that describes a collision
between Mr. Dombey's manager, Carker, and a railway engine (chap.
55). Dombey witnesses the event and faints at the sight—it is not an
"accident" but the physical embodiment of a terrible obsession. When
we next encounter Dombey (chap. 58) he is superintending the bankruptcy of his firm which results from Carker's secret machinations and
which he will do nothing to avert. He is alone in the world, for he has
driven away his gentle daughter Florence, and he is a "ruined man."
With gruesome immediacy he thinks of suicide, but just before the
knife strikes, his daughter rushes in, a great reconciliation and redemp-
tion occurs, and Mr. Dombey, no longer worth five thousand or very
much of anything a year, is at last a good man. For all his inventive
energy Dickens cannot make clear the relation between the departure
of Carker from this world and the moral conversion that Mr. Dombey

[22] See K. Tillotson, *Novels of the Eighteen-Forties*, p. 318.

then undergoes. But this number of *Dombey and Son* together with the contemporaneous number of *Vanity Fair* suggests the extreme lengths to which two of the most sensitive minds of the mid-century were driven in their effort to reconcile the mysterious power of finance capitalism with the requirements of private morality. "Sell yourself" still meant the worst degradation, but the time was approaching when it would become a formula for "success."

In *Vanity Fair* at any rate Becky's bankruptcy offers no clearer connection between villainy—or goodness—and loss of credit than does the situation of Old John Sedley that Osborne so ruthlessly categorizes. The thoroughness with which Thackeray has covered his tracks suggests that no single transaction, not even payment by adultery, is at issue here. The kind of credit upon which the Crawleys lived so well in London and Paris is beyond the power of any act or value to overtake, for it is the social version of that system in which the perpetual promise to pay is taken for the perpetual fact of payment. "The truth is, when we say of a gentleman that he lives well on nothing a year, we use the word 'nothing' to signify something unknown" (chap. 36, p. 374). It may be that Rawdon and Becky are "wicked," but their wickedness will not account for their credit as they pursue the fashionable life. Just as the war that so mysteriously yet inevitably ruined John Sedley was, as Thackeray tells us, a lucky accident interrupting the endless double- and triple-dealing among nations (chap. 28, pp. 279–80), so for Becky an accident interrupts the double-dealing and counter double-dealing of the scramble for social power. The perspectives here are indeed almost endless; they are certainly beyond the limits of innocence or guilt. Even Rawdon, who experiences something like conversion or reform as Becky's career reaches its height, is not quite secure. His one assertion to Becky after the battle is an ironic fulfillment of Steyne's accusation: "You might have spared me a hundred pounds, Becky, out of all this—I have always shared with you" (chap. 53, p. 556).[23] And the last words he speaks in the novel are as ambiguous as any question from the narrator:

> "She has kep money concealed from me these ten years," he said. "She swore, last night only, she had none from Steyne. She knew it was all up, directly I found it. If she's not guilty, Pitt, she's as bad as guilty, and I'll never see her again, never." (chap. 55, p. 579)

It is hardly possible to find the outrage of manly honor in these exactly

[23] For a quite different interpretation, see Tillotson, *Novels of the Eighteen-Forties,* pp. 248, 251 [pp. 81, 83 above].

struck last words. The distinction between "guilty" and "as bad as guilty" would be the final viciousness if it were not the final irrelevance.

But, again, is this what Thackeray means, and is it the *all* that he means? We can believe so only by acknowledging that the easy confidence between reader and writer promised at the beginning has been renounced, for we are here outside the domain of laziness, benevolence, or sarcasm. If the renunciation were the deliberate act of a supreme ironist who turns and rends us for our naive acceptance of his confidential detachment, Thackeray would indeed have created a masterpiece. But in the crucial scene and in portions of the chapters that lead to it Thackeray has exposed us to violent emotions that no politeness can conceal. The enmity between Little Rawdy and Lord Steyne, for example, is an extension of Becky's neglect of her child that erupts into physical violence: Becky boxes his ears for listening to her on the stairs as she entertains Lord Steyne (chap. 44, p. 460). The child indeed makes his first speaking appearance in the same chapter as that in which Lord Steyne also first appears, grinning "hideously, his little eyes leering towards Rebecca" (chap. 37, p. 389). The juxtaposition is emphasized when little Rawdon is apostrophized:

> O thou poor lonely little benighted boy! Mother is the name for God in the lips and hearts of little children; and here was one who was worshipping a stone. (p. 392)

The appeal is no mere instance of competing with the creator of little Paul Dombey, as everyone who has read Thackeray's letters to his own mother will know. It is an appeal similar to many others in the narrative of Amelia, although there Thackeray is more characteristically reticent. When Amelia and her mother are reunited after her marriage, though Thackeray begins by referring to "How the floodgates were opened," he adds, "Let us respect Amelia and her mamma whispering and whimpering and laughing and crying in the parlour and the twilight." And when Amelia retreats to meditate in "the little room" with its "little white bed" in her old home, Thackeray desists:

> Have we a right to repeat or to overhear her prayers? These, brother, are secrets, and out of the domain of Vanity Fair, in which our story lies. (chap. 26, pp. 262, 264)

Even—especially—if we construe this scene and its secrets as an expression of Amelia's first awareness that she is to be a mother herself, it still involves relationships and sentiments outside the "domain" that Thackeray so thoroughly explored. It is a domain bounded by the "politeness" invoked in that early address to the reader in which the narrator promises "to love and shake by the hand" his "good and kindly" characters, "to laugh confidentially in the reader's sleeve" at the "silly" ones, but "to abuse in the strongest terms that politeness admits of" all those who are "wicked and heartless" (chap. 8, p. 79). Such terms of abuse for the wicked and love for the good are for the most part so polite that we accept them with all the detachment guaranteed by the Manager of the Performance. But the limits of this detachment—its very bankruptcy—can be shown only as we glimpse the howling wilderness outside, where the secrets of private feelings are violently confused with public forces of huge and mysterious dimensions, and where there is neither lucidity nor truth.

What Thackeray does then exhibit within the domain of the Fair is the impossibility of self-knowledge and, in the fullest sense, dramatic change. The most intimate experiences of the self, whether in prayer or in love, in disappointment or in outrage, must be kept outside. Becky's "I am innocent" is no more an articulation of the truth than it is the lucid exposure of a lie. But to put us where we cannot know "What *had* happened" and to face us with the bewildering irrelevance of our polite detachment, Thackeray was driven to an extreme that no style of his could control. He could not be clear without being untruthful, and he could not be truthful without being obscure. He tried to recover himself, it is true, in the subsequent chapters by returning to the conception of Becky that most saves his book. The most interesting feature of her characterization is not that she begins from the ambiguous social position of the orphan and governess— " 'I don't trust them governesses, Pinner,' says the Sedley housekeeper with enormous assurance, 'they're neither one thing nor t'other. They give themselves the hairs and hupstarts of ladies, and their wages is no better than you nor me' " (chap. 6, p. 60). Thackeray is concerned with much more than the favorite Victorian example of social mobility. The greater truth about Becky is that she is a mimic, that she trades on the difference between fantasy and society, between the role and the fact. But the truth of endless mimicry is much too large for the domain of the lucid. It is larger than any drawing room, park, or square of Vanity Fair, and it could be forced in only by an act of violence that darkened lucidity and concealed truth. The casuistry upon which *Vanity Fair* rests is unique, and the responses of many thousands of readers for a hundred years to this much-read book must constitute one of the most erratic subterranean currents of our moral history.

Neoclassical Conventions:
Vanity Fair, Pendennis, The Newcomes

by John Loofbourow

"They say he is like Fielding: they talk of his wit, humour, comic powers. He resembles Fielding as an eagle does a vulture," Charlotte Brontë wrote of *Vanity Fair.* "His wit [bears] the same relation to his serious genius, that the mere lambent sheet-lightning playing under the edge of the summer-cloud, does to the electric death-spark hid in its womb." [1] Thackeray's "wit," finding new and unexpected formulations for romanticism, was an alien quality in the nineteenth-century novel. Miss Brontë deprecates the comparison with Fielding, but what she calls "the Greek fire of [Thackeray's] sarcasm" was his legacy from the eighteenth century. The literary resources of neoclassical objectivity—pastoral to parody poetic artifice, mock-epic to satirize heroic exaltation—were, for Thackeray, valid perspectives on nineteenth-century reality.

In the mid-nineteenth century, romanticism faltered at social fact, and pure rationalism could not interpret the intuitive aspects of experience. In 1870, Cardinal Newman expressed his sense of the ambivalence of perception and reality: "this universal living scene of things is after all as little a logical world as it is a poetical; and, as it cannot without violence be exalted into poetical perfection, neither can it be attenuated into a logical formula." [2] It was this awareness of the relativity of reality that Thackeray recognized in *Pendennis* (Ch. LXI)—"I see truth in that man, as I do in his brother, whose logic drives him to quite a different conclusion," the hero remarks of the two

"Neoclassical Conventions: *Vanity Fair, Pendennis, The Newcomes.*" From *Thackeray and the Form of Fiction,* by John Loofbourow (Princeton, N.J.: Princeton University Press, 1964), pp. 51–72. Copyright © 1964 by Princeton University Press. Reprinted by permission of the author and the publisher.

[1] Charlotte Brontë, *Jane Eyre* (preface to the second edition).

[2] John Henry Cardinal Newman, *An Essay in Aid of a Grammar of Assent,* Longmans, Green and Co., New York, 1947, p. 204, ch. 8.

Newmans. During the years when *Vanity Fair* was being published, there were signs that the romantic experiment would not succeed, but a retreat to neoclassical certitudes was no longer possible. New combinations of perception and expression were needed to express contemporary experience, as in the Renaissance, whose literature has been called "the register of a violent effort to catch up with the expanding conditions of life. With its realization that certain themes are still untreated goes the feeling that certain techniques are becoming outmoded. . . . A transitional sense of disproportion makes itself felt . . . mock-epic, which magnifies vulgarity, applying the grand manner to commonplace matters; and travesty, which minimizes greatness, reclothing noble figures in base attire." [3] So Thackeray, expressing a new sense of the multiplicity of reality, experiments with literary hybrids: chivalry mates with mock-epic, pastoral is paired with romance, sentiment is crossed with satire. If the adaptation of romance in Thackeray's novels was an unconventional development, his assimilation of pastoral and mock-epic represents an equally unexpected phenomenon —the unforeseen specialization and the improbable vigor of Augustan modes in a Victorian habitat.

Since neoclassical conventions were initially antagonistic to Thackeray's other narrative modes, it took him longer to weave them into the continuous fabric of his prose. In *Vanity Fair,* the neoclassical genres are not integral narrative textures; pastoral and mock-epic are pastiches, like the patches of fashionable parody in earlier novels. These unfused passages are easy to recognize; there are concentrated sequences in *Vanity Fair,* one of pastoral, one of mock-epic, and these compressed examples of Thackeray's basic methods make good subjects for analysis. But the use of neoclassical modes as part of sustained narrative must be explored in Thackeray's later novels—*Pendennis, The Newcomes.*

Pastoral

Thackeray most often practiced pastoral in the Augustan manner— the mode was popular with the romantics, but Thackeray borrowed their effects only for secondary resonance. His Arcadian harmony was essentially neoclassical—and the neoclassical mode was never quite serious; it premised an impossibility and parodied itself. If Thackeray

---

[3] Harry Levin, "The Example of Cervantes," *Contexts of Criticism,* Harvard University Press, Cambridge, Mass., 1957, p. 86.

found in pastoral an image of improbable innocence, it was a result of eighteenth-century usage; and to appreciate the charm and irony that characterize the mode in *Vanity Fair* it is helpful to consider the development of the Augustan convention.

Eighteenth-century pastoral was purely Arcadian. The Renaissance had produced magnificent Christian hybrids, but Augustans admitted only the image of innocence that was envisioned in Sannazaro's *Arcadia*—"one of the great dreams of humanity." [4] Simplicity was the essence of this Augustan pastoral—not the simplicity of undisciplined nature, but a formal, though spontaneous, decorum; a pattern, like neoclassical nature, of original grace. So Dryden, describing Theocritus, remarks that "A simplicity shines through all he writes: he shows his art and learning, by disguising both," and Pope accepts Dryden's analysis of what is "becoming of a pastoral," [5] which has, he says, "the general moral of innocence and simplicity." [6]

But innocence and simplicity, artfully imitated, turned into insipid artifice; it was this quality that discredited the pastoral Thackeray knew. Early in the eighteenth century the mode became suspect; the porcelain muse began to titter her lines and Augustans, unable to alter the decorum they had established, agreed that pastoral was unfit for serious company—Steele ridicules the religious connotation in *The Guardian*: "Damon, or sometimes the god Pan, is dead. This immediately causes . . . [the shepherd] to make complaints . . . his friend interrupts him, and tells him that Damon lives, and shows him a track of light in the skies to confirm it; then invites him to chestnuts and cheese." [7] The pastorals of Pope's early years primly conform to Augustan precept and warble that "The Groves of *Eden*, vanish'd now so long, Live in Description, and look green in Song." [8] But the reflections of the original Garden that shimmer through his youthful Arcadia are eventually replaced by a caricature of the pastoral paradise: "The suff'ring eye inverted Nature sees, Trees cut to Statues, Statues thick as trees"; and in the *Moral Essays*, Pope's pastoral lovers, like Steyne

---

[4] C. S. Lewis, *English Literature in the Sixteenth Century*, Clarendon Press, Oxford, 1954, p. 334.

[5] John Dryden, "Preface to Sylvae," *Essays of John Dryden*, ed. W. P. Ker, The Clarendon Press, Oxford, 1900, I, 265.

[6] Alexander Pope, "A Discourse on Pastoral Poetry," *The Poems of Alexander Pope* (The Twickenham Edition), General Editor, John Butt, Methuen & Co., Ltd., London and Yale University Press, New Haven, 1939–61, I, 32.

[7] Richard Steele, "On Pastoral Poetry," *The Guardian*, No. 30.

[8] Alexander Pope, "Windsor Forest," ll. 7–8; this and subsequent citations of Pope's poetry refer to the text of The Twickenham Edition, cited above.

and Rebecca in *Vanity Fair,* hardly pretend to believe in their idyllic roles:

> Arcadia's Countess, here, in ermin'd pride,
> Is there, Pastora by a fountain side.
> Here Fannia, leering on her own good man,
> Is there, a naked Leda with a swan.[9]

The pastoral disenchantment continued throughout the century. Dr. Johnson remarked that pastoral was "not to be considered the effusion of real passion."[10] The "great dream of humanity" had become a sentimental joke. So, in Carlyle's translation, the pastoral imagery in *Wilhelm Meister* is an emblem of adolescent nostalgia: "The stuffed bunches of wool denominated lambs, the waterfalls of tin, the paper roses, and the one-sided huts of straw, awoke in him fair poetic visions of an old pastoral world."[11]

Through Carlyle and Johnson as well as the Augustans, Thackeray inherited the whimsical neoclassical convention, with a range that extended from silver-toned mockery to discordant satire. Of Gay's pastorals, he wrote: "They are to poetry what charming little Dresden china figures are to sculpture . . . and die of despair or rapture, with the most pathetic little grins and ogles."[12] In *Catherine,* romantic pastoral parodies "fashionable" fiction's purple passages; in *Pendennis,* Arcadian motifs represent the willful sentimentality of the factitious lovers. Thackeray used pastoral for compassion or ridicule but almost never to idealize his characters; and his expressive, if not his narrative, technique is fully developed in *Vanity Fair.*

One of *Vanity Fair's* extended scenes is predicated upon the pastoral metaphor. In this Arcadian sequence, Rebecca flirts with the Marquis of Steyne, while her husband, Rawdon, unconscious of deception, plays high stakes with Lord Southdown. Pastoral imagery is smuggled in disguised as a "sheep-dog"—"I mean a *moral* shepherd's dog," Rebecca explains, "A dog to keep the wolves off me . . . A companion."

"Dear little innocent lamb, you want one," said the Marquis; and

---

[9] Pope, *Moral Essays,* "Epistle IV: Of the Use of Riches," ll. 119–20; "Epistle II: Of the Characters of Women," ll. 7–10.

[10] Samuel Johnson, "Milton," in *Works,* Talboys and Wheeler, and W. Pickering, London, 1825, VII, 119.

[11] Johann Wolfgang von Goethe, *Wilhelm Meister's Appenticeship and Travels,* in the translation by Thomas Carlyle, S. E. Cassino & Co., Boston, 1882, I, 58.

[12] *The Works of William Makepeace Thackeray* (The Biographical Edition), Harper and Brothers, New York, 1899–1903, VII, 530–31. (*The English Humourists of the Eighteenth Century,* "Prior, Gay, and Pope.")

his jaw thrust out, he began to grin hideously, his little eyes leering towards Rebecca.

The great Lord of Steyne was standing by the fire sipping coffee. The fire crackled and blazed pleasantly. There was a score of candles sparkling round the mantelpiece, in all sorts of quaint sconces, of gilt and bronze and porcelain. They lighted up Rebecca's figure to admiration, as she sate on a sofa covered with a pattern of gaudy flowers. She was in a pink dress, that looked as fresh as a rose; her dazzling white arms and shoulders were half covered with a thin hazy scarf through which they sparkled; her hair hung in curls round her neck; one of her little feet peeped out from the fresh crisp folds of the silk: the prettiest little foot in the prettiest little sandal in the finest silk stocking in the world.

Here, a charming Dresden figure is set forth in a rhetoric whose pastoral decorum is barely disordered by the realistic images of crackling fire, coffee, and the ersatz blossoms on the town-nymph's meadow—"a sofa covered with a pattern of gaudy flowers." The tinkling pleasantry is more seriously disturbed by the aggressive wit of Arcadia's own Silenus as Steyne begins to crack jokes, grinning "hideously, his little eyes leering":

"And so the Shepherd is not enough," said he, "to defend his lambkin?"

"The Shepherd is too fond of playing at cards and going to his clubs," answered Becky, laughing.

"Gad, what a debauched Corydon!" said my Lord—"what a mouth for a pipe!"

"I take your three to two," here said Rawdon at the cardtable.

"Hark at Meliboeus," snarled the noble Marquis; "he's pastorally occupied too: he's shearing a Southdown: What an innocent mutton, heh? Damme, what a snowy fleece!"

The Marquis' innuendoes are unmistakably indecorous. His jibe "what a mouth for a pipe" runs pastoral riot from derisive suggestions of shepherd's flute and lamb's bleat to a jeer at Rawdon's barracks-room smoking habits. When Steyne identifies Rawdon with the dubious Virgilian lover, Corydon, he impugns the virility of this military "Meliboeus" (" 'How is Mrs. Crawley's husband?' Lord Steyne used to say to him. . . . He was Colonel Crawley no longer. He was Mrs. Crawley's husband.") The aristocratic Silenus' wit is insufferable, and the Shepherdess takes his latest conceit as an invitation to riposte. Sharpening the Marquis' quip about Southdown's "snowy fleece," she turns it into a pastoral pun that pierces the Marquis' Jason-image (knight of the order—seducer of his hostess—hero of the golden fleece) and quivers in Steyne himself: "Rebecca's eyes shot out gleams of scornful humour. 'My Lord,' she said, 'you are a knight of the Order.' He had the collar round his neck, indeed—a gift of the restored Princes of Spain." With Becky's allusion to the nobleman's Golden Fleece, the imputation of foul play ("shearing a Southdown") is diverted from Rawdon, and the aristocrat's sneer at the gambling fraternity is returned with interest, for Rebecca's "knight of the Order" refers as well to the Marquis' former membership in that fraternity:

> Lord Steyne in early life had been notorious for his daring and success at play. He had sat up two days and two nights with Mr. Fox at hazard. He had won money of the most august personages of the realm: he had won his marquisate, it was said, at the gaming table; but he did not like an allusion to those bygone *fredaines.* Rebecca saw the scowl gathering over his heavy brow.
>
> She rose up from her sofa, and went and took his coffee cup out of his hand with a little curtsey. "Yes," she said, "I must get a watchdog. But he won't bark at *you.*" [13]

Thackeray's phrasing is as sure as Rebecca's in this silken transition from Arcadian artifice to narrative present; reality emerges in commonplace details—"sofa," "coffee cup," "watchdog"—that relate the pastoral coda to the imagery of the exposition. The scene's relevance to *Vanity Fair* as a whole is apparent: given a knowledge of the characters it stands for itself, an integral, appropriate allegory.

And yet, it is this quality of independence that marks the passage as immature. The scene is a beautiful embroidery, but it does not assist event; nothing is suggested that was not already premised, and pastoral imagery is not developed during the rest of the novel. The sequence remains pastiche like the parody in *Catherine,* but the expressive method is established, and Thackeray is ready now to integrate this mode into his narrative medium.

As *Pendennis* followed *Vanity Fair,* pastoral fused with dramatic continuity. In *Pendennis,* Arcadian motifs characterize the hero's flirtation with a questionable heroine in graceful parody of artistic and social pretense. There are no profound insights here, nor are they intended; the sequence is a succession of witty water colors, like Thackeray's drawings for the satirical ballet scenes in *Flore et Zephyr.* But, in contrast to the isolated tableau in *Vanity Fair,* the pastoral sequence in *Pendennis* moves freely through dramatic event, pastoral motifs creating as well as ornamenting the action; the metaphor is no longer

[13] *Works,* I, 362–64, ch. 37.

confined to a brilliant cadenza but participates in the flow of narrative prose.

Early in *Pendennis*, allusive imagery discloses a mock-Arcadia of rural English brooks and gardens, the desultory hero, Pendennis, in the role of pastoral swain to Blanche, "the pretty little fish which played round his fly." [14] A coy prelude leads to a conventional pas-de-deux: "Under a piece of moss and a stone, he used to put little poems, or letters equally poetical, which were addressed to a certain Undine, or Naiad who frequented the stream, and which, once or twice, were replaced by a receipt . . . written in a delicate hand, in French or English, and on pink scented paper . . . whilst the tree was reflected into the stream, and the Brawl went rolling by." [15] As in *Vanity Fair*, Thackeray follows the neoclassical practice of satirizing pastoral artifice by introducing commonplace details—"letters equally poetical," "a receipt," "scented paper." But the romantic modulation of subsequent phrases—"the tree was reflected into the stream, and the Brawl went rolling by"—suggests an ironic reference to the Biblical Garden which the Arcadian idyll reflects, and the hint is reinforced a few pages later, when the first phase of this flirtation ends, by a semi-satiric recollection of the "Tree of Life which, from the beginning, has tempted all mankind." [16]

The hero's initial dalliance is inconclusive; other events supersede the artificial love affair and pastoral motifs fade away. The scene shifts to London: Blanche re-enters in a fashionable drawing-room; and Arcadian imagery reappears, altered by the urban context to a decorator's fantasy, like the pastoral setting in *Vanity Fair*—"the carpets were so magnificently fluffy that your foot made no more noise on them than your shadow: on their white ground bloomed roses and tulips as big as warming-pans: about the room were . . . chairs so attenuated that it was a wonder any but a sylph could sit upon them . . . there were Dresden shepherds and shepherdesses . . . light-blue poodles and ducks and cocks and hens in porcelain; there were nymphs by Boucher, and shepherdesses by Greuze, very chaste indeed." [17] The sylph's attenuated chairs prepare this spurious Arcadian setting for the pseudo-heroine, who has now become a "sylphide." [18] The quality of the pastoral artifice is measured by the shopkeeper's unctuous phrase "very chaste indeed."

[14] *Works*, ii, 217, ch. 22.
[15] *Ibid.*, p. 238, ch. 25.
[16] *Ibid.*, p. 246, ch. 25.
[17] *Ibid.*, p. 365, ch. 37.
[18] *Ibid.*, p. 366, ch. 37.

After this central sequence, the pastoral continuity is again diffused into narrative event; but the caricature of civilized Arcadia has prepared for a recapitulation of pastoral themes near the end of the novel. When the ostensible lovers meet again in the country, their eulogy of rural pleasures precedes an inadvertent confession of pretense:

> "And do you really like the country?" he asked her, as they walked together.
> "I should like never to see that odious city again . . . one's good thoughts grow up in those sweet woods and calm solitudes, like those flowers which won't bloom in London, you know. The gardener comes and changes our balconies once a week." [19]

The Arcadian settings, like the idyllic "thoughts" of the pastoral couple, are synthetic—"The gardener comes and changes our balconies once a week." Pursuit of artifice has led to anti-paradise; a rhetorical coda satirizes the decorous affectation: "What took place? O ringdoves and roses, O dews and wild-flowers, O waving greenwoods and balmy airs of summer! Here were two battered London rakes, taking themselves in for a moment, and fancying that they were in love with each other, like Phyllis and Corydon." [20] Corydon, the epithet of Rawdon's displacement in *Vanity Fair,* identifies the present Arcadian hero, and in this epicene role the actor concludes his flirtation. *Pendennis's* pastoral episode is a divertissement, but its allegory is part of the novel's continuous action. From idyllic illusion and the acceptance of artifice to sterility in the ineffectual garden, the Arcadian metaphor has been assimilated into *Pendennis's* expressive textures, and pastoral convention has shared in the novel's continuity, creating, rather than interrupting, dramatic event.

Mock-Epic

Mock-epic in *Vanity Fair,* like pastoral, is a stylistic digression; but if pastoral is a charming arabesque, mock-epic is an intense, purposeful parable. In pastoral costume, Rebecca is only a decorative version of her usual self. In mock-epic, she is a less familiar personification. The novel's mock-epic metaphor, which has complex symbolic connotations, is also irreproachable shorthand for Becky's sexual behavior after her break with Rawdon:

[19] *Ibid.,* p. 634, ch. 63.
[20] *Ibid.,* p. 634, ch. 63.

I defy any one to say that our Becky, who has certainly some vices, has not been presented to the public in a perfectly genteel and inoffensive manner. In describing this siren, singing and smiling, coaxing and cajoling, the author, with modest pride, asks his readers all round, has he once forgotten the laws of politeness, and showed the monster's hideous tail above water? No! Those who like may peep down under waves that are pretty transparent, and see it writhing and twirling, diabolically hideous and slimy, flapping amongst bones, or curling round corpses; but above the water-line, I ask, has not everything been proper, agreeable, and decorous, and has any the most squeamish immoralist in Vanity Fair a right to cry fie? When, however, the siren disappears and dives below, down among the dead men, the water of course grows turbid over her, and it is labour lost to look into it ever so curiously. They look pretty enough when they sit upon a rock, twanging their harps and combing their hair, and sing, and beckon to you to come and hold the looking glass; but when they sink into their native element, depend on it those mermaids are about no good, and we had best not examine the fiendish marine cannibals, revelling and feasting on their wretched pickled victims.[21]

This flaunting decorum is not a prudish expedient—quite the reverse. Charlotte Brontë pointed out that Thackeray's "hint is more vivid than other men's elaborate explanations, and never is his satire [so keen as when] he modestly recommends to the approbation of the public his own exemplary discretion." [22] *Vanity Fair's* mock-epic rhetoric is gilded to attract attention, and its traditional allusions are whimsically mixed. Homer's sirens—bodiless melodies that paralyzed their victims—were not carnivorous water creatures. Perhaps the present mermaids acquired their tails and harps in Thackeray's favorite classical source, "Lempriere's delightful Dictionary": "Some authors suppose that they were monsters who had the form of a woman above the waist, . . . The sirens are often represented holding, one a lyre, a second a flute, and the third singing." In *Odyssey* xii, Circe describes the Homeric sirens; but in Book x, she has sent Odysseus to Hades, and the full context of Homer's Circe-sequence, coalescing with the *Odyssey's* siren-image, suggests elements in the composition of Thackeray's mermaids. The sirens in *Vanity Fair* are amphibious creatures who "dive below" into "turbid water," and this imagery recalls, not Circe's description, but the "vast waters, strange currents" that Odysseus must fathom on his underworld journey; the present sirens'

---

[21] *Works*, I, 624–25, ch. 64.
[22] Charlotte Brontë, *Jane Eyre* (preface to the second edition).

sojourn "among dead men" reflects an image from Agamemnon's speech in Hades: "all around, men slaughtered like white-tusked swine." The swine-image, however, also recalls Circe's domain; and *Vanity Fair*'s mermaids, "feasting on their victims," reflect as well the scene of Odysseus' return to the island where his men are "imprisoned in airless dens like swine." So, Circe herself becomes part of Thackeray's picture; in this setting, she presently gives the Homeric description of the sirens: "melodious hypnotists—for those whom the sirens on the moist grass pierce with song no wife and children wait." Unfathomed waters and carnage in Homeric Hades are the "turbid" "native element" of Thackeray's mermaids; and Circe's predatory aspect fuses with the sirens' lethal image in *Vanity Fair*'s "marine cannibals." Thackeray's "agreeable and decorous" style ("twanging" harps, "about no good," "fiendish cannibals," "pickled victims") is neoclassical—a mock-epic diminution of rhetorical decorum by means of incongruous epithets.

And there is another aspect to *Vanity Fair*'s mock-epic evocation, one of mythic suggestion. The classical metaphor's mocking hints of sexual promiscuity not only convey realistic aspects of Becky's experience but suggest a dimension of primordial sensuality, a reptilian concupiscence "writhing and twirling," "flapping amongst bones or curling round corpses"—an amoral Becky, a prehuman form, only "diabolical" and "fiendish" in its "coaxing," "cajoling," feminine impersonation when it becomes a "monster's hideous tail"—a fish out of water.

In Thackeray's later novels, *Vanity Fair*'s mock-epic experiment developed, like pastoral, into a sustained narrative mode; in *Henry Esmond,* the heroic metaphor is fundamental. The significance of epic in *Esmond* will call for analysis later on; here, however, the less intense but fully integrated use of epic in *The Newcomes* will exemplify Thackeray's mature method. But before discussing *The Newcomes,* it will be necessary to look at the literary background of the heroic techniques with which Thackeray was familiar; their history is longer than that of Thackeray's other modes, and his use of them is complex.

Renaissance burlesque had a fine tradition—Chaucer, Shakespeare, and Cervantes parodied pastoral and chivalry—but the mock-epic mode is a more recent phenomenon. True mock-epic is comic amplification; preserving the stylistic decorum of heroic convention, it elevates base materials while it satirizes their insufficiency. Conversely, travesty and burlesque discredit their models. Dr. Johnson makes the point in his Life of Butler: "Burlesque consists in a disproportion between the style and the sentiments, or between the adventitious sentiments and the fundamental subject. It, therefore, like all bodies compounded of heterogeneous parts, contains in it a principle of corruption. . . . . We admire it awhile as a strange thing; but, when it is no longer strange, we perceive its deformity." [23] In Thackeray, burlesque, which accompanies mock-epic, needs no annotation; its techniques have remained the same from Petronius to Evelyn Waugh. But his mock-epic method is a legacy from the neoclassical satirists who were the first to discriminate among the different kinds of heroic imitation.

If Boileau is not indisputably mock-epic's creator, he is probably the first to discuss it critically; and he is very conscious of innovation. In the preface to *Le Lutrin* he announces his achievement: "C'est un burlesque nouveau, dont je me suis avisé en notre langue: car, au lieu que dans l'autre burlesque, Didon et Énée parloient comme des harengères et des crocheteurs, dans celui-ci une horlogère et un horloger parlent comme Didon et Énée." [24] This first critical recognition of mock-epic makes a special point of the factor of amplification. Dryden pursues the argument in his "Discourse Concerning Satire": "[Boileau] writes . . . ['Le Lutrin'] in the French heroic verse, and calls it an heroic poem; his subject is trivial, but his verse is noble. I doubt not but he had Virgil in his eye, for we find many admirable imitations of him, and some parodies. . . . This, I think, my Lord, to be the most beautiful, and most noble kind of satire. Here is the majesty of the heroic, finely mixed with the venom of the other; and raising the delight which otherwise would be flat and vulgar, by the sublimity of the expression." [25] Dryden's distinction between "imitations" and "parodies" is important; in true mock-epic, the mode is imitation not caricature—incongruity is confined to the content of the chosen subject.

It was Johnson who most convincingly argued that "noble verse" and dramatic conventions suitable to "an heroic poem" could be adapted to elevate a "trivial subject." The idea is expressed in his discussion of *The Rape of the Lock:* "Pope brought into view a new race of beings, with powers and passions proportionate to their operation. The sylphs and gnomes act, at the toilet and the tea-table, what more terrifick and powerful phantoms perform on the stormy ocean, or the field of battle. . . . New things are made familiar, and familiar things are made new. . . . The subject of the poem is an event below the common

[23] Samuel Johnson, "Butler," *Works*, VII, 155–56.
[24] Boileau, "Au Lecteur," Preface (1st printed 1674) to "Le Lutrin," *Oeuvres Complètes*, Garnier Frères, Paris, 1872, II, 405.
[25] Dryden, "A Discourse Concerning the Original and Progress of Satire," *Essays*, II, 107–8.

incidents of common life . . . yet the whole detail of a female day is here brought before us invested with so much art of decoration, that, though nothing is disguised, every thing is striking." [26] Unlike burlesque, mock-epic reveals the triviality of its subject only in the contrast between elevated manner and undignified matter. The derogatory rhetoric of burlesque is never appropriate in mock-epic, where the nobility of the heroic language should sustain the epic decorum, while implicit contrast both satirizes the inadequacy of the content and suggests the presence of the ideal in the commonplace.

The opening lines of Pope's *Dunciad*, for instance, like many mock-epic passages in Thackeray, are rhetorically unexceptionable. They are comic rather than heroic epic by a process of induction alone—"The mighty mother, and her son, who brings The Smithfield muses to the ear of kings." "Smithfield" is not inherently satiric, although its incidental absurdity is a useful cue to readers; only the cunning precision of the epithets ("mighty" with mother, none with son) suggests cumbrous despotic Dullness and the servile Grub Street Poet. A slight alteration in these epithets would subvert the humor and turn the lines into pompous eulogy, while the use of indecorous diminutives would result in travesty. Later passages in *The Dunciad*, however, include both "parodies" and mock-epic "imitations"—the "grossness of its images," Dr. Johnson remarked, turns many lines into burlesque[27]—

> Why should I sing, what bards the nightly Muse
> Did slumb'ring visit, and convey to stews; . . .
> How Henley lay inspir'd beside a sink,
> And to mere mortals seem'd a Priest in drink.[28]

"Nightly" is felicitous satire, but most of the rhetoric is indecorous. "Stews," "sink," and "Priest in drink" debase the epic convention; both concept and content become farcical. "But even this fault," Johnson points out, "may be forgiven for the excellence of other passages." [29]

In Thackeray, burlesque, mock-, and heroic epic co-exist: his early journalistic comments on Greece, for example, combine farcical derision—"Think of 'filling high a cup of Samian wine' . . . Byron himself always drank gin"; comic diminution—"of the Temple of Jupiter . . . I declare with confidence that not one [column] is taller than our own glorious Monument on Fish Street Hill"; and sober reverence: "You and I could not invent—it even stretches our minds

[26] Johnson, "Pope," *Works*, VIII, 332–33.
[27] *Ibid.*, p. 339.
[28] Pope, "Dunciad," Book II, ll. 421–26.
[29] Johnson, "Pope," p. 339.

painfully to try and comprehend part of the beauty of the Parthenon
—ever so little of it,—the beauty of a single column,—a fragment of
a broken shaft lying under the astonishing blue sky there, in the midst
of that unrivalled landscape." [30] In Thackeray's early novels, burlesque
heroics are progressively revised towards the "agreeable and decorous"
mock-epic of *Vanity Fair.* Predictably, Thackeray, like Dr. Johnson,
disparages Pope's reliance on farce; *The Dunciad*'s abusive rhetoric,
"gin, cowheel, tripe," he comments, "is so easy to write." [31] But Johnson's praise of the "stately numbers which dignify the concluding paragraph" [32] is tepid to Thackeray's eulogy of "that wonderful flight with
which the 'Dunciad' concludes . . . the loftiest assertion of truth, the
most generous wisdom illustrated by the noblest poetic figure." [33]

In comparison with neoclassical genres, Thackeray's epic has no
fixed categories. The Augustans distinguished between heroic and mock-
epic by rhetorical subject. The "great Argument" of "Eternal Providence" was asserted in *Paradise Lost;* conversely, *The Rape of the Lock*
described "What mighty contests rise from trivial things." Mock-epic
itself was differentiated from more farcical burlesque only by rhetorical
technique. But, though rhetoric is a variable index, *The Dunciad* is not
hard to distinguish from *Hudibras.* Thackeray's textures, by contrast,
are ambiguous; burlesque, comic, and heroic epic are juxtaposed in
novels like *Henry Esmond*—the fluctuating modality expresses an
awareness of the multiple aspects of experience. Within this relativistic
context, however, Thackeray's epic modes can often be distinguished
by the idiomatic variations that indicate a serious or satiric emphasis.
Mock-epic is his habitual mode, and instances of his mock-epic manner
vary from quasi-burlesque to quasi-heroic, depending on the farcical
or decorous quality of the satire. In Thackeray's cursive rhetoric, the
language is contemporary and unexceptional—"Miss Newcome has a
great look of the huntress Diana"; in semi-farce, it is often colloquial—
"Diana and Diana's grandmother"; in decorous satire, the epithet is
frequently a compressed allegory—"Diana whose looks were so cold
and whose arrows were so keen." Heroic epic is characterized by more
oblique, suggestive allusion, often by Greek or Latin quotation—"In
Miss Ethel's black hair there was a slight natural ripple, as when a fresh
breeze blows over the *melan hudor*"—and by tacit personification—
"Ethel, severe nymph with the bright eyes." In more intense moments,

[30] *Works*, v, 625–27 ("A Journey from Cornhill to Cairo"); *Works*, vi, 80 ("Wanderings of Our Fat Contributor," in "Contributions to Punch").
[31] *Works*, vii, 555 (*The English Humourists*, "Prior, Gay, and Pope").
[32] Johnson, "Pope," p. 339.
[33] *Works*, vii, 555–56 (*The English Humourists*, "Prior, Gay, and Pope").

the metaphor's immediate dramatic application is often equivocal. Thus, a passage of classical imagery in *The Newcomes* that seems to be a poetic digression, becomes in the event a prophetic emblem of the protagonists' future suffering: "I was looking, of late, at a wall in the Naples Museum, whereon a boy of Herculaneum eighteen hundred years ago had scratched with a nail the figure of a soldier. . . . Which of us that is thirty years old has not had his Pompeii? . . . You open an old letter-box and look at your own childish scrawls, or your mother's letters to you when you were at school; and excavate your heart." [34]

In *The Newcomes*, mock-epic develops into sustained polyphony as does pastoral in *Pendennis*. The mode is most frequently associated with a Diana-motif that characterizes the heroine, and this metaphor sustains one of the novel's major themes—a satiric parable on the Victorian marriage market. The fable begins with the hero's apostrophe to the statues of Venus and Diana at the Louvre: "O Victrix! O lucky Paris! . . . How could he give the apple to any else but this enslaver, —this joy of gods and men? at whose benign presence the flowers spring up, and the smiling ocean sparkles, and the soft skies beam with serene light! . . . Did you ever see my pretty young cousin, Miss Newcome, Sir Brian's daughter? She has a great look of the huntress Diana. It is sometimes too proud and too cold for me. The blare of those horns is too shrill, and the rapid pursuit through bush and bramble too daring." [35]

Ethel Newcome is as yet an innocent, self-centred young girl. She is not aware of the marital commerce that controls the society in which she lives. But the satiric point is already implicit in the classical imagery —Venus, the sexual quarry, is paired with Diana, the virgin huntress, and the mercenary chase is on. Although mock-epic rhetoric seems to contrast the two divinities, their conjunction in the hunt is suggested by Thackeray's substitution of the aggressive epithet "Victrix" in the paraphrase that begins the quoted passage for Lucretius' original "Genetrix! Delight of Gods and men, sweet Venus" for whom "earth bears scented flowers . . . oceans smile . . . serene skies glow with soft radiance." [36] The pride and purity of Diana are real attributes of the heroine in this early phase of her experience, but their potential

[34] *Works*, VIII, 286, ch. 28.
[35] *Ibid.*, p. 216, ch. 22.
[36] Lucretius, *De Rerum Natura*, Book I, ll. 1–2. Citations from the Latin text refer to the Loeb Classical Library edition; the present author's free translations are indebted to William Ellery Leonard's version in The Modern Library (New York, 1950).

distortion into hostile, predatory qualities is conveyed by echoes of the *Iliad*'s Diana-epithets, "fond of hunting," "piercing, noisy."

As the novel continues, Ethel becomes increasingly aware of her commercial value in the Victorian market; she admits it at first with bitter resentment—"when we are exhibiting, [we] ought to have little green tickets pinned on our backs, with 'Sold' written on them." [37] Thackeray's classical imagery, shading from travesty to pathos and recurrently invoking the initial Lucretian allusion, traces the emotional course of the heroine's career. In Lucretius, the invocation to Venus is followed by the sacrifice of Iphigenia: "As once at Aulis, the elected chiefs . . . defiled Diana's altar, virgin queen, with Agamemnon's daughter, foully slain. . . . A parent felled her on her bridal day, making his child a sacrificial beast." [38] So, in *The Newcomes*, the Diana-motif woven into Thackeray's initial paraphrase of the Venus-metaphor leads, though a series of satiric allusions ("a virgin sold," "funeral pile," "the deadly couch") to a restatement of Lucretius' Iphigenia-image in a passage of pure mock-epic, where the "decorous painter" both elevates and satirizes contemporary codes by introducing delicate fashionable overtones into the classical rhetoric: "let us pity Lady Iphigenia's father when that venerable chief is obliged to offer up his darling child; but it is over *her* part of the business that a decorous painter would throw the veil now. Her ladyship's sacrifice is performed, and the less said about it the better." [39] The heroine's scruples are gradually removed; Victorian beauty ("O Victrix"), under the tutelage of her grandmother, is persuaded to seek a desirable match with the Marquis of Farintosh. As Ethel's participation in the marital chase grows more ardent and purposeful, she comes to resemble the *Odyssey*'s "chaste goddess with gentle, lethal arrows"—"other Mayfair nymphs were afraid of this severe Diana, whose looks were so cold, and whose arrows were so keen." [40] Eventually, the Homeric huntress undergoes a further metamorphosis and the imagery suggests a feminine scavenger, searching for marital spoil: "we must compare the Marquis of Farintosh to a lamb for the nonce, and Miss Ethel Newcome to a young eaglet. Is it not a rare provision of nature . . . that the strong-winged bird can soar to the sun and gaze at it, and then come down from heaven and pounce on a piece of carrion?" [41]

[37] *Works*, VIII, 289, ch. 28.
[38] Lucretius, Book I, ll. 84–99.
[39] *Works*, VIII, 288, pp. 291–92, ch. 28.
[40] *Ibid.*, p. 245, ch. 24.
[41] *Ibid.*, p. 486, ch. 46.

At last the scene reverts to Paris, where the hero's original apostrophe to Venus and Diana initiated the heroine's epic personifications. There, Ethel receives a proposal from her eligible Marquis, and the Victorian fable concludes with a diminutive apologue: "I was not present when Diana and Diana's grandmother hunted the noble Scottish stag of whom we have just been writing; nor care to know how many times Lord Farintosh escaped, and how at last he was brought to bay and taken by his resolute pursuers. Paris, it appears, was the scene of his fall and capture." [42] From the Paris of idealized classical art to a Paris of pseudo-heroic social competition, the mock-epic mode has defined the progress of Thackeray's heroine; the isolated parable of *Vanity Fair* has become a dramatic sequence in *The Newcomes.*

And there is another aspect of Thackeray's expressive integration in *The Newcomes* which is worth considering, since it is major element in the technique of his mature novels. This is the fusion of his full range of allusive modes—fashionable, romance, pastoral, epic—in passages where the novel's figurative themes meet and intersect. Such a passage occurs in the central part of *The Newcomes.* It opens with a typical instance of Thackeray's rhetorical revision towards true mock-epic decorum—the alteration of an early burlesque of Ariadne, who "consoled herself with drinking," [43] to the present classical image of the Marquise Ariane, "who had taken to Bacchus as a consolation." The scene is Baden, a continental resort where the hero and heroine meet:

> There was not one woman there who was not the heroine of some discreditable story. It was the Comtesse Calypso who had been jilted by the Duc Ulysse. It was the Marquise Ariane to whom the Prince Thésée had behaved so shamefully, and who had taken to Bacchus as a consolation. It was Madame Médée who had absolutely killed her old father by her conduct regarding Jason; she had done everything for Jason; she had got him the *toison d'or* from the Queen Mother, and now had to meet him every day with his little blonde bride on his arm! J.J. compared Ethel, moving in the midst of these folks, to the Lady amidst the rout of Comus. There they were, the Fauns and Satyrs: there they were, the merry Pagans: drinking and dancing, dicing and sporting. . . . He did not know, in the first place, the mystery of their iniquities. . . . The world was welcome to him; the day a pleasure; all nature a gay feast . . . Clive's happy friendly nature shone out of his face; and almost all who beheld it felt kindly towards him. As those guileless virgins of romance

[42] *Ibid.,* p. 559, ch. 53.
[43] *Works,* VI, 64 ("Wanderings of Our Fat Contributor," in "Contributions to Punch").

and ballad, who walk smiling through dark forests charming off dragons and confronting lions, the young man as yet went through the world harmless; no giant waylaid him as yet; no robbing ogre fed on him; and (greatest danger of all for one of his ardent nature) no winning enchantress or artful siren coaxed him to her cave, or lured him into her waters—haunts into which we know so many young simpletons are drawn, where their silly bones are picked and their tender flesh devoured.[44]

In this passage, Thackeray's multiple expressive modes create a varied series of imaginative perspectives. Classical reference is modified by fashionable idiom—"jilted," "behaved so shamefully," "absolutely killed her father"—and is rephrased as mock-epic in the pseudo-heroic modern epithets—"Marquise Ariane," "Prince Thésée," "Madame Médée," "*toison d'or.*" The central reference to *Comus* diffuses pastoral imagery through the passage's mock-classical and fashionable textures—"fauns," "satyrs," "merry Pagans." A free transition evokes the hero's biblical innocence—"He did not know . . . the mystery of their iniquities"—and anticipates, in an ironic image—"nature a gay feast"—the sardonic resolution of the predatory metaphor—"tender flesh devoured." The mode modulates to the chivalric convention— "guileless virgins of romance"—and romance motifs—"dragons," "giants," "ogres"—are fused with classical allusion as the "winning enchantress" is paired with the "artful siren" in language that rephrases *Vanity Fair*'s mock-epic imagery ("marine cannibals," "pickled victims") and resolves the polyphonic modulations in a prophetic figuration of the hero's marital tragedy and the heroine's role as scavenging Diana: "no winning enchantress or artful siren coaxed him to her cave, or lured him into her waters—haunts into which we know so many young simpletons are drawn, where their silly bones are picked and their tender flesh devoured."

[44] *Works*, VIII, pp. 284–85, ch. 28.

Henry Esmond as an Historical Novel

by Georg Lukács

Thackeray is an outstanding critical realist. He has deep ties with the best traditions of English literature, with the great social canvases of the eighteenth century, which he treated at length in several interesting critical studies. Consciously, he has no interest in separating the historical from the social-critical novel, that is in turning the historical novel into a genre of its own, which was generally the objective result of this development. However, he does not base himself on the classical form of the historical novel, that is on Scott; instead, he attempts to apply the traditions of the eighteenth century social novel to a new type of historical novel. We have said before that eighteenth century historical events were included in the English realist novel particularly in Fielding and Smollett, however only insofar as they came into direct contact with the personal lives of the heroes; thus from the standpoint of the general conception and artistic tendencies of this period, only episodically and never really affecting the chief problems of the novels.

Thackeray, then, consciously takes over this manner of portrayal in his historical novels, but his outlook and artistic aim are quite different from those of the eighteenth century realists. *The approach of the latter towards historicism* grew in a natural way out of their social-critical, realist tendencies. It was one of the many steps towards that realistic conception of history, of social and natural life, which reached its apex in Scott or Pushkin. In the case of Thackery this *return* to the style and structure of the novels of the eighteenth century stems from a quite different ideological cause, from a deep and bitter disillusionment with the nature of politics, with the relations between social and political life in his own time. This disillusionment expresses

"*Henry Esmond* as an Historical Novel" (editor's title). From *The Historical Novel*, by Georg Lukács, trans. from the German by Hannah and Stanley Mitchell (London: The Merlin Press, Ltd., 1962; Boston: Beacon Press, 1963), pp. 201–206. Copyright © 1962 by The Merlin Press, Ltd. Reprinted by permission of the publishers.

itself satirically. By resuming the style of the eighteenth century Thackeray wishes to expose contemporary apologetics.

He, therefore, sees the dilemma in the portayal of historical events as a choice between public pathos and private manners, the glorification of the one or the realistic depiction of the other. Thus when his hero, Henry Esmond, telling his own story—at the turn of the seventeenth to eighteenth centuries—polemically counters the official histories with the novels of Fielding, when in a discussion with Addison he defends the rights of realism in describing war against poetic embellishment, his language—the language of the memoir—captures the tone of the period beautifully, yet at the same time it expresses Thackeray's own artistic convictions. The basis of this style is the exposure of false heroism, in particular the reputed heroism fostered by historical legend. Esmond speaks of this, too, very vividly and finely: "What spectacle is more august than that of a great king in exile? Who is more worthy of respect than a brave man in misfortune? Mr. Addison has painted such a figure in his noble piece of *Cato*. But suppose fugitive Cato fuddling himself at the tavern with a wench on his knee, a dozen faithful and tipsy companions of defeat, and a landlord calling out for his bill; and the dignity of misfortune is straightway lost." Thackeray requires this exposure in order to strip history of its periwig, in order to deny that English and French history took place only at the courts of Windsor and Versailles.

Of course, it is Esmond who says all this and not Thackeray himself, and the novel is not meant to be an objective picture of the time, but simply the hero's autobiography. But apart from the fact that this relationship between private manners and historical events is very similar, say, to that in *Vanity Fair,* with a writer as important and conscious as Thackeray the composition of *Henry Esmond* cannot be accidental. The memoir is an appropriate form for Thackeray's exposure of pseudo-greatness. Everything can be seen from the proximity of everyday private life and, shown in this microscopic way, the false pathos of the artificial, self-imagined hero collapses. And this is what is intended. The hero has seen Louis XIV in old age. Louis, says Esmond, was perhaps a hero for a book, for a statue, for a mural, "but what more than a man for Madame Maintenon, or the barber who shaved him, or Monsieur Fagon, his surgeon?" Proximity destroys the alleged greatness of Marlborough, the Stuart Pretender and many others. And when every great man swindle of history has been exposed, there remains just the honesty of simply, slightly above average men capable of real sacrifice like the hero himself.

This picture is remarkably consistent. But is it a real picture of the time, as Thackeray intended? Thackeray's answer to his own dilemma is right enough. But the dilemma itself is narrow and wrong. There is a third way: what, in fact, the classical historical novel does. Admittedly, the epoch following the "Glorious Revolution" and ending with the establishment of the House of Hanover on the throne of England is certainly not one of the most heroic of periods; especially as regards the behaviour and activity of the supporters of Stuart Restoration. But we recall that Scott, too, had portrayed these Stuart restoration attempts (in *Waverley* and, for a later period, in *Rob Roy* and *Redgauntlet*), and had neither idealized nor indeed spared either the dynasty or its followers. Nevertheless, the picture of history he produced was grand, dramatic and rife with deep conflict in every phase. The secret of these grand dimensions is easily discoverable. Scott gives a broad and *objective* picture both of the historical forces which lead to the Stuart rebellions and of those which inevitably foredoom them. At the centre of this picture are the Scottish clans, driven to desperation by economic and social circumstances and misled by adventurers. The fate of the Pretender himself is tragi-comic in Scott, the fate of his English adherents either comic or pathetic. The latter are dissatisfied with the Hanoverian régime, yet keep quiet because they are too cowardly and irresolute to act, because they do not dare jeopardize their material well-being; because the growth of capitalism in England has levelled out the former distinctions between feudal and capitalist land-ownership. But since the background to the action is the real suffering and real heroism (however untimely and misguided) of a people, the events lose all their trivial, mean and haphazard qualities, all that is purely individual and private about them.

Thackeray, however, does not see the people. He reduces his story to the intrigues of the upper classes. Of course, he knows perfectly well that these trivialities are confined to the class he describes and tell us nothing of the real historical process. It is not by chance that every so often the Cromwell age, the heroic period of the English people, casts its shadow in discussions. But this period seems to have wholly disappeared, and the life which is described is given over entirely to trivial and private goings-on. The people's attitude to what happens is never revealed. Yet it was at this time that those who had fought the battles of the Civil War, above all the middle farmers, yeomanry and city plebeians were undergoing economic and moral ruin as a result of the tempestuous development of capitalism. Only much later did the new heroes, the Luddites and Chartists, arise from the soil made fertile by their blood. Of this tragedy, which is the real basis of the tragi-comedies and comedies occurring "on top" Thackeray sees nothing.

But he thereby dispels historical objectivity, and the more compellingly he motivates his characters psychologically, the subtler this private psychology, the more haphazard it all appears in an historical perspective. The psychology is not wrong, on the contrary it very subtly shows the accidental nature of the political standpoints of the characters. But this accidentality can only appear truly false, if placed within an objective class context where it becomes a factor of historical necessity. Scott's Waverley also joins the Stuart Rebellion by accident; but he is simply there as a foil to those for whom the revolt is a social-historical necessity. The perspective in which Thackeray shows Marlborough, however, is purely private. His hero, he says, has become a bitter enemy rather than an enthusiastic follower of Marlborough simply because of bad treatment at a levée. The resulting caricature is such that Thackeray himself feels compelled to counter his own subjectivism with supplementary corrections and notes to his memoirs. But these corrections lessen the one-sidedness only theoretically, they cannot give the figure of Marlborough any objective-historical relief.

This subjectivism degrades all the historical figures who appear in the novel. We see only the "all-too-human" side of Swift, so that we should have to regard him as a petty intriguer and careerist, if we did not have a different picture of him from *his own* works. But even characters whom Esmond describes with obvious sympathy, such as Steele and Addison, the well-known writers of the epoch, are objectively degraded, because their personalities reveal no more than the normal, sociable habits of everyday private life. What made them into important representatives of the epoch, into ideologists of big social changes is excluded from the story by Thackeray's general conception. The influence of their journal *The Spectator,* which extended over the whole of educated bourgeois Europe, is sufficiently well-known in both history and the history of literature, as well as the fact that it was largely due to the use of everyday events as a basis for arguing and demonstrating the new, triumphant morality of the rising bourgeoisie. *The Spectator* turns up in *Henry Esmond,* too; the hero uses his personal friendship with the editors in order to ridicule the frivolous coquetry of the woman with whom he is in love and so exert a beneficial moral influence upon her. No doubt such articles did appear in the journal. But to reduce its historical role to private episodes of this kind means, objectively, the distortion of history, its degradation to the level of the trivial and the private.

Thackeray undoubtedly suffered as a result of this discrepancy. In another historical novel (*The Virginians*) he gives voice to his dissatisfaction. He argues that it is not possible for the present-day writer to show his characters in the context of their professional lives, their actual work etc. The writer has to confine himself to the passions —love or jealousy—on the one hand and to outward forms of social life (in the superficial "worldly" sense) on the other. Thackeray herewith states very tersely the decisive failing of the period of the nascent decline of realism—though without understanding the real social causes and their artistic consequences. He does not see this failing as the result of a narrowed-down and one-sided conception of man, of the fact that characters have come adrift from the main currents of popular life and hence from the really important problems and forces of the age.

The classic realist writers were able to portray these sides of human life poetically and plastically, because in their works all social forces still took the form of human relationships. An important reversal such as the threatened bankruptcy of old Osbaldiston in *Rob Roy* enables Scott to draw from the social-human drama of the situation the various commercial practices of the Glasgow merchants without any ponderous descriptions of *milieu*. In Tolstoy, the different attitudes to professional army life on the part of Andrei Bolkonsky, Nikolai Rostov, Boris Drubetskoy, Berg etc., the differing views on agriculture and serfdom on the part of old and young Bolkonsky are organic integral components of the story, and of the human and psychological development of these characters.

As attitudes towards society and history become more and more private, so such vividly seen connections vanish. Professional life appears dead; everything human is submerged under the desert sands of capitalist prose. The later naturalists—even Zola—seize upon the prose and place it at the centre of literature, but they only fix and perpetuate its withered features, limiting their picture to a description of the "thing-like" *milieu*. What Thackeray, with the right instinct, though from a false situation, declared unportrayable, they leave as it is, replacing portrayals by mere descriptions—supposedly scientific, and brilliant in detail—of things and thing-relationships.

Thackeray is too conscious a realist, too strongly tied to the traditions of true realism for him to take this naturalist way out. Hence he escapes back beyond the classical and for him unattainable form of the historical novel to an artificial renewal of the style of the English Enlightenment. This archaism, however, can only lead to problematic results, as it does elsewhere. The quest for a style leads to stylization, bringing the weaknesses in Thackeray's general conception of social life garishly to the surface, stressing them much more strongly than he would consciously intend. His only wish is to expose false greatness, pseudo-heroism, yet the effect of his stylization, as we have seen, is to show every historical figure, whatever his importance, in a disparaging and sometimes thoroughly destructive light. He wishes to counter this with the genuine, inner nobility of simple morality, but his stylization turns his positive characters into tedious, insufferable paragons of virtue. True, the literary traditions of the eighteenth century lend cohesion to his works and this has a beneficial effect at a time when naturalism is beginning to break up narrative form. Still, this cohesion is only a stylistic one, it does not touch the depths of the portrayal; hence at most it can only cover up the "problematic" which arises from the making private of history, but not solve it.

The Love Theme of *Henry Esmond*

by *John E. Tilford, Jr.*

I

The first chapter of *Henry Esmond* opens with the meeting of young Henry and Rachel Esmond, Viscountess Castlewood, and their complex relations provide the major thematic integration of the novel. For most readers, however, the love interest centers in Henry's chronic courtship of Beatrix, Rachel's daughter. In modern criticism of the novel, allusions to the love of Henry and Rachel are usually perfunctory, often indicating little more than that, after the decline and fall of Beatrix, they were wed—a union which distressed many Victorian critics because of its disquieting implications of incest. For a century there has been no widespread perception of Thackeray's intentions regarding this pervasive love theme.[1]

Thackeray himself was markedly reticent about his thematic intentions, both during the composition of *Esmond* (as Lady Ritchie recalls) and after its publication in October 1852. He mentioned it many times in his letters, but said almost nothing about the love theme. One reason, without doubt, was that *Esmond* reflected an intensely personal part of his own life—his love for Jane Brookfield—which came to a sad crisis in September 1851, shortly after he had begun writing the novel; and he repeatedly remarked that his painful feelings during this period affected the tone of his "grave and sad" book. Several recent studies have examined the ways in which the characters, the plot, and Esmond's commentary shadow forth the Brookfield affair.[2]

"The Love Theme of *Henry Esmond*" by John E. Tilford, Jr. From *PMLA*, LXVII (1952), 684–701. Copyright 1952 by the Modern Language Association. Reprinted by permission of the author and the Modern Language Association.

[1] For a brief survey of pertinent criticism, see my " 'Unsavoury Plot' of *Henry Esmond*," *Nineteenth-Century Fiction*, VI (Sept. 1951), 121–130.

[2] Gordon N. Ray, Introd. to *Henry Esmond*, Modern Library Coll. Ed. (New York, 1950); J. Y. T. Greig, *Thackeray: A Reconsideration* (London, 1950), Chap. XIV; Lionel Stevenson, *The Showman of Vanity Fair* (New York, 1947), p. 246, and Introd. to *Henry Esmond*, Harper's Modern Classics (New York, 1950); and Lambert

Another reason for Thackeray's reticence was probably the daring nature of the story itself; though faced by much critical disapproval, he apparently felt that he had best keep quiet. (He had already experienced ugly publicity when rumors had identified him as the Rochester of *Jane Eyre*.) His curt remark to Mrs. John Brown that it was not he who had married Henry and Rachel, "They married themselves," suggests his unwillingness to discuss the matter even with close friends. But it also suggests his intentions regarding the relations of his characters, and it is a plausible statement.

Thackeray's reactions to two reviews give some further indication of how he felt and what he had intended. George Brimley, in the *Spectator* (6 Nov. 1852), lauded the novel in every respect and particularly admired the characterization of Henry and Rachel. He observed that Henry's "life is throughout a record of his attachment to one woman, towards whom his childish gratitude . . . grows . . . into a complex feeling, in which filial affection and an unconscious passion are curiously blended." Thackeray's "consummate skill" not only saved these relations "from becoming ridiculous, or offensive, or both," but gave "rise to beauties which a safer ambition would have not dared to attempt." This review, wrote Thackeray from America (in late 1852), "brought tears into my eyes—I think it will into some folks at home—a few, a few—and who would have many?" [3] But the review in the *Times* (23 Dec. 1852) wholeheartedly attacked the novel, the worst thing of all being the concluding marriage: "Esmond, the importunate and high-souled, the sensitive and delicate-minded, marries his own 'dear mother'!" Of this review, Thackeray wrote a few weeks later: "I was pleased—The man cannot understand what I am writing any more than poor Jack Forster; and it's quite as right that they should speak and think ill of my writing, as that I should

---

Ennis, *Thackeray: The Sentimental Cynic* (Evanston, Ill., 1950), pp. 176–183. See also Malcolm Elwin, *Thackeray* (London, 1935), pp. 209–211; H. N. Wethered, *On the Art of Thackeray* (London, 1938), p. 114; John W. Dodds, *Thackeray: A Critical Portrait* (New York, 1941), Chap. viii; Howard O. Brogan, "Rachel Esmond and the Dilemma of the Victorian Ideal of Womanhood," *ELH*, XIII (Sept. 1946), 223–232; and Lady Ritchie's Introd. to the Centenary Biographical Edition of *Esmond* (London, 1911). See *The Letters and Private Papers of William Makepeace Thackeray*, ed. Gordon N. Ray, 4 vols. (Cambridge, Mass., 1945–46), for Thackeray's remarks about *Esmond*, esp., passim, II, 708–815; III, 15–47, 181–390; IV, 125, 429–437. Letters dealing with Thackeray and Jane Brookfield are found in II, 802 ff.; III; and IV, esp. 418 ff.

[3] *Letters*, III, 135. The review is reprinted in George Brimley, *Essays*, ed. W. G. Clark (London, 1882), pp. 226–235.

continue on my way. May God help us to say the Truth alway." [4] It would be perilous to conclude that Thackeray's remarks referred exclusively to the treatment of the love theme by the reviews, but as each had expressed strongly contradictory judgments of it, we may reasonably infer that he approved Brimley's interpretation.

The biographical approach to literature is a tempting and popular one, and it has much value if the literature itself is not lost sight of. As Gordon N. Ray says, "No doubt *Esmond* stands firm without the support of biographical exegesis, yet much can be learned about the novel by studying it in connection with . . . 'the Brookfield affair'." [5] We do indeed learn much from Ray's judicious exegesis. But fascinating as it is to contemplate *Esmond* as a symbolic expression of Thackeray's spiritual tribulations, our final concern is with the book as a work of art. For however much Thackeray was sublimating his personal grief, he was primarily, we may believe, writing a novel to be understood and enjoyed in itself, to be judged by its merits alone. We know of his intensive labor on the book and of his repeated conviction that it was his best work, by which he "should like to stand or fall." He did not demand that his contemporary readers know the details of his private life in order to make sense of his story; nor can that demand be made today. That Rachel and Henry are in many ways drawn from Jane Brookfield and Thackeray, and that the relations of the former in the novel suggestively parallel those of the latter in life, are ultimately irrelevant. As a novel *per se* it is neither better nor worse thereby, any more than it would be if it were anonymous.

II

Many readers today, like the Victorian reviewers, are agitated when Henry Esmond announces his marriage to his "dear mistress." They have not clearly seen that he "had been in love with the mother, as well as with the daughter, all along," that "she did not exactly wait to be a widow before she fell in love with him," [6] and particularly

---

[4] *Letters,* III, 175. The *Times* review is reprinted in *Littell's Living Age,* XXXVI (Jan.–Mar. 1853), 277–280. Thackeray later wrote, not accurately, that "the sale [of *Esmond*] was absolutely stopped by a Times article" (*Letters,* IV, 125). Forster's unsigned review (identified by Ray) appeared in the *Examiner,* 13 Nov. 1852, pp. 723–726, but Thackeray said he did not read it (see *Letters,* III, 135, 155, 175, 250). Forster, though generally hostile, was surprisingly accurate in recognizing the main outline of Rachel's attachment to Henry; but he could not be induced "to accept or tolerate such a set of incidents as these."

[5] Introd. to *Henry Esmond,* p. xi.

[6] George Saintsbury, *A Consideration of Thackeray* (London, 1931), p. 196.

that Thackeray had long foreshadowed the eventual marriage. Pelham Edgar observes that even the first meeting of the pair in Chapter i "has more value than appears on the surface, for it adjusts our point of view at the outset to the charm and graciousness of Rachel, and to the precocious gravity of the boy. . . . The author's problem will be to lead us through the subsequent years of Esmond's infatuation for the daughter to his marriage with the mother; and infinite and almost successful are the pains he takes to accommodate us to this strange adjustment of his affections." ⁷ Actually, Thackeray begins adjusting our point of view in the Preface to the memoirs, supposedly written by Henry's daughter. There, besides revealing much that Henry could hardly tell, the daughter presages some of the most important elements of the story—the extraordinary youthfulness of Henry's wife ("At sixty . . . she still looked young"); her "extreme devotion" to him, "passionate and exclusive"; her pathological jealousy; and even the end of the "future bishop's lady" (i.e., Beatrix).⁸ We are not told that Henry's wife is named Rachel (though his daughter's having the same name is a broad hint); still, her most apparent characteristics are emphasized, and her final relations to Henry implicit. The crucial question is whether Thackeray's pains are only "almost successful" in accommodating us to "this strange adjustment."

Though it is not possible here to trace all the ramifications of the love theme, Thackeray's intentions and methods can be clarified by focusing attention on two key scenes. In each there is crisis, and from each the love theme takes a new turn. The first of these is at Castlewood when Henry brings smallpox to his benefactors. To prepare specifically for this revelation of Rachel and Henry's relations, Thackeray allows only two of the first seven chapters. The first (i, i) sets forth Rachel's kindness to young Henry and his wholehearted gratitude. (The following five chapters deal with the Esmond family and Henry's unhappy childhood.) The second (i, vii) stresses Henry's nature: "He . . . had a fond and affectionate heart, tender to weakness, that would fain attach itself to somebody"—the somebody of course being Rachel, for whom he soon feels "a devoted affection and passion of gratitude, which entirely filled his young heart. . . . It cannot be called love, that a lad of twelve . . . felt for an exalted lady, his mistress: but it was worship." Then follows a summary of the next

---

⁷ *The Art of the Novel* (New York, 1934), pp. 114–115. Brimley, Trollope, E. A. Baker, Dodds, Brogan, and Ray are among the other critics who have noted these preparations by Thackeray.

⁸ Citations from *Esmond* are from the Harper's Modern Classics edition, ed. Stevenson.

three years, during which their associations and sympathies grow ever closer, and hints of her marital troubles appear. Thackeray again gives one of his countless foreshadowings of the end: Henry vows "that no power should separate him from his mistress," and adds, "Now, at the close of his life . . . , he can think, not ungratefully, that he has been faithful to that early vow." Thackeray also has Henry occasionally hint at Rachel's feelings—for instance, she sighs apprehensively at the idea of his eventually leaving Castlewood, divining "his thoughts with her usual jealous watch and affection."

The reader who has noted such preparations is better able to interpret Rachel's almost hysterical vituperation of Henry in the first key scene (I, viii), which reflects both her natural fears of the smallpox and her jealousy of Henry (now sixteen), who has been seeing Nancy Sievewright. "Revelations of her love," says Howard O. Brogan, "are always involuntary, the effect of surprise, naïveté, or enormous emotional pressure." [9] Thackeray carefully insinuates not only Rachel's inner tensions but also her recognition of their nature and danger. This is notably seen in her apologies to Henry—the first a tacit admission of her jealousy:

> "I beg your pardon, Henry," she said; "I spoke very unkindly. I have no right to interfere with you—with your"—My Lord broke into an oath. "Can't you leave the boy alone, my Lady?" She looked a little red, and frankly pressed the lad's hand as she dropped it.

Later she apologizes again "in a hard, dry voice," and her entire speech, though ostensibly innocent, is an ironic intimation of her feelings. Henry must perceive, she says, that he cannot "continue to stay upon the intimate footing in this family" he has enjoyed and should go on to the university:

> ". . . I did not press this matter, thinking you a child, as you are, indeed, in years—quite a child; and I should never have thought of treating you otherwise until—until these *circumstances* came to light. And I shall beg my Lord to dispatch you as quick as possible: and I will go on with Frank's learning as well as I can (I owe my father thanks for a little grounding, and you, I'm sure, for much you have taught me),—and— and I wish you a good night, Mr. Esmond."

The strangely formal behavior ("Mr. Esmond"), the repetitions and hesitations, the double meanings ("these *circumstances*"), all signify awareness of her passion for Henry—even, perhaps, the acknowledg-

[9] *ELH*, XIII, 230.

ment for what he has taught her, which is not only languages but the fact that her love for him is no longer innocent. (If one thinks too much is being read into this dialogue, let him recall that later—ii, vi —Rachel indicates that she deliberately sent Henry away in order to thrust temptation from her.)

Thackeray's methods of conveying this intelligence to the reader need emphasis, for they are his principal means of setting forth Rachel's central problem hereafter. Because Henry is the narrator, Thackeray is restricted to dramatic presentation: the hero must report Rachel's dialogue and actions, but his interpretive comment must be carefully controlled, or, for one thing, the story would be given away directly. Thus Henry's memoirs must show, as Brogan puts it, that Rachel's love gradually changes from "motherly affection for a waif" into love of "unlawful strength"—a love which she recognizes but which few others do, including Henry (and many readers). And while other characters in time "half suspect the truth" about their love, says Brogan, "the nature of her love for Henry is doubtful right to the end." [10] But however doubtful it may be to others, *it is never doubtful to Rachel herself.* Hence Thackeray must try to make clear Rachel's private conflicts, which the hero-narrator does not then fully comprehend himself; and he must make the hero, at the same time, indicate his own mixed feelings.

III

Following the first key scene are many events, culminating in Viscount Castlewood's death and Henry's imprisonment. But these are primarily significant with relation to the love theme, which Thackeray never allows us to forget. Henry matures, and the sympathies between him and Rachel increase because of various circumstances (including the Viscount's philandering). Henry observes "that a secret care . . . was weighing upon her"—apparently her concern about her crumbling marriage, which was really no secret, but implicitly her anxiety about her attraction to Henry. When she donates a small inheritance to send him to the university, the feelings of both are pointed up (i, ix). She looks at Henry "with sad penetrating glances," while he hangs back "abashed," protesting that if she wished he would stay forever. Her agitation and ambiguous utterances make even the simple Viscount uneasy:

[10] *ELH*, xiii, 229, 231.

"Curse me, Rachel, if I know now whether thou art in earnest or not," said my Lord.

"In earnest, my Lord! . . . Is there much subject here for joke?"

She gives "a stately look to Harry Esmond, which seemed to say, 'Remember; you understand me, though he does not'." She seems "rejoiced to lose him" and cuts short "his protests of love and his lamentations." " 'Indeed, you are best away,' said my Lady, laughing, as she put her hand on the boy's head for a moment." And her calling him her "knight" makes him blush, for that is his thought too. So, by such word-play and hinting, otherwise gratuitously meaningless, Thackeray continually suggests her struggles and Henry's own nebulous feelings.

Often, however, Thackeray's methods are more apparent. For example, Henry's attempt to reconcile his patrons is met with inexplicable sarcasm from Rachel (I, xii).

". . . What wrong have I done you that you should wound me so, cruel woman?"

"What wrong!" she said, looking at Esmond with wild eyes. "Well, none —none that you know of, Harry, or could help. Why did you bring back the smallpox," she added, after a pause, ". . . You could not help it, could you? Which of us knows whither fate leads us? But we were all happy, Henry, till then."

Her first exclamation, her "wild eyes," her "none that you know of, Harry," her pause, the allusions to fate and unhappiness—all these could only signify her continuing spiritual perturbation, his innocence of its causes, and her recognition of that innocence. And there is no doubt of Thackeray's desire to keep us mindful of the theme when he makes Mohun say to Henry (I, xiii): "By the Lord, I believe thou hast an eye to the pretty Puritan thyself, Master Harry. . . . Whisper, Harry, art thou in love with her thyself? . . ." Harry protests that he loves her as a mother and worships "her as a devotee worships a saint," which, we must believe, is what he honestly thinks, at the time. A few minutes later, when her husband cries that "Harry" (Mohun) has been killed, she, thinking of Harry Esmond, screams and faints.

To one who has overlooked these implications of Rachel's emotional state in Book I, her behavior toward Henry in prison, as Book II opens, would be almost meaningless. For her speech here is that of one profoundly distraught for reasons greater than the loss of a husband she no longer loved (though she now protests adulation of him). She says that her misfortunes are "a just judgment on my wicked heart

—my wicked jealous heart," but, as in the smallpox scene, blames Henry for everything. "And, young as you were . . . there was evil, I knew there was evil, in keeping you," she says, and again reproaches Henry for bringing the smallpox, presumably because it injured her beauty and alienated the Viscount. But it is altogether clear now that, undone by a tragedy for which she feels responsible, she is overwhelmed by a profound feeling of guilt, though she distorts the reasons for that feeling. Thus is explained her obsession with the smallpox, which had the important dual effects on her life not only of increasing her husband's lack of interest in her, but of bringing into the open her passion for Henry. Her feeling of guilt, we now know, is not due to jealousy; it is due to loving Henry beyond maternal bounds. The "evil" in him is not that he brought smallpox but that he aroused fearful desires in her. (In this scene Thackeray employs a clumsy little device to indicate, finally, that even as she harangued Henry she really loved him: while he is unconscious she purloins from his sleeve a button, which, the last line of the novel tells us, "she wore ever after . . . on the tenderest heart in the world.") And Thackeray again emphasizes Rachel's feelings of guilt when Steele reports to Henry her remarks (ii, ii): religious counsel, she tells Steele, bids her "to part from [Henry], and to see him no more," though in future years, "when our knees and our tears and our contrition have changed our sinful hearts, we may meet again." Such counsel could follow only from confession of her "guilty" love. And when she adds that "Mr. Esmond will find other—other friends," her hesitation, as usual, signifies.

Thus throughout the episodes following the first manifestation of the love theme, Thackeray continually implies how things stand with his principals. He emphasizes Rachel's problems; but he does not neglect to remind us that Henry has some too, if less excruciating. And again as a pointer, he makes the Dowager Viscountess, like Mohun, suspect Henry of being in love with Rachel (ii, iii), though Henry merely replies that he takes no shame in loving and honoring her "before all the world."

IV

The second key scene presents the reunion of Henry and Rachel at Walcote (ii, vi). With respect to the love theme, it is the most significant event in the novel. In this intensive short chapter Thackeray at-

tempts three important things which must be understood before much
can be made of the major characters or of the ensuing narrative. Using
the dramatic technique, he clarifies much of what has gone before, indicates the present feelings of Rachel and Henry, and prepares for
what is to come.

The scene is set with masterly skill. Henry has been driven to Walcote, despite Rachel's interdiction, by indignation (though it looks
more like jealousy), for he has heard that Tom Tusher might marry
her. The date is the 29th of December, memorable for both Henry and
Rachel (who celebrate it as his "birthday"; on it long ago he saved
young Frank's life, for which, she said, "she would love him all her
life"—I, xi). They meet at Winchester cathedral, a solemn and suggestive setting. More than half the chapter is dialogue, with almost no
interpretive comment by Henry; and though the conversations seem to
move naturally, the matter is highly compressed, as in a play.

"It was a rapture of reconciliation," says Henry, and Rachel weeps
with gladness. After summarizing his past attitudes toward her, Henry
introduces a mutation that prepares for what happens later in the
chapter and beyond:

> Brighter eyes there might be, and faces more beautiful, but none so
> dear—no voice so sweet as that of his beloved mistress, who had been
> sister, mother, goddess to him during his youth—goddess now no more,
> for he knew of her weaknesses; and by thought, suffering, and that
> experience it brings, was older now than she; but more fondly cherished
> as woman perhaps than ever she had been adored as divinity.

During the talk Rachel says much that enlightens. It was her "selfishness" that made her wish Henry to be the chaplain at Castlewood, so
that he might be near her. She elaborates on her feelings of guilt and
sin, and, though by indirection and pointed ellipsis, makes clear the
nature of that sin. She says "it was God's will that [she] should be
punished," and acknowledges "how wicked [her] heart has been" and
how she has suffered. "I confessed to Mr. Atterbury—I must not tell
any more." To do so would be to declare openly her love for Henry
and its effect on her life. Her religious counselor's advice (to which she
refers here) that she should try to see Henry no more could be meaningful only in this implied context.

Besides furnishing a striking background, the cathedral reflects Rachel's strong religious nature (she is the daughter of a clergyman) and
gives Thackeray a means of leading to another of her revelatory out-
bursts. The symbol for this is Psalm 126, which is being chanted when
she first sees Henry. Overcome with emotion after the service, she

smiles "an almost wild smile" and recalls the date: "She burst into a wild flood of weeping as she spoke; she laughed and sobbed on the young man's heart, crying out wildly, 'bringing your sheaves with you —your sheaves with you!' " By now even Henry, who has hitherto been made to be rather dully oblivious of her deeper feelings, is allowed to comprehend what is going on; and he remarks that "the depth of this pure devotion (which was, for the first time, revealed to him) quite smote upon him, and filled his heart with thanksgiving." His next speech specifies this revelation (and foreshadows much), for here he first proposes to her—hesitantly and obliquely, but nonetheless proposes:

"If—if 'tis so, dear lady . . . why should I ever leave you? If God has given me this great boon—and near or far from me, as I know now, the heart of my dearest mistress follows me, let me have that blessing near me, nor ever part with it till death separate us. Come away—leave this Europe. . . . Begin a new life in a new world. . . . that land in Virginia. . . . Frank will give us that. . . ."

Marriage, it is true, has not been named, and Brogan thinks that "one is not certain whether Henry wishes to take her away in the capacity of mother or wife"; but the wording of the proposal, with its echo of the marital vows, and especially the context seem clearly to imply "wife" (Henry's cherishing her as a "woman," his recognizing "the depth" of her "devotion," and the way he presses the matter and her reasons for refusing). Her immediate objections show understanding of his meaning: "And my children—and my duty—and my good father, Henry? . . ." When he wonders why, if he "would leave all to follow" her, she cannot "be as generous," she suddenly retreats back to her maternal role, for the first time in the chapter: " 'Hush, boy!' she said, and it was with a mother's sweet plaintive tone and look that she spoke." Moreover, she says, again bringing up the subject, she has "been so weak and sinful" she must "pray out an expiation." Then Thackeray has her add, by way of emphasis:

". . . But I would love you still—yes, there is no sin in such a love as mine now—and my dear lord in heaven may see my heart; and knows the tears that have washed my sin away—and now—now my duty is here, by my children, whilst they need me, and by my poor old father, and"—

"And not by me?" Henry said.

"Hush!" she said again, and raised her hand up to his lip.

Once more she refers to her sin and its horrors, and when Henry seeks to interrupt, she gives the final reason for her refusal: ". . . Be silent! let me say all. You never loved me, dear Henry—no, you do not now, and I thank heaven for it. I used to watch you, and knew by a thousand signs that it was so." Thus Rachel, realizing that Henry has never "loved" her, i.e., erotically, believes that his proposal was inspired rather by strong feelings and his duty as a gentleman than by a sincere desire to have her to wife. She thanks heaven, perhaps, because she knows that if his love were erotic, she would likely yield. And that would involve her sense of sin again, as her next words indicate: because she sent him (i.e., temptation) away to college, she received "absolution" from two clergymen—Mr. Atterbury and her father.

Henry comprehends the general tenor of this enigmatic dialogue, for as the chapter ends he rather easily acquiesces to her apparent desire to re-establish the old relationship: " 'I think the angels are not all in heaven,' Mr. Esmond said. And as a brother folds a sister to his heart; and as a mother cleaves to her son's breast—so for a few moments Esmond's beloved mistress came to him and blessed him." Because of the relations tacitly agreed upon, the way is left open not only for Henry's pursuit of Beatrix (beginning in the next chapter), but for the continuation of Rachel's conflicts in considerably modified circumstances. Whether Henry really comprehends her terrible struggles is not certain—presumably he does so only dimly. But when John W. Dodds complains that in this scene Henry "is a confused blend of son and lover," he is overlooking the fact that that is just the point.

The focus of the chapter, however, is not Henry but Rachel. Her speeches not only clarify her feelings but prepare for her future behavior and, ultimately, for her acceptance of Henry as her husband. Her momentary loss of control and her preoccupation with her sin manifest attempted suppression, but by no means eradication, of her passionate desire for Henry. It is difficult, as Dodds points out, to reconcile her speaking "with a mother's sweet plaintive tone and look" and her saying that "there is no sin in such a love as mine now." [11] In one sense, indeed, she could mean: "Because I have repented loving you before my husband died, my (erotic) love is not now sinful." But both her deliberate behavior and her speech seem rather to make the meaning: "As I have exorcised my passion for you, my love is maternal now and hence sinless." She seems to be attempting to convince Henry, as well as herself, that her love is and will be henceforth maternal (or sisterly); and certainly what she later

[11] *Thackeray,* pp. 170–171.

says and does is meaningful only in the light of this inner struggle.[12]
As if to make sure that his reader does not overlook the significance
of this unusual scene, Thackeray accentuates its major ideas in the
several following chapters. For instance, just after Beatrix has smitten
Henry with her beauty (II, vii), Thackeray has Frank, in the midst of
a long speech, say to Henry: ". . . mother's in love with you,—yes, I
think mother's in love with you. She was always praising you, and always talking about you; and when she went to Southampton, to see
the ship, I found her out. But you see it is impossible. . . ." And a few
pages later (II, viii), Rachel, warning Henry ("my son") of Beatrix's
weaknesses, alludes to the now familiar subject: "I know you both,
and love you: need I be ashamed of that love now? No, never,
never. . . ."

This chapter (II, viii) ends with a statement of Henry's unsettled
feelings about Rachel: "and as for his mistress, 'twas difficult to say
with what a feeling he regarded her. 'Twas happiness to have seen
her; 'twas no great pang to part; a filial tenderness, a love that was
at once respect and protection, filled his mind as he thought of her,
and from that day until now, and from now till death is past, and
beyond it, he prays that sacred flame may ever burn." This is indeed
ambiguous and one feels like asking, with Dodds, "Come now,
Esmond, *what* flame? Your 'filial tenderness,' long before this writing,
must have been sublimated at the marriage altar." [13] In part, at least,
it should have been. But might not Thackeray have been attempting
a compressed statement that moves in two dimensions of time? The
first part of the passage expresses Henry's feelings at the time of action. The second suggests how those feeings, with modifications, have
extended to the present time, i.e., of the writing of the memoirs. Thus
the "sacred flame" may waver and even feed on different fuels, but
it never goes out; so that the implication is one of transition and
continuity. The closing lines of the following chapter (II, ix) deal
with Henry's feelings from another angle: off to the wars again, he

[12] Trollope states in his *Thackeray* (New York, 1879), p. 128, that here Rachel
"herself does not know that her own heart is seeking his with all a woman's love"—
but that, of course, is exactly what she does know. And Brogan's belief that Rachel
"gives him up to Beatrix without a struggle" at Walcote (*ELH*, XIII, 230) does not
take into account the reasons for the apparent relinquishment, involving struggle
enough, or the continuation of the struggle during the remainder of the story. Some
readers (like the reviewer in the *Times*) have been annoyed by Rachel's "hypocrisy"
later on, as she appears to advance Henry's suit with Beatrix while wanting him herself; but they have failed to understand the nature of her "sin" and her attempts
to expiate it.
[13] *Thackeray*, p. 170.

ponders his hopeless passion for Beatrix; then—"And as, before the blazing sun of morning, the moon fades away in the sky almost invisible, Esmond thought, with a blush perhaps, of another sweet pale face, sad and faint, and fading out of sight, with its sweet fond gaze of affection: such a last look it seemed to cast as Eurydice might have given, yearning after her lover, when fate and Pluto summoned her, and she passed away into the shades." In both passages is reflected the delicate situation: Rachel, loving Henry passionately but trying to suppress her love and sublimate it into a "sinless" one; Henry, loving Rachel in a somewhat different way (and now infatuated with her daughter), but, though outwardly conforming to the filial relation, vaguely aware of disturbing elements in his own feelings that he is as yet unable to isolate and analyze. Orpheus and Eurydice, however, were lovers.

V

If the remainder of *Esmond* is analyzed in terms of the Walcote scene, much that otherwise seems puzzling or irrelevant is clarified.

The most obvious part of Thackeray's design in the love theme, as Trollope and others have seen, is stressing Rachel's youthful beauty, a preparation extending from the Preface to Henry's own remark at the end that "the tender matron" was "as beautiful in her autumn, and as pure as virgins in their spring." [14] And Thackeray concurrently disparages Beatrix. Henry constantly makes such declarations as: "Beautiful as she [Beatrix] was, he had heard people say a score of times . . . that Beatrix's mother looked as young, and was the handsomer of the two," and "my lady Castlewood, though now almost forty, did not look to be within ten years of her age." Technically more disarming are the many similar remarks of others, including those of Steele (ii, ii), Bolingbroke (ii, xv), the Pretender (iii, ix), and occasionally even Beatrix—"Does not mamma look charming?" (iii, iii). Simultaneously, Henry is being made older—"Why, you are old enough and grave enough to be our father," says Beatrix (iii, iii).

More important than this assiduous "romantic adjustment" are Thackeray's continual efforts to keep the reader ever mindful of his characters' problems—by scores of references, often in dialogue and

---

[14] As Edgar puts it, "Having damaged her beauty to achieve her husband's complete alienation, the author has to mend it again like Amelia's broken nose in Fielding's story" (*The Art of the Novel*, p. 115).

without comment, as well as by innumerable, almost hidden, allusions. Rachel's jealousy is ever present. It is shown, for example, by her impatience when she finds Henry kissing Beatrix's foot (III, ii), by her often meeting Henry when he leaves Beatrix, implicitly by anxious design, and by Beatrix's dialogue (III, vii). Likewise, Thackeray repeatedly makes Rachel manifest her suppressed love through her tender solicitousness toward Henry, her acute sensitivity to his feelings, and her keen glances at him when Beatrix is present or discussed. Sometimes her emotions break through her self-imposed maternal role, and then Henry's own bewilderment is likely to be reflected—as, for instance, when she comforts him (II, x): " 'I am your mother, you are my son, and I love you always,' she said . . . : and he went away comforted and humbled in mind, as he thought of that amazing and constant love and tenderness with which this sweet lady ever blessed and pursued him." But the love she expresses, we feel sure, is not wholly maternal. The final chapter of Book II (which is saturated with references to Rachel's beauty and charm) particularly marks the relations of the two principals. Rachel, calling Henry her son and Beatrix his sister, talks of the latter's weaknesses: " 'I thought you might cure yourself of your passion,' my lady added fondly." His confusion is seen in his reply, ". . . You are a thousand times better: the fondest, the fairest, the dearest of women. . . . But she is my fate . . . *Je l'aime.*" And when Rachel says, "I wish she would have you," Thackeray allows us to determine her sincerity for ourselves. But when she says, "You are such a treasure that the woman who has your love, shouldn't change it away against a kingdom, I think," who can doubt what she means? It is peculiar love-making, but it is a peculiar situation; and Thackeray treats it with amazing adroitness. A more obvious instance occurs when Henry formally renounces his claim to the Castlewood title (III, ii) and Rachel kneels and kisses his hands "in an outbreak of passionate love and gratitude," saying, "in a wild way": "Don't raise me. . . . Let me kneel—let me kneel, and—and—worship you." (Henry is made to report scenes like this with a straight face!)

Rachel's sense of sin is not forgotten, either. Once (III, iii) this is brought out by the candid Beatrix: "Oh, how good she is, Harry! . . . She has had a great sorrow in her life and a great secret; and repented of it. It could not have been my father's death. She talks freely about that; nor could she have loved him very much—though who knows what we women do love, and why?" His reply ("What, and why, indeed") is vapid, to be sure; but he could hardly have been allowed to remark the implications, as he could not have been a few moments later when Beatrix observes that her mother "loves you, sir, a great deal too much; and I hate you for it."

Finally, as very pointed preparation for the ending, Thackeray again selects Beatrix as a means. "You and mamma are fit for each other," she says to Henry (iii, iii); and again (iii, iv), "Mamma would have been the wife for you, had you been a little older, though you look ten years older than she does. . . ." And, just before the plot to restore the Pretender (iii, vii), Beatrix returns the family jewels to Henry: "You will give them to your wife, Cousin. . . . My cousin, your wife has a lovely complexion and shape." The allusion to Rachel is unmistakable. But Henry, though he reflects occasionally on his own emotions, is never allowed to appear fully aware of the crucial issues between him and Rachel—as if his passion for the daughter, plus the tacit agreement at Walcote, have made him obtuse to those issues.

As the final scenes approach, Thackeray has but to fulfill what he has been so long preparing for. In the last chapter (iii, xiii) he quickly kills Henry's desire for Beatrix ("The love was dead within him"); destroys her beauty ("The roses had shuddered out of her cheeks; her eyes were glaring; she looked quite old"); and makes Henry rather lamely wonder "that he could ever have loved her." Then, with a sentimental prelude about that "happiness . . . of its nature sacred and secret" and "the truest and tenderest and purest wife ever man was blessed with," Thackeray allows him to announce "that my dear mistress became my wife."

Though these few citations can hardly convey Thackeray's subtleties of technique or the cumulative effect of the whole, they indicate the nature of his "infinite pains" in developing his love theme: to keep before his readers the feelings of his characters, especially Rachel's, as the story proceeds and circumstances change, and to prepare for the marriage which, we cannot doubt, he wished to appear the natural and inevitable result of all that had gone before.

VI

The evident pattern of the love theme makes Thackeray's intentions unmistakable. He wished, as George Brimley pretty well saw in his review, to show the growth of an unusual kind of devotion, beginning as that of a dependent-son-brother of twelve and a protector-mother-sister of twenty, and ending primarily as that of lovers twenty years later. But it is not first one thing exclusively and then another thing exclusively, as is often assumed; rather it is a gradual development, with the relation continually modifying for each character until at the end it is not a simple, conventional love, but a complex one, cumulatively grown. The cohesive tension is ever Rachel's suppressed passion for Henry, attended by conflicting feelings of guilt and desire —tension continually interacting with Henry's own fluctuating and uncertain affection for her.

Yet a large number of readers have failed to see the manifestations of the theme or have appeared only vaguely cognizant of them. Hence we must return to the question of whether Thackeray was only "almost successful" in fulfilling his intentions. If we assume that he was not being wilfully obscurant, then we must admit that communication between author and readers has been imperfect.

There are several probable causes. The reader today may overlook the development of the love theme simply because he does not expect to find such an anomalous treatment of passion in a Victorian novel (though, ironically, many Victorians found it readily enough), and because he likely approaches the book as no more than a conventional "historical romance"—once Beatrix descends the stair, he understandably expects her to pair off with Henry at the end. And to the reader who has missed Thackeray's manifold preparations, the ending may well appear capriciously sudden.[15]

There are more consequential reasons, however, in addition to Thackeray's natural restraint in treating an unusual and delicate subject. Despite the persistence of the thematic ideas, they are overshadowed by other elements of the story—the long accounts of Henry's military campaigns, the ten-year courtship of Beatrix, the elaboration of the historical background, and, finally, the excitement of the restoration plot. Moreover, the reader does not find in *Esmond* the authorial help he has become accustomed to in Thackeray and his contemporaries. With a few exceptions (like Emily Brontë) Victorian novelists oversimplified, slanted, and generally interpreted to the extent that hardly a reader could fail to understand. So it had been in *Vanity Fair* and *Pendennis*. But *Esmond*, though plain enough when it deals with Rachel's beauty or Marlborough's improbity, contains almost no

---

[15] As it did to the reviewer in the *Athenaeum*: "The *finale* . . . is painfully disappointing. The reader who has been hoping throughout that Beatrix would at last flower into virtue for Esmond's reward, is shocked to find her finally flung away like a withered weed, and Esmond's affections abruptly transferred from the daughter to the mother" (6 Nov. 1852, p. 1199).

interpretive comment about the love theme. Its presentation is preponderantly dramatic; the meanings are implicit rather than explicit; and the reader must do his own interpreting. The failure to appreciate this quality of Thackeray's technique in *Esmond,* I believe, is a major cause for uncertainty about his intentions.

The technical problems of Thackeray's narration are not often considered. In form *Esmond* is ostensibly a memoir, written by Henry for his grandsons and other descendants, who may be presumed to know already the general outline of the story, including the outcome. But *Esmond* is also a novel: hence there must be suspense, and information that would not in reality be withheld from the grandsons must be withheld from the reader. Furthermore, Henry is writing decades after the action, when presumably he comprehends the meaning of what he reports; but simultaneously he must appear not to understand certain parts of it as of the time of action. Hence Thackeray's difficulties in keeping his work looking like an ingenuous memoir. His problems do not differ essentially from those of other novelists whose heroes tell the story, except perhaps in the unorthodox kind of love to be depicted and in the curious use of the third person, which gives the narrator the similitude of the omniscient author without his prerogatives. Henry must necessarily be limited in awareness from time to time (as Copperfield must be with respect to Agnes and to Steerforth); but he must be limited, or at least is limited, to the degree that he perforce appears naïve, a bit dull, and occasionally a little stupid. Yet if Thackeray should allow him to understand, the plot would have to be drastically altered, the narration would become extremely complicated, and much of the sense of immediacy would be impaired. Hence, even when Beatrix mentions her mother's "great secret," Henry gently passes it by.

Dodds thinks that to delineate relations like those of Henry and Rachel "requires an absolute certainty of touch, and it is at just such moments that Thackeray is likely to be confused by conflicting impulses. We are never sure, during the growth of this strange affection, just what it means at any given moment. It is not improbable that Rachel and Esmond themselves should at certain times be uncertain of the exact nature of their feelings for each other, but certainly Thackeray should know, and it is not clear that he did." [16] No one would hold that Thackeray had "an absolute certainty of touch," yet it is not implausible to claim that, considering his obstacles, he evinced a re-

---

[16] *Thackeray,* p. 170. Dodds's perceptive essay is one of the few analyzing in detail the technical problems in *Esmond.*

markable certainty until the very end. And as Henry himself tells the story, it would be extremely difficult for Thackeray to make clear that he, the author, knows "the exact nature" of his characters' feelings, particularly Rachel's. If he had "conflicting impulses" about the love theme, they were perhaps rather those of technique than of understanding—rather of trying to determine just how much ought to be shown and how to show it.

The depiction of Rachel is of paramount importance in an interpretation of the love theme. Indeed, the story is not so much Henry's as hers: the history of a passionate and imperfect woman who long suffers what she thinks to be a sinful love—a history told by the object of her passion. Henry's emotional problems are perplexing enough, but, except when concerning his infatuation with Beatrix, they are rarely as sharply set forth as Rachel's. Always it is Rachel who is the restrained aggressor, who has long believed that he does not "love" her in her sense of the word. And it is the presentation of her character, rather than Henry's, which has most disturbed readers. Especially have some been distressed by the contradiction between Henry's constant praise of her virtues (hence, they conclude, implying Thackeray's own approval) and the many less admirable qualities she displays, such as jealousy, haughtiness, and dissemblance. As Lord David Cecil says: "Lady Castlewood . . . moves through *Esmond* to a sort of organ accompaniment of approbation; in speaking of her Thackeray's colloquial tone takes on a religious enthusiasm that makes it resemble something between a chat and a chant. . . . Yet her actions reveal her as a most unamiable character. . . ."[17] But Cecil credits Thackeray with no dramatic ability and seems to forget that it is Henry who is supposed to be writing his memoirs. Henry could hardly be expected to call his grandsons' attention pointedly to their grandmother's weaknesses (though he occasionally does); besides, he is a gentleman of sentimental loyalty writing about his wife, whom in his fashion he loves. Still, as Thackeray must make him portray her accurately in action and speech, in this fictional memoir the apparent discrepancy is hardly avoidable. Brogan well observes that Henry's views are not necessarily his creator's, calling readers "overly serious . . . who take at face value everything that Henry says." But Brogan thinks "that with minor reservations, Thackeray was in essential agreement with Henry," the dilemma being explained by the fact that Rachel's faults exemplify real virtues "carried to excess."[18] Brogan develops his argu-

[17] *Early Victorian Novelists* (London, 1934), p. 96.
[18] *ELH*, XIII, 224, 231.

ment ingeniously, but, again, the explanation minimizes Thackeray's dramatic technique and its implications. Are not Henry's praise—itself often wryly ironical—and Rachel's actions implicit commentaries on both their characters? And cannot Thackeray be given credit for deliberately using these means of character portrayal and revelation? He was no novice at fiction.

A final concern is Thackeray's treatment of the incestuous implications of the love theme, and especially his resolution of the problems involved; for it is this resolution which has helped cause misapprehension of his intentions. It would be unrealistic to complain that, writing in the 1850's, he was not highly explicit in dealing with these implications. But there is hardly doubt that they are to be understood as part of Rachel's "sin," intensifying her humiliation at what happened—she not only fell in love with a poor dependent while her husband lived, but did so with one who in many ways was like a son. Her almost pathological preoccupation with her sin, her religious adviser's belief that she should not see Henry again (otherwise, why should she not, after her husband's death and after her repentance and absolution?), and her desperate attempt to restore and maintain her maternal relation to him—all these indicate Thackeray's intention for his reader to be aware that she was troubled by some feeling of incest. Henry never speaks of similar doubts, though his own mixed feelings derive in part from the continual difficulty of adjusting his first strong love for Rachel as a "mother" or "sister" to a love for her as a desirable woman. But how does Rachel overcome her sense of sin as well as her belief that Henry does not love her in the appropriate way? And Henry's misgivings about his feelings for her—how are they dispelled? We are never told. The vague ending may have been due to Thackeray's disinclination or temperamental inability to probe openly a matter that might be distasteful to his readers, even though he had deliberately built his love story around it, or to his feeling that, because of the elaborate preparations, the reader's imagination could fill in as necessary. It may even have been that he could not decide how to handle the problem.[19] But whatever the reason, the gap is there;

[19] Haste may help account for the ending: the publisher's deadline was long past, and Thackeray grew increasingly impatient to finish his book. (See *Letters*, III, 15–47; and Stevenson, *The Showman of Vanity Fair*, pp. 246–254.) Stevenson thinks that the prospect of Thackeray's American tour, which "took positive form" during the last weeks of composition, influenced "the unexpected removal of his hero and heroine to Virginia" (p. 254), though that possibility had been foreshadowed when Henry first proposed to Rachel (II, vi) and later when he addressed his "grandson" who lives by the "Rappahannoc" (III, v).

and even readers who sympathetically follow the love theme will not
find the conclusion satisfying and will feel that he did not carry out
his responsibility to them—that of giving *his* idea of the resolution of
those problems which would establish the ending as clear and con-
vincing. He did not, therefore, completely fulfill his intentions; and
his novel must take the artistic consequences. The evasive resolution
—if it be a resolution at all—is the major artistic flaw, and a grave
one, in the novel.

The high praise *Esmond* has received has rarely included recognition of the full significance of the love theme, though it is that theme
on which the novel largely depends for meaning. The scope of this
study forbids an attempt to evaluate *Esmond* as a whole—there is
too much else to consider. But when the love theme, rigorously
isolated here for analysis, is integrated into the full body of the novel,
Thackeray's entire accomplishment can be more justly appraised;
and, despite serious weaknesses, it will, I think, appear more astonishing than has been supposed. If we must admit that he did not entirely
succeed in fulfilling his intentions, we must concede that his readers
have not always seen what he put there for them. Those who are unhampered by presuppositions, however, and who are willing to grant
Esmond the attention they give later symbol-fraught novels, will be
rewarded by an ironically perceptive interpretation of an uncommon
human relationship. They will also find one of the most provocative
and subtle portraits of a lady in nineteenth-century English fiction.
And they may even be willing to forgive Thackeray his final artistic
blemish.

The Newcomes

by Gordon N. Ray

In writing *The Newcomes* Thackeray set the pattern for all his later fiction except *Denis Duval*. A tired and sick man, increasingly weary of story-telling, he had seen his effort to write a tautly organized and carefully finished work of art in *Esmond* received by the public with relative indifference. He determined henceforth, instead of striving for unwanted perfection, to fall back into the comfortable pattern of serial improvisation which twenty years as a journalist had made second nature to him. But he did not find this an inspiriting decision. The engaging "overture" with which *The Newcomes* begins is a defence against the charges of repetitiousness and cynicism which he foresees will be levelled against the novel,[1] and his private comments were at first desponding enough. The "new book . . . won't be a good one," he wrote, "not a step forward . . . a retreat rather." "I can't but see it is a repetition of past performances, and think that vein is pretty nigh worked out in me."[2]

But as Thackeray advanced with *The Newcomes*, his confidence returned. He kept the pace of his narrative very slow, limiting himself to two incidents at most in each monthly number,[3] and "filling in"

"*The Newcomes.*" From *Thackeray: The Age of Wisdom, 1847–63*, by Gordon N. Ray (New York: McGraw-Hill Book Company, Inc., 1958; London: Oxford University Press, 1958), pp. 236–49. Copyright © 1958 by McGraw-Hill Book Company, Inc. Reprinted by permission of the author and the publishers.

[1] See *The Oxford Thackeray*, ed. George Saintsbury, 17 vols. (London, 1908), XIV, 1–6. Hereafter referred to as *Works.*

[2] *The Letters and Private Papers of William Makepeace Thackeray*, ed. Gordon N. Ray, 4 vols. (Cambridge, Mass., 1945–46), II, 283, 287.

[3] This point may be illustrated from a synopsis, unique among Thackeray's surviving papers, for Parts 16 to 24 of *The Newcomes*: "XVI. The Colonel comes back, and proposes to Barnes for Ethel for Clive. Rupture between the Colonel & Barnes. XVII. Announcement of her engagement to Lord Farintosh, death of Lady Kew. XVIII. Clive's marriage. Binnie's Nunc Dimittis. XIX. Elopement of Lady Clara. Ethel's revolt. XX. The Election. Height of Clive's prosperity. Bitterness at home. XXI. Failure of the B. B. Mrˢ Mack comes to live with the young people. XXII. Retreat of the Colonel before her. His resolve and its execution. XXIII. IV. Orme's History of India. Too late. The Colonel's Ethanasia." (Edgcumbe) Thackeray adhered closely to this plan, though certain incidents were deferred for one number.

the remainder of his thirty-two pages. As in *Vanity Fair*, he devoted a maximum of attention to preparing for revelations of character, a minimum to preparing for turns in the plot.[4] This enabled him to deal chiefly in what came to him most easily: authentic detail about his characters and general commentary suggested by his narrative. Such commentary flowed more readily after it occurred to him to make "Mr. Pendennis . . . the writer of his friend's memoirs," a device which he borrowed from Bulwer Lytton's *My Novel*. "Under that mask and acting, as it were, I can afford to say and think many things that I couldn't venture on in my own person, now that it is a person, and I know the public are staring at it." When Bradbury and Evans complained after publishing four monthly parts, "the public has found that the story does not move," Thackeray remained undisturbed, offering only the facetious assurance that future numbers "will be immense—bland passionate and deeply religious."[5] He finished his novel persuaded that he had done his best. "I can't jump further than I did in the Newcomes," he told Elwin.[6]

And indeed *The Newcomes* is in some respects the richest, not only of Thackeray's books but of all Victorian fictions. Sixty years later Henry James found the characteristic note of the Edwardian novel to be the degree of "saturation" that its writers achieved, their "state of inordinate possession."[7] Yet *Clayhanger*, *Tono-Bungay*, and *The Man of Property* (a book directly comparable in theme and subject matter) seem the work of frivolous impressionists when placed beside *The Newcomes*. As Saintsbury observed, the novel is "scarcely even a microcosm; it is almost the world itself."[8] Thackeray's plan is to follow an English family in all its ramifications through four generations. His scores of characters all have their place, because as "connexions of the most respectable Newcome family" they are entitled "to a page or two in these their memoirs."[9] With interest thus dispersed, the novel, particularly during its first third, seems almost suicidally discursive

---

[4] Thackeray's assertion that the "story" of *The Newcomes* was "revealed" to him near Berne shortly after he began the novel has caused some critical bewilderment. He no doubt meant that he then conceived the two incidents that were to bring his tale to an end, the discovery of Sophia Newcome's lost letter about her will in Orme's *History of India* and the Colonel's seeking refuge at Grey Friars as a poor brother, careful preparation for which is made early in the novel. See *Works*, XIV, 42, 970–973; 86–87, 1007.

[5] *Letters*, III, 297–298; IV, 436; III, 346–347, 351.

[6] *Some Eighteenth Century Men of Letters*, 2 vols. (London, 1902), I, 156.

[7] "The Younger Generation," *Times Literary Supplement*, 19 March 1914, pp. 133–134.

[8] *Works*, XIV, xxvi.

[9] The same, XIV, 589.

and moves with glacial slowness.[10] But in the end Thackeray's long preparation justifies itself. The reader who persists comes to know the Newcomes as well as any family in fiction.

James complained that the Edwardian formula of "saturation" left the reader with no "centre of interest . . . or sense of the whole." This is not true of *The Newcomes*, but the book is held together by its theme rather than by its plot. If Thackeray was bored by story-telling, he was still profoundly concerned with moral life. As is suggested by his subtitle, "the memoirs of a most respectable family," he is conducting an inquiry into the nature of "respectability" as the governing code of the upper and middle classes of Victorian England, "the most polite, and most intelligent, and best informed, and best dressed, and most selfish people in the world." [11] Though his theme is closely related to that of *Vanity Fair*, and even of *The Great Hoggarty Diamond*, his focus is rather different from that in these earlier books. In *The Newcomes* he desired to display "the heartlessness of London—which is awful to think of—the most godless respectable thing. . . . That world is base and prosperous and content, not unkind—very well bred—very unaffected in manner, not dissolute—clean in person and raiment and going to church every Sunday—but in the eyes of the Great Judge of right & wrong what rank will those people have with all their fine manners and spotless characters and linen? They never feel love, but directly it's born, they throttle it and fling it under the sewer as poor girls do their unlawful children—they make up money-marriages and are content—then the father goes to the House of Commons or the Counting House, the mother to her balls and visits—the children lurk upstairs with their governess, and when their turn comes are bought and sold, as respectable and heartless as their parents before them." [12]

Thackeray had long detested and suffered from this code. For fifteen years after he lost his fortune, he lived beyond the pale of "carriage company" as an impecunious painter and writer. As late as 1846 he had lost a house that he wished to rent because his bankers, Lubbock, Forster and Company, *"refused to answer to my respectability."* [13] And after he had achieved fame and success, he found himself a particular target for "the wrath of the Pharisees." [14] They

---

[10] Thackeray often apologizes for his seeming irrelevance. See, for example, XIV, 135, 160–161, 296–297.
[11] The same, XIV, 320.
[12] *Letters*, III, 296–297.
[13] The same, II, 225.
[14] Anonymous review of *The Newcomes*, *Spectator*, 18 August 1855, p. 860.

objected to the morality of his books, though, as he pointed out to Elwin: "the vanity of success &c of all but Love and Goodness—is not that the teaching of Domini Nostri?" [15] They took him to task for defending all means of innocent enjoyment, for praising cakes and ale against the protests of the virtuous. Hence he determined to justify himself by anatomizing the respectability of the consciously virtuous in a "philosophical novel." [16]

That England in the 1850's urgently required to be so anatomized is beyond question. Self-righteous conformity to a narrow and bigoted standard of conduct was a besetting sin of the decade, just as an addiction to cant and humbug had been a besetting sin of the 1830's. *The Newcomes* anticipates Mill's *On Liberty*, indeed, just as *Esmond* had anticipated his *Subjection of Women*. Though Thackeray did not share Mill's cult of the exceptional person and alarm at "collective mediocrity," his subject too is "Individuality, as one of the elements of well-being." Like Mill, Thackeray felt that "mankind are not infallible; that their truths, for the most part, are only half-truths." He too urged that "from the highest class of society down to the lowest, every one lives as under the eye of a hostile and dreaded censorship," that "the man, and still more the woman, who can be accused of doing 'what nobody does,' or of not doing 'what everybody does,' is the subject of as much depreciatory remark as if he or she had committed some grave moral delinquency." And both men agreed that the iron yoke of conformity was made the more onerous through being shaped by the prevailing evangelical theory of life, which by suppressing natural feeling makes for the dominance of a "pinched and hidebound type of human character." [17]

The Newcomes are an upstart family, as their name suggests, and display the respectable code in all its rawness. They stem from a foundling, named for the town in which he has his obscure origin, who becomes Sheriff of London and marries into a banking firm, "a most respectable house of many years' standing, and doing a most respectable business, especially in the dissenting connexion." [18] His sons, Brian and Hobson Newcome, become pillars respectively of the aristocracy and the upper middle class, and provide themselves with a genealogy dating from the battle of Hastings which allows them to believe that the

---

[15] *Letters*, III, 467.
[16] James Hannay, *"The Newcomes," Leader*, 8 September 1855, p. 870.
[17] *On Liberty* (London, 1859), pp. 119, 101, 110, 123, 112.
[18] *Works*, XIV, 58–59.

town of Newcome is in fact named for their family. This "respectable family dwelling in the world" provides Thackeray with examples of nearly all the anomalies in the "tariff of British Virtue" when judged by Christian ethics. "Virtue is very often shameful according to the English social constitution, and shame honourable. Truth, if yours happens to differ from your neighbour's, provokes your friend's coldness, your mother's tears, the world's persecution. Love is not to be dealt in, save under restrictions which kill its sweet healthy free commerce. Sin in man is so light that scarce the fine of a penny is imposed: while for woman it is so heavy, that no repentance can wash it out." Aligning himself with the sinners and publicans, Thackeray is "true to his party," asking "who can tell the mischief which the very virtuous do?" and "is it the sinners who are the most sinful?" From his picture of Sophia Newcome, darkening all of Thomas Newcome's younger life by her unjust severity, to that of Mrs. Hobson Newcome, constantly pluming herself on the misfortunes of others as if they "were designed for the special warning and advantage of her private family," Thackeray does not spare the "Unco Guid." Nor does he forget the "getting and keeping scoundrel" whom he had first portrayed in Brough of *The Great Hoggarty Diamond*. This proliferating figure, who found the code of respectability a protective shield under which he could violate with impunity every social decency, was the target of most of the great Victorian novelists; but he is nowhere so brilliantly exposed as in Barnes Newcome, who despite his "natural propensity to darkness and evil," remains "as scrupulously whited as any sepulchre in the whole bills of mortality." [19]

The offences of respectability are seen most clearly, however, in that fashionable society from which its code is imitated. This aspect of English life is Thackeray's principal subject during the middle third of the novel, while Colonel Newcome is recouping his fortune in India. As we have seen, he had come to know the great world intimately after 1847, and the direct, detailed picture which he draws of it in *The Newcomes* is substantially different from the oblique, impressionistic sketch which he had provided in *Vanity Fair*. In his earlier novel, he could not conceal an intermittent imaginative sympathy with the Disraelian view of society, expressed in *Coningsby* and other novels, as "a world where people want to get on and be amused, where birth and money and beauty and wit all have their place as com-

[19] The same, XIV, 502, 360, 368, 246, 716, 103.

modities; and where no one behaves, or is expected to behave, with disregard for material values," [20] even while he specifically disowned this view. During the intervening years, as he acquired an expert, first-hand knowledge of fashionable life, his judgment of it became increasingly disillusioned. Thackeray had promised in his "overture" to *The Newcomes* that, "while every justice is done to the peacocks themselves, the splendour of their plumage, the gorgeousness of their dazzling necks, and the magnificence of their tails, exception will yet be taken to the absurdity of their rickety strut, and the foolish discord of their pert squeaking." [21] But in the event he somewhat slighted the glamour of fashionable life; and whereas in *Vanity Fair* the balance is held even between admiring artist and disapproving moralist, in *The Newcomes* the moralist has the upper hand. [22]

The Newcome family gains its foothold in the great world through Brian Newcome's marriage to Lady Ann Kew. This alliance with one of the most ancient families in the peerage brings them under the dominance of the dowager Lady Kew, who is the "wicked fairy" of *The Newcomes*, [23] a symbolic figure in this novel, as her lamented brother, the Marquis of Steyne, never is in *Vanity Fair*. The Newcomes are schooled by her to subdue their generous impulses to the demands of respectability. Thackeray particularly emphasizes two of their resulting prejudices.

They follow fashionable society in their contempt for art. "The Muse of Painting is a lady whose social station is not altogether recognized with us as yet," Thackeray explains. "The polite world permits a gentleman to amuse himself with her, but to take her for better or for worse! forsake all other chances and cleave unto her! to assume her name! Many a respectable person would be as much shocked at the notion as if his son had married an opera dancer." So it is that when Clive Newcome becomes a painter, his uncle Hobson, though by no means a precisionist, finds his choice of profession humiliating for the whole family: "I don't care what a fellow is if he is a good fellow. But a painter! hang it—a painter's no trade at all." And even the

[20] Anthony Powell, introduction to *Novels of High Society from the Victorian Age* (London, 1947), p. viii.

[21] *Works*, XIV, 5–6.

[22] It may be mentioned that Thackeray's disillusionment with the great world seems either to have inspired or to have coincided with a mood of general disgust in the early 1850's. It has its artistic counterpart, for example, in Dicky Doyle's "friezes" of London society in the British Museum and in Millais's drawings of the seamy side of fashionable life. See Robin Ironside, *The Pre-Raphaelite Painters* (London, 1948), Plates 58 and 59.

[23] *Works*, XIV, 538.

Colonel and Ethel, despite their love for Clive, can only regard his devotion to art as a bewildering aberration. To this prejudice Thackeray opposes his own conviction, "felt in the blood, and felt along the heart," that those who have the keys of "that fair Art-World" are the happiest of mortals. This is true both of Clive, whose talents are modest, and of the young genius, "J. J." Ridley. Clive says of the latter, indeed, "Of all pieces of good fortune which can befall a man, is not this the greatest: to have your desire, and then never to tire of it?" [24] Thackeray's lively and authoritative picture of the joys of the artist's life, like his sketches of the writer's world in *Pendennis,* not only attracted recruits to the profession, but also enhanced its status in the eyes of the world. "Respectability?" exclaimed Edward Burne-Jones after reading the novel. "When shall we awake from this nightmare and phantom to acknowledge the true dignity of work of any kind, . . . and particularly of work that gives its doer most happiness?" [25]

Of all society's usages, however, the marriage of convenience involves the Newcomes in most distress. So large does it loom in their lives, indeed, that one reviewer conceived Thackeray's "central purpose" to be an analysis of that "social disease, unhappy wedded life." [26] As we have seen, he had ample opportunity to observe the workings of the marriage mart in London and elsewhere. The thought that such favourites of his as Blanche Airlie and Sally Baxter, who both served as models for Ethel Newcome,[27] might so sacrifice themselves to Mammon had long moved him to indignant remonstrance. Certainly in *The Newcomes* the subject elicits from him some of his most eloquent commentary, and he is at pains to give it comprehensive dramatic embodiment as well. The loveless marriages of Léonore de Blois, of the Colonel, and of Clive are all shown to be painful enough, but Thackeray's central exhibits are the histories of Ethel and of Lady Clara. Tempted by Lady Kew, Ethel narrowly avoids a *mariage de convenance,* first with Lord Kew and afterwards with the Marquis of Farintosh, though she loves Clive all the while. She sees her position clearly enough. On one occasion, indeed, she exasperates Lady Kew by appearing at a family dinner as a *tableau-vivant* with a little green ticket marked "Sold," which she has brought home from the Water-Colour Exhibition, pinned to her dress. Yet she is sufficiently infected by

[24] The same, XIV, 339, 245, 160, 661.

[25] "Essay on The Newcomes," *Oxford and Cambridge Magazine,* I (January, 1856), 56–57.

[26] The same, I, 55.

[27] Transcript of manuscript letter from Mrs. George Jones to her sister, 8 July 1855 (Fuller).

respectability to feel that a grand marriage must be better than love in a cottage, and particularly during her second campaign she so obviously pursues Farintosh that "the young fellows were making an 'event' of Ethel's marriage, and sporting their money on it." In the end Ethel is saved from "marrying without love, . . . to fall into it afterwards." But Thackeray is careful to complete his picture with the story of Lady Clara Pulleyn, who after several miserable years as Barnes Newcome's wife, elopes with Jack Belsize, a tale that Thackeray contrives to relate candidly enough despite the restrictions of "modern conventionalism." [28] Contemporary reviewers took this aspect of the novel very seriously, most of them agreeing with the *Examiner*'s reviewer, that "the theme is worthy of the power spent on it." [29] It is not surprising that a veteran of the London world like Lord Stanley of Alderley, anxious to inculcate received opinions in his daughters, should have forbidden them "to read Thackeray on the ground that the picture of London society in his novels was too accurate to be good for young girls." [30]

Most of Thackeray's characters succumb at least partially to the code of respectability. But there is a saving remnant moved by the promptings of the heart rather than by the counsels of the world, by "Right and Love" rather than by "Self and Ambition and Advancement." Colonel Newcome is the chief of these, of course, and it is by his simplicity and rectitude that the others are tried and found wanting. But Clive and Ethel also struggle through to salvation in the end. And in the background there is "J. J.," the frail sickly boy who by some magic charm is able to forget "the vulgar life-track, and the light of common day" in the splendid world of art. He had a particular fascination for the first readers of the novel, and in its last pages Thackeray announced: "J. J.'s history, let me confidentially state, has been revealed to me, and may be told." [31]

But *The Newcomes* is too vast and complex a work to be discussed exclusively in the light of its dominant theme. The novel has its distinctive emotional colouring, which faithfully reflects Thackeray's state of mind during the years 1853–1855. While he was writing its final chapters, he made some significant confidences regarding "his heart

[28] *Works*, XIV, 361–362, 595, 501, 442.
[29] 1 September 1855, p. 548.
[30] *The Amberley Papers*, ed. Bertrand and Patricia Russell, 2 vols. (London, 1937), I, 14.
[31] *Works*, XIV, 502, 160, 1008.

troubles" and their impression on his book to a Boston friend, Mrs. George Jones, who was visiting Paris. "I should judge he had arrived at that stage of calm despair when one is left almost without regret or hope," wrote Mrs. Jones. "He loves another, but seeks in the rigid discharge of his duty to his family to shut out the dangerous contemplation of what might be his happiness. He has been, one can see, a thoroughly disappointed man." In particular Thackeray called her attention to a letter from Mme. de Florac to Colonel Newcome, which had "more in it than met the eye." [32] And in fact Thackeray here recaptured the rhetoric of his now forbidden letters to Jane Brookfield:

> How well I remember me of every one of those days, though there is a death between me and them, and it is as across a grave I review them. Yet another parting, and tears and regrets are finished. *Tenez,* I do not believe them when they say there is no meeting for us afterwards, there above. To what good to have seen you, friend, if we are to part here, and in Heaven too? . . . When the end comes with its great absolution, I shall not be sorry. One supports the combats of life, but they are long, and one comes from them very wounded; ah, when shall they be over? . . . I live but of the past; and play with its souvenirs as the detained caress little birds, little flowers, in their prisons. I was born for the happiness; my God! I have learned it in knowing you. In losing you I have lost it.[33]

But whereas in *Esmond* the reflection of the Brookfield affair is concentrated in one set of relationships, those between Henry and Lord and Lady Castlewood, in *The Newcomes* it is diffused throughout the novel. The true love of finer spirits is everywhere destined to frustration or at best to "brief fruition." [34] The careers of Clive and the Colonel, of Mme. de Florac and Ethel, alike illustrate the pathos of renunciation and self-sacrifice.[35] As the end of the novel approached, Thackeray was besieged by appeals to unite his hero and heroine, and finally he brought himself to assure his readers "that in fable-land somewhere Ethel and Clive are living most comfortably together." [36]

[32] Transcript of manuscript letter to her sister, 8 July 1855 (Fuller).
[33] *Works*, XIV, 701–702.
[34] The same, XIV, 29.
[35] See, for example, the same, XIV, 200–201, 387–388, 735, 765.
[36] The same, XIV, 1008. Even so there was discontent because Thackeray had not elaborated on his happy ending. A journalist named James Hain Friswell went so far as to write a supplementary chapter for *Sharpe's Magazine* "in compassion for the many people who wished to share in the joys of Clive and Ethel." "Here for three-and-twenty months," Friswell explained, "has the hand of the mighty master

But with his novel attuned throughout to a minor key, Thackeray knew that this was "an artistic blunder," [37] just as Dickens did when he brought Estella and Pip together at the end of *Great Expectations*. In Thackeray's treatment of his central character, however, there is no such damaging concession. Indeed, Colonel Newcome is the supreme example of his creator's conviction (which Henry James was later to make his own) that nobility of character is best displayed in defeat and resignation. During the first third of the novel, Thackeray portrays the Colonel in prosperity and hopefulness as the perfect embodiment, for all his eccentricities, of the gentlemanly ideal. By the time he departs for India he has taken his place beside Parson Adams and Dr. Primrose, on whom he was partially modelled, as one of the great imaginative embodiments of manly simplicity. Thackeray brought the Colonel back into the last third of his novel with the far more demanding objective of offering him as a pattern of Christian humility. "The strong and eager covet honour and enjoyment for themselves," Thackeray wrote; "the gentle and disappointed (once they may have been strong and eager too), desire these gifts for their children." The Colonel has always been one of "the gentle and disappointed," but his misguided ambition for Clive leads him into a headlong career of vindictive folly. Disaster, when it comes, is his salvation.

> He that is down need fear no fall,
> He that is low no pride.

Only after his defences are utterly swept away, after his heart has become "as that of a little child," does his true grace of character appear. He is then seen as the supreme example of Thackeray's doctrine of charity in all human judgment, since "the Judge who sees not the outward acts merely, but their causes, and views not the wrong alone, but the temptations, struggles, ignorance of erring creatures, we know

---

held us spell-bound in such a mixture of wonder, pity, and delight; such an April passion of gentle smiles and tears; such a tremor of indignation or soft gush of love at or for Ethel Newcome,—and now, at the moment when he has so nobly rescued his heroine, when he has made our hearts spring forth again with an after-crop of affection, so strong, so fresh, and so enduring that it will last the winter of our lives, we are to be disappointed in hearing how it was done." This must not be, Friswell felt, and he accordingly supplied the missing picture of newly-wed happiness in a ludicrously faithful pastiche of Thackeray's manner.

[37] *Letters of James Russell Lowell*, ed. Charles Eliot Norton, 2 vols. (New York, 1894), I, 239. Thackeray explained to Lowell: "What could a fellow do? So many people wanted 'em married. To be sure, I had to kill off poor little Rosey rather suddenly, but shall not a man do what he will with his own? Besides, we can hope they won't have any children."

has a different code to ours," and of submission to "the Divine Will, which ordains these trials, these triumphs, these humiliations, these blest griefs, this crowning Love." [38]

The Newcomes offers many of Thackeray's most successful characters. In this discussion there has been no opportunity to touch upon the dreadful "Campaigner," the most elaborate of that series of portraits of Mrs. Shawe which led one reader of Thackeray's fiction to complain "that odious novelists had frightened mothers-in-law out of their daughters' homes," [39] such delightful eccentrics as Frederick Bayham, James Binnie, and Paul de Florac, or such collaterals of the Newcome clan as that quintessential spinster, Martha Honeyman, and her precious and affected brother Charles. The novel also presents some of Thackeray's finest scenes, beginning with the opening glimpse of the Colonel in the Cave of Harmony, which one would choose before almost any other to illustrate the full range of his genius, and going on from strength to strength to the moving final episodes of his purgatory and euthanasia. Thackeray's style was never more supple and elegant. Consider, for example, the vignette in which he brings together Clive and Jack Belsize at Baden in hopeless attendance on the ladies whom they love:

> They lapse into silence, during which Jack's cigar glimmers from the twilight corner where Clive's bed is; whilst Clive wafts his fragrance out of the window where he sits, and whence he has a view of Lady Ann Newcome's windows to the right, over the bridge across the little rushing river, at the Hotel de Hollande hard by. The lights twinkle in the booths under the pretty lime avenues. The hum of distant voices is heard; the gambling palace is all in a blaze; it is an assembly night, and from the doors of the conversation-rooms, as they open and close, escape gusts of harmony. Behind on the little hill the darkling woods lie calm, the edges of the fir-trees cut sharp against the sky, which is clear with a crescent moon and the lambent lights of the starry hosts of heaven. Clive does not see pine-robed hills and shining stars, nor think of pleasure in its palace yonder, nor of pain writhing on his own bed within a few feet of him, where poor Belsize was groaning. His eyes are fixed upon a window whence comes the red light of a lamp, across

---

[38] *Works*, XIV, 673, 1007, 807, 956. For a fuller development of this view of Colonel Newcome, see *Buried Life*, pp. 108–116. That Thackeray did all this without sacrificing his customary fidelity to actual life is amply attested. Chartres Biron writes, for example, "Colonel Newcome is often voted too unworldly, but if you read Lord Roberts' Indian reminiscences, you realize what a very accurate picture he is of an Indian Colonel before the Mutiny" (*Pious Opinions*, London, 1923, p. 216).

[39] Berdmore, *Scratch Team of Essays*, p. 179.

which shadows float now and again. So every light in every booth yonder has a scheme of its own: every star above shines by itself; and each individual heart of ours goes on brightening with its own hopes, burning with its own desires, and quivering with its own pain.[40]

Concerning the commentary with which Thackeray accompanies his narrative in *The Newcomes,* there has been sharp critical disagreement. During the earlier part of the book Thackeray's device of telling the story through Pen is acceptable enough, since Pen is for all intents and purposes his *alter ego.* One is grateful for such delicious pages as those beginning Chapter 9, in which after an account of the delights of Brighton the proposition is developed that "the true pleasure of life is to live with your inferiors," [41] no matter who the supposed author may be. But one becomes uneasy at prolonged explanations of how Pen has come into possession of the story he tells.[42] And the appearance in Chapter 49 of "dear Laura"—safely immured, one had hoped, in the pages of *Pendennis*—elicits a stronger response than uneasiness. When she is on the scene, Thackeray's protective sense of the ridiculous, which usually restrains him from sentimental excess, operates only intermittently. The praise of her infallible rectitude, the accounts of her "sauciness," and the coy periphrases in which her displays of conjugal affection are described make for an atmosphere of domesticity at once cloying and factitious. One can only endorse the complaint of Thackeray's friend Whitwell Elwin: "There is a pragmatic assumption about her goodness, an air of prudery and self-conceit—the strings by which she leads her pliant husband, who esteems her the more for her pretension—but which render the praises bestowed upon her, and the general confidence reposed in her, somewhat distasteful." [43]

The Newcomes raised Thackeray's contemporary reputation to its apex. Indeed, in their discussions of the book critics were hard put to it to find fresh aspects of characters whom the public knew "as well as it does the faces of Disraeli and Lord John Russell, and has been much more interested about them for two years past. What can we say that has not been said over hundreds of dining-tables, in countless drawing-rooms, students' chambers, under-graduates' rooms?" [44] They united in praising the Colonel, whose character was seen as triumphantly vindi-

[40] *Works,* XIV, 378.
[41] The same, XIV, 114–119.
[42] See, for example, the same, XIV, 296–297, 319.
[43] *Quarterly Review,* XCVIII (September, 1855), 360. In some moods Thackeray himself endorsed this criticism. See *Letters,* III, 438n, 469.
[44] *Spectator,* 18 August 1855, p. 859.

cating Thackeray from whatever residue of the charge of cynicism might have remained after *Esmond*. By creating so noble a figure Thackeray had removed the last obstacle that prevented the great public from taking him to its heart, and he was henceforth seen as one of the foremost Victorian worthies. Nor had he sacrificed any part of his vogue with the *élite* in the process. During most of *The Newcomes'* run, Dickens had offered in competition only *Hard Times*, about which Macaulay's judgment of "disagreeable & overstrained" [45] was representative; and Thackeray was conceived by many members of the intellectual classes to have passed his great rival in the race for pre-eminence. So in 1857 George Eliot thought Thackeray, "as I suppose the majority of people with any intellect do, on the whole the most powerful of living novelists." [46] There were critical reservations certainly, on the ground of repetitiousness in subject matter and theme and a "strong family likeness" [47] in characters when compared with his earlier fiction, but these were unimportant.

The Newcomes long held a favoured position among Thackeray's novels. As late as 1908 Saintsbury could contend that it had been on the whole "Thackeray's most popular book." [48] More typical today is Elizabeth Bowen's dismissal of it as the "shell of a great novel." [49] Certainly of all Thackeray's novels it is the one which benefited most from the circumstances of serial issue. As it appeared in twenty-four monthly parts, it seemed to many readers the "masterpiece of all novel writing." [50] Such an audience was not disturbed by its slow beginning, by the "seated mass of information" which requires a sixth of the novel before the narrative proper begins. This prolonged exposition is necessary preparation for the rest, in which, as Thackeray promised, "there's plenty of action & passion too";[51] but only slow, concentrated attention, such as serial readers were prepared to give, could ensure its proper assimilation. So equipped one sees *The Newcomes*, not as an inept book, like many Victorian serials, but as an expert one in a difficult mode. "The artful trick of keeping two stories going like a juggler's ball," Edith Wharton points out, "is entirely different from the attempt to follow the interior movement of typical social groups, as

[45] Manuscript journal, 13 August 1854 (Trinity College, Cambridge).
[46] *The George Eliot Letters*, ed. Haight, II, 349.
[47] *Spectator*, 18 August 1855, p. 859.
[48] *Works*, XIV, xvi.
[49] "English Novelists," in *The Romance of English Literature*, ed. Turner (New York, 1944), p. 250.
[50] Burne-Jones, I, 51.
[51] *Letters*, III, 349.

The Adventures of Philip

by Joseph E. Baker

Very early in his career, Thackeray published his *Catherine* (1839–40) as part of *Fraser's Magazine*'s campaign against fiction that glamorized criminals and sinners. In a note to Chapter i, he singled out for criticism Bulwer's *Ernest Maltravers* because it "opens with a seduction; but then it is performed by people of the strictest virtue on both sides; there is so much religion and philosophy in the heart of the seducer, so much tender innocence in the soul of the seduced, that —bless the little dears!—their very peccadilloes make one interested in them; and their naughtiness becomes quite sacred, so deliciously is it described." In *Fraser's*, August 1832, Bulwer had been accused of parallel confusions: "having to paint an adulterer, you describe him as belonging to the class of country curates, among whom, perhaps, such a criminal is not met with once in a hundred years." [1]

Thackeray's *Philip* appeared in *The Cornhill Magazine,* Jan. 1861– Aug. 1862. In this novel, written at the end of his life, the author has a woman chloroform a clergyman and rob him of his property, a "bill" he is said to have "purchased." [2] How many times in a hundred years could we find such a person as "Hunt, the clergyman"? He is described as: "needy, greedy, treacherous, unscrupulous,"—a blackmailer—"such a low, graceless, friendless vagabond, that if he comes in for a few kicks . . . we need not be very sorry." [3] Notice that one thing that makes him contemptible is that he is "friendless"; we are to rejoice when Philip gets what he wants in the world through having prosperous friends.

"The Adventures of Philip" (originally entitled "Thackeray's Recantation") by Joseph E. Baker. From *PMLA*, LXXVII (1962), 586–94. Copyright © 1962 by the Modern Language Association. Reprinted by permission of the author and the Modern Language Association.

[1] VI, 68 (in "Elizabeth Brownrigge," sometimes erroneously ascribed to Thackeray).

[2] So Philip's father reports at the end of Ch. xxxvi.

[3] Ch. xi. *Works of W. M. Thackeray, Special Biographical Edition* (N.Y. and London, 1898–1900), XX, 208–209. This edition is used for volume and page references throughout the text of this paper.

We are expected to love Mrs. Brandon, who robbed the clergyman. She is Caroline of *A Shabby Genteel Story*, seduced by Philip's father before he married Philip's mother. But—bless the little dear! We may say, there is "so much tender innocence in the soul of the seduced," that her "naughtiness"—or at least her theft—"becomes quite sacred, so deliciously is it described." Thackeray insistently refers to her as the Little "Sister" or nurse, for as a nurse she makes a living. She having lost her child and Philip his mother, she has mothered him all his life; and now that he is a married man with children, following a profession or two, she would like to exercise more prerogatives than the wife would allow. As she goes about laying her trap for the clergyman, baited with herself, this is how it is "deliciously" described, peccadilloes and all:

> To rescue Philip, to secure the fatal bill, to go with it to Charlotte, and say, "There, Mrs. Philip, there's your husband's liberty [from having to pay it]." It would be a rare triumph, that it would! And Philip would promise, on his honour, that this should be the last and only bill he would pay for that wretched old father. With these happy thoughts swelling in her little heart, Mrs. Brandon made her way to the familiar house in Thornhaugh Street, and would have a little bit of supper, so she would. And laid her own little cloth; and set forth her little forks and spoons, which were as bright as rubbing could make them . . . And, with her bit of supper, after a day's work, our little friend would sometimes indulge in a glass—a little glass— of something comfortable. . . . I am sure she said a grace before her meat.

In this paragraph the word "little" occurs a dozen times, besides other words and phrases declaring all this to be very cute. Mrs. Brandon is not presented as grandmotherly, but almost as a rival to Philip's wife; she proves very attractive in the clergyman's eyes:

> "Won't you step in and sit down to it, and take something?" asks the smiling hostess.
> Of course, Hunt would take something. And the greasy hat is taken off his head with a flourish, and he struts into the poor Little Sister's little room, pulling a wisp of grizzled hair, and endeavoring to assume a careless fashionable look. (XXI, 576–577)

Is Thackeray trying to make us say, "the dirty fly! the poor little spider"? She speaks "meekly" and "in her gay artless way." She looks "pretty, and rosy, and bright. Her cheeks are like apples, her figure is trim and graceful, and always attired in the neatest fitting gown." If in *Henry Esmond* "psychological incest . . . is present" when Henry

"marries his own 'dear mother,' "[4] we should not be surprised that
Thackeray would write as follows, after Philip, a great hulking fellow, threw the clergyman down the steps: "She liked to see him just
now standing over her enemy, courageous, victorious, her champion
. . . And she passed her little hand down his arm, of which the muscles
were all in a quiver from the recent skirmish . . . she fondles him
. . . It is a wonder how she prattles on . . . the innocent Delilah
coaxing and wheedling this young Samson" (xx, 218).

And Thackeray gives another Biblical story a rather unholy application when he writes, "the poor Little Sister proffered her mite,
her all, to Philip" (xx, 273). This reference to the widow's mite is appropriate, since the great religious principle which justifies any crime
she may commit is that she pets Philip, spoils him, and makes him
her god, as the mother of Pendennis "worshipped" her son (*Pendennis*,
Ch. ii, iii, 14).

In discussing Thackeray, we must consider such matters important,
for, as Gordon Ray says, "The moral life was Thackeray's overwhelm-
ing preoccupation." [5] And I have myself pointed out how close his
Vanity Fair is to a central Christian and Platonic tradition.[6] Yet when
we examine *Philip* closely we discover moral obtuseness, or perversity.
Las Vergnas finds *Barry Lyndon* characterized by virility, *Vanity Fair*
by profundity, and *Philip* by "le sermon." [7] If so, what does the sermon
preach? Critics seem to have been so much struck by the manner of
the novel—the *least* direct narrative of any novel before the twentieth
century—or simply so bored by its prolixity, that they have not focussed
attention on its most puzzling qualities. Perhaps this novel more than
any other illustrates what Lambert Ennis calls Thackeray's "ambiva-
lences" and his "preoccupation with masks." [8] But no one has tried to
remove the masks of this novel. If we do, what do we see behind them?

Thackeray was often profound in his treatment of all kinds of vices
and virtues; but in the field of ethics his specialty was snobs and their
converse, the true gentleman. Early in *The Book of Snobs* (Ch. ii) he
says, "*He who meanly admires mean things is a Snob*—perhaps that is

---

[4] J. E. Tilford, Jr., "The 'Unsavoury Plot' of *Henry Esmond*," *Nineteenth-Century Fiction*, Sept. 1951, p. 122. The second phrase is quoted by Tilford from the
Times, 23 December, 1852.
[5] "Epilogue," *Thackeray, the Age of Wisdom, 1847–1863* (N.Y., 1958). As for the
title of this book, see Gordon Ray's "Preface."
[6] "*Vanity Fair* and the Celestial City," *Nineteenth-Century Fiction*, Sept. 1955, pp.
89–98.
[7] W. M. Thackeray, *L'Homme—Le Penseur—Le Romancier* (Paris, 1932), p. 299.
[8] *Thackeray, the Sentimental Cynic* (Evanston, Ill., 1950), pp. 1, 2.

a safe definition"; and "What is it to be a gentleman? It is to be honest, to be gentle, to be generous, to be brave, to be wise, and, possessing all these qualities, to exercise them in the most graceful outward manner." Now the gentleman-hero of this novel is rough, lacks a graceful outward manner, and is not always wise. He is generous to his own scoundrel father, but not to his wife's mother. He is less likely to be generous to others than to spend for what he wants to enjoy. There is no occasion for bravery. He certainly is not gentle; he is "as rude as a bear" (xxi, 516). Usually his violence is made to seem justified. But not always. Thackeray has not made it that easy for us. He may be patting Philip on the head, but he is not whitewashing him. Consider this incident: Philip's employer Mugford has him and his wife to dinner with the Woolseys. Woolsey is "a wealthy tailor"; his wife had been an actress.

> Now, more worthy and honourable people do not live than Woolsey and his wife . . . Mrs. Woolsey is loud. Her *h*'s are by no means where they should be; her knife at dinner is often where it should not be . . . I do not say that this was an elegant woman, or a fitting companion for Mrs. Philip [Firmin]: but I know that Mrs. Woolsey was a good, clever, and kindly woman, and that Philip behaved rudely to her . . . the truth is, he treated her, her husband, Mugford, and Mrs. Mugford, with a haughty ill-humour which utterly exasperated and perplexed them.

(A significant question can be asked: If the wife of Philip, or of Pendennis, or of Thackeray, had been treated that way, by a nobleman, would the author have been content to write merely that it "exasperated and perplexed them"?)

> About this poor lady, who was modest and innocent as Susannah, Philip had heard some wicked elders at wicked clubs tell wicked stories in old times . . . On an ordinary occasion Philip would never have cared or squabbled about a question of precedence . . . But when Mrs. Woolsey in crumpled satins and blowsy lace made her appearance, and was eagerly and respectfully saluted by the host and hostess, Philip remembered those early stories about the poor lady: his eyes flashed wrath, and his breast beat with an indignation which almost choked him. Ask that woman to meet my wife? he thought to himself . . .
>   Philip, then, scowling at the newly-arrived guests, turning his great hulking back upon the company, and talking to his wife, presented a not agreeable figure to his entertainer. "Hang the fellow's pride!" thought Mugford.

At the end of the evening, ready to depart, "in a sudden gust of passion, Philip stepped out of the carriage, and stalked up to his host

. . . 'I am come back, sir,' said Philip, glaring at Mugford, 'to ask how you dared invite Mrs. Philip Firmin to meet that woman?' " Notice Thackeray's keen psychology: it is Philip's own name that is being given a rank too low; this is not chivalrous defense of his lady, who is horrified at the outburst. So Mugford fired Philip. Philip was sorry for this income "thrown away," but felt "still keener remorse" when he found that Mrs. Woolsey "was a most respectable and honourable woman," against whom "he had cast a sidelong stone of persecution." (The Biblical allusion to the casting of stones at a woman makes us ask if Thackeray is really employing Christ's teaching; that is, would it have been *correct* to cast the stone if she had proved to be a *guilty* woman?) And we notice again the emphasis on what is, at first glance, irrelevant: the social fact of the low position of tailors: " 'I should like to go, sir, and grovel before her,' Philip said, in his energetic way. 'If I see that tailor, I will request him to put his foot on my head, and trample on me . . . shall I never learn charity towards my neighbours, and always go on believing in the lies which people tell me?' " (XXI, 533–536).

Thus Philip mentions, only to pass over, his lack of charity, and interprets it as a matter of his having been deceived. He would like to chastise the scoundrel who lied to him about Mrs. Woolsey. And so he remains as proud as ever. "Philip's roughness and frankness did not displease Tregarvan," his next employer (XXI, 539). How much does it displease the author? How does Thackeray the moralist *judge* what Thackeray the artist and social psychologist so mercilessly portrays? "I daresay not a just man, but I have met juster men not half so honest" (XX, 270–271). What the writer especially liked about Philip was his rude frankness, his saying what he felt, wearing no mask. Thackeray himself often wears a mask; even in this novel he pretends that its author is Pendennis. But this time the authorial mask is so thin that we are convinced that the judgments of "Pendennis" are those of Thackeray.

II

Philip was Thackeray's last completed full length novel; *Barry Lyndon* was his first (1844). A comparison of the two is disturbing. In both books the ostensible writer, Barry or Pendennis, describes, with moral insensitivity and even admiration, deeds, words, and attitudes that are reprehensible and arrogant, however much the sins may differ in

degree. Barry is complacent about the crimes of his hero, who is himself; Pendennis and Philip are both complacent about the pain caused
by the hero Philip. Yet in the latter novel, Thackeray has clearly endorsed the evaluations made by "Pendennis" and expects the reader to
agree with him. Moreover, he has ascribed to Philip many of his own
experiences and preferences, so that the novel is largely autobiographi-
cal.

In both novels there is emphasis upon mere luck as the determinant
of rewards in this world. In neither novel does the narrator look upon
worldly prosperity as merely a "Vanity Fair." The title preferred by
Thackeray for the first novel was not *Memoirs* but *The Luck of Barry
Lyndon.* Some chapters carry such titles as "More Runs of Luck" and
"In which my Good Fortune Begins to Waver." In a note to Chapter
xvii, Thackeray (not Barry) adds that Lyndon is not the only man who
"has passed for 'nobody's enemy but his own': a jovial good-natured
fellow . . . not, we repeat, a hero of the common pattern; but . . . Do
not as many rogues succeed in life as honest men? more fools than men
of talent?" Yet this is the situation we are to be pleased with in *Philip,*
for it enables the hero to be rewarded. And here appears a chapter
entitled, "In which the Luck Goes Very Much against Us," followed
soon by one in which a stroke of luck gives a fortune to Philip. The
wife of the narrator identifies these good strokes of luck as the provi-
dential actions of a Supreme Power. Against this the writer offers an
amused protest (xxi, 529). Later she says, "with a self-satisfied air, 'Was
I not certain that succour would come?' " (xxi, 560). And, with prayer,
succour did come—after that same believer in Providence had, by the
practice of some hypocrisy, provided another employer for Philip: "Go,
Delilah! I understand your tricks! . . . My wife humbugged that
wretched Member of Parliament [Tregarvan] in a way that makes me
shudder" (xxi, 538). Pendennis-Thackeray fairly gloats over the irra-
tionalities by which a gentleman can be kept afloat and enabled to provide meals for his "wife, children, guests, servants, charwoman" (xxi,
537).

We cannot judge Thackeray from the point of view of his own total
achievement if we stay within the terms accepted on the surface of
this novel. The question of Philip's honesty has been raised. We seem
to be *told* that he is honest. What are we *shown?* Making his living as
a journalist, he writes London letters for a New York journal in which
he tells lies about the doings of the European aristocracy. He signs
them "Philalethes"—Lover of Truth—"and, as nobody was wounded
by the shafts of our long-bow, I trust Mr. Philip and his friends may

be pardoned for twanging it." [9] Tregarvan, an MP, needs an editor for his *European Review*, established to publicize his opinions on tariff, income tax, and the designs of Russia, about which Philip knows nothing. Philip is for sale and takes the job gratefully, without any thought as to the damage such journalism might do the nation. In later days, reminiscing, he says, "Under great suffering I have met with supreme consolation . . . I bow my head in thanks and awe . . ." He mentions, "an article of my own, and a very dull one, on a subject which I knew nothing about. 'Persian politics, and the intrigues at the Court of Teheran.' It was done to order . . . I breakfasted with Tregarvan in the Albany, the facts (we will call them facts) and papers were supplied to me, and I went home to point out . . . the atrocious intrigues of the Russian Court" (xxi, 530).

When Thackeray himself was a young Radical, he got his start working for the Tory *Fraser's Magazine*. But I am not aware of any case where he is known to have prostituted his profession to give the public "information" that he did not himself believe in. Utter indifference to the truth is the worst crime that can be imputed to a journalist as journalist, especially in dealing with international affairs. Now Thackeray expects us to feel that this is part of Philip's charm.

A moralist—Victorian or not—would surely hold this truth to be self-evident: that lack of integrity in one's profession is bad enough in any individual. Not quite so contemptible, but perhaps more significant, sociologically, is the practice of a profession for which one has no ability or training. Philip had a chance to study law, and Chapter xvi recounts indulgently how he frittered that time away. At the end of Chapter xxxiii he is regretting "that he had been idle . . . Had he studied for the bar, he might have made that profession now profitable." But when he was really in need of money to maintain his upper-class status, "a shower of gold was poured out" on him: through the influence of his friends he was offered a brief, to his surprise; after this one, others followed, until he "positively had money in bank." He was induced to accept this work by the Little Sister, and her snobbish remarks are extremely illuminating; they open a glimpse into the class structure of British society as it has developed in modern times:

> "Now there's this opening, you must take it, my dear," she said. "Suppose you don't know much about law . . ."
> "Much! nothing," interposed Philip. "You might ask me to play the piano; but as I never happened to have learned—"

[9] xxi, 515. (In the previous volume, p. 212, Thackeray equates his phrase "pulled the long-bow" with "twanged a famous lie out." It is a euphemism for lying.)

"La—don't tell me! You mustn't show a faint heart. Take the business, and do it as best you can. You'll do it better next time, and next. The Bar's a gentleman's business. Don't I attend [as nurse] a judge's lady, which I remember her with her first in a little bit of a house in Bernard Street, Russell Square; and now haven't I been to her in Eaton Square, with a butler and two footmen, and carriages ever so many? . . . A gentleman like Mr. Philip oughtn't to have a master. I couldn't bear to think of your going down of a Saturday to the publishing office to get your wages like a workman."

"But I *am* a workman," interposes Philip.

"La! But do you mean to remain one for ever? I would rise, if I was a man! . . . I'd have more spirit than to live in a second floor—I would!" (xxi, 552–553)

Willingly accepting her position as a member of a lower class, she thus whole-heartedly endorses the principle by which the best things in life are to be the prerogative of a relatively small class of "gentlemen," including opportunities for gain in professions they have not been trained for, and have no aptitude for. The reader is expected to be reverently grateful that the hero and his lady can be taken care of in this way. "A gentleman," says the nurse elsewhere, "ought not to live in a two-pair lodging; he ought to have a house of his own" (xxi, 555). But the novel has only scorn for a *woman's* "selling herself," when the "tempter . . . showed her a purse and *three* fine houses" [italics mine].[10]

Philip, though temporarily embarrassed in paying for servants and wine, indubitably *belonged* to this privileged class: "Here's a fellow born with a silver spoon in his mouth," [11] born son of a gentleman (who stole); with noble relatives (whom he rightly scorns); "in right of the heiress, his poor mother, Philip might quarter the Ringwood arms on his carriage" (xxi, 542). He had attended the right kind of school (whose educational methods Thackeray considered quite wrong); he had influential friends; he was potentially heir to enough money to save him from having to work for anybody; he married the daughter of a general. In their worst extremity, he and his lady thought of letting lodgings. When the nurse heard of this project, "she was in a fury. *She* might let lodgin's, but it wasn't for Philip to do so . . . and the way she scolded Mrs. Firmin was not a little amusing." The scolding did not anger Philip's wife. "She liked the scheme as little as

[10] xxi, 601, referring to Agnes Twysden, who turned from Philip to marry Woolcomb.

[11] xx, 262; General Baynes says it to the writer, after they have heard Philip speaking of his own future prospects "in his lordly way."

Brandon" (xxi, 622). It takes the lower classes to keep the upper from
lowering themselves. Since we know something of the masses of sick
and poor who, even when ill-fed, were working long hours daily in
Victorian London, the passage which follows (still within the same
paragraph) is interesting in showing how the "best people" can be
taken care of:

> Everybody who could, made away for a holiday, whilst poor Philip
> remained at his work, snipping and pasting his paragraphs, and doing
> his humble drudgery. A sojourn on the sea-shore was prescribed by Dr.
> Goodenough, as absolutely necessary for Charlotte and her young ones,
> and when Philip pleaded certain cogent reasons why the family could
> not take the medicine prescribed by the Doctor, that eccentric physician
> had recourse to the same pocketbook which we have known him to pro-
> duce on a former occasion . . . [saying] "Pooh! Pay me when you are a
> rich man!" And this Samaritan had jumped into his carriage, and was
> gone, before [they] could say a word of thanks . . . So Philip and his
> young folks came down to Periwinkle Bay . . .

The non-gentleman Mugford, Philip's employer whom he had so insulted and ridiculed, did Philip's work for him "whilst the latter enjoyed his holiday" (xxi, 623). Poor Philip? Does it make any difference
whether or not Philip measured up to the new definition of "gentleman" which Thackeray more than anyone else had been urging upon
the English-speaking people for half a generation? Has Thackeray
completely abandoned his protest against rank and privilege?

Perhaps we should interpret the protest in his earlier work to be
restricted to mean only that a man of the *upper* middle class (or lower
gentry), seeing anyone *above him* in rank or wealth, is justified in
saying, "I would like to see all men equal, and this bloated aristocracy
blasted to the wings of all the winds . . . Oh for a few enlightened
Republicans, men to say their say honestly, and dare to do and say the
truth." This was written to his mother in 1840, while he was writing
for the Tory *Fraser's*. He explains, "I'm not a Chartist, only a Republican," i.e., not a monarchist. And he had just written: "Thank God
that the Chartists have not a man of courage at their head who might
set the kingdom in a blaze. With their views about equalizing property
—robbery, in fact—" (vii, xxviii, xxix). But what if a man of lower
origin has money enough (not birth or background) so that the middle-
class gentleman cannot look down upon him for economic reasons?
What then? How does Philip act?

One sign that he is a gentleman I did not list: He speaks the variety of English that has recently been designated as "U" (i.e., "upper-class," actually most carefully cultivated by the upper *middle* class, in the southern half of Britain). Those who express themselves in Non-U are assumed to be socially inferior. At the time Philip was retailing to a New York journal more or less false tittle-tattle about aristocratic society, his chief job was that of sub-editor for Mr. Mugford. He argues that to accept friendship with Mugford would be "to make friends with the mammon of unrighteousness," and to prove it he ridicules Mugford's pronunciation and that of kind-hearted Mrs. Mugford:

> "A good father, a good husband, a generous host, and a most tremendous bore, and cad . . . Well, Mugford has yellow satin sofas in the 'droaring-room'—"
>
> "Oh, Philip!" says a lady [the writer's wife], and two or three circum-jacent children set up an insane giggle, which is speedily and sternly silenced.
>
> "I tell you she calls it 'droaring-room.' . . . She is a good woman: a kind woman. . . . But how can Char frankly be the friend of a woman who calls a drawing-room a droaring-room? With our dear little friend in Thornhaugh Street, it is different. [He is referring to nurse Brandon, his mother-substitute.] She makes no pretence even at equality. Here is a patron and a patroness, don't you see? When Mugford walks me round his paddock and gardens and says, 'Look year, Firmin;' or scratches one of his pigs on the back, and says, 'we'll 'ave a cut of this fellow on Satur-day' "—(explosive attempts at insubordination and derision on the part of the children again are severely checked by the parental authorities)— 'we'll 'ave a cut of this fellow on Saturday,' I feel inclined to throw him or myself into the trough over the palings . . .
>
> "I can no more be that man's friend que celui du domestique qui vient d'apporter le what-d'-you-call-'em? le coal-scuttle (John entered the room with that useful article during Philip's oration—and we allowed the elder children to laugh this time, for the fact is, none of us knew the French word for coal-scuttle . . .)." (xx, 513–514)

This passage shows how children are "educated" to be ladies and gentlemen with a proper contempt for the lower orders, in spite of the liberal and "Radical" and sometimes Christian theories voiced by their elders. In this paper I have said little about Thackeray's artistry; but notice the terrifying literary efficiency with which he has produced this piece of sociology—so smooth and swift that we hardly notice what has happened. Indeed, we get the impression that Thackeray himself did not know what he had revealed! Compare the "Concluding Ob-servations," the last chapter of his *Book of Snobs* (whose subtitle was, *By One of Themselves*):

We can apply the Snob test to him, and try whether he is conceited and a quack, whether pompous and lacking humility—whether uncharitable and proud of his narrow soul . . . How does he comport himself in the presence of his Grace the Duke? and how in that of Smith the tradesman? And it seems to me that all English society is cursed by this mammoniacle superstition . . . I can bear it no longer—this diabolical invention of gentility which kills natural kindliness and honest friendship. Proper pride, indeed!

Does Thackeray's treatment of Philip show that his position has changed in the fifteen years since he wrote the *Snob* papers; or is he saying the same thing more quietly? Thackeray was himself born into the British aristocracy in India, lost a fortune, and lived much of his life as a Bohemian among gentlemen, a gentleman among Bohemians. In the last part of his life he worked hard—writing *Philip*, for instance —with the set purpose of raising his fortune back up to a point from which it had fallen. His efforts were crowned with success, which included an expensive house and a number of servants, not to mention a supply of wine of choice vintages. Has Thackeray's "anxiety to make a fortune for his daughters" brought his last novel in line with his later letters, "filled with recantations of what he had come to regard as his earlier cynicism"? [12] Using recent terminology, should we say that Thackeray became a pillar of "The Establishment" after having started out as an "Angry Young Man"?

III

So far, we have looked at Philip who is sometimes like Thackeray; or at "the writer," ostensibly Pendennis. The "Pendennis" mask is very thin, and we have assumed that Thackeray is speaking, but when can we be sure? We can, at least, ascribe to Thackeray full responsibility for the title and subtitle of the novel; and this turns out to be quite revealing. It runs thus: *The Adventures of Philip on His Way through the World, Showing Who Robbed Him, Who Helped Him, and Who Passed Him By.* This is a reference to the parable of the Good Samaritan, which is mentioned explicitly again and again in the novel. Verbally he has kept the reference all the closer by saying, "Who Robbed Him," not "Who Attempted to Rob Him," though the latter would cover more of the novel's incidents. And there is no stress on robbery anyway, but rather on *loss*. Clearly, Thackeray used that

[12] Gordon Ray, *The Buried Life* (Cambridge, Mass., 1952), p. 118.

phrase for its Biblical echo; it is the last two clauses that he is really interested in, especially, "Who helped him." Who did? What moral can be drawn? Certainly not Christ's. "Go, and do thou likewise,"—showing mercy and loving the stranger "as thyself"—that is by no means the point of the novel; rather, "Thank God that gentlemen like you will receive financial assistance and a ladylike wife." In words from Chapter xv, entitled "Samaritans," and referring to "Philip fallen among thieves" (i.e., cheated by his own father): "Ah, thanks to Heaven, travellers find Samaritans as well as Levites on life's hard way!" [13] Thackeray has strangely emphasized the social exclusiveness of his sympathies by repeated reference to a parable originally directed *against* the pride and self-sufficiency of the in-group.

Thackeray has kept this parable before us, without any recognition that it does not say what he is saying. As told in the Bible, it illustrates that a man who is *not* "one of us," a man from a group looked down upon by "us," acted in humane kindness and proved himself more admirable than those from our own inner circle, our own priests and Levites. Hereditary Levites might be parallelled to hereditary aristocrats, like Philip himself, or the baronet and the earl, his relatives, from whom he inherits his two fortunes. Throughout, Philip is aided by people of his own class, gentlemen, and by "good friends" immediately identified as examples of "your good Samaritan" (xxi, 530). While temporarily in distress, or what might seem like distress to a born gentleman—for he must go to work—Philip receives aid from his best friends, and, " 'By George!' he swore, 'it is worth being ruined to find such good people in the world' " (xx, 271). Contrast the parable, where the "man from Jerusalem" finds that those who might be expected to be helpful "passed by on the other side," while he received kindness from an outsider, and a despised outsider at that, a man of Samaria, not a real Jew of Judaea.

What attitude does this novel take towards outsiders (i.e., towards "Samaritans" in the Biblical sense)? It is clear that the author is *not* in favor of integration between the "race" of English gentlemen and other classes. Those who think they believe in equality are deceiving themselves; in one brief sketch, Sir John Ringwood is satirized for considering himself "a staunch Liberal," even a "republican," and talking about "natural equality and the outrageous injustice of the present social system" (xxi, 543–544). One should speak kindly to servants; but to pretend to more of the democratic spirit is presented as the sign

[13] xx, 267. And near the end of the novel, he mentions "the Samaritans who came to Philip's help in these his straits" (xxi, 617).

of a harsh self-deceiver. It is the duty of a servant to subordinate himself to the master class. At the time of writing *Philip*, Thackeray wrote in one of the *Roundabout Papers*, published in his *Cornhill Magazine*, an incident concerning a servant who, all through dinner, was waiting.

> The champagne was properly iced, the dinner was excellently served; every guest was attended to; the dinner disappeared; the dessert was set; the claret was in perfect order, carefully decanted, and more ready. And then Henry said, "If you please, sir, may I go home?" He had received word that his house was on fire; and having seen through his dinner, he wished to go and look after his children, and little sticks of furniture.[14]

But Thackeray is not preparing to say, "What an abject snob; why didn't he act like a man and treat the suffering of his children as a matter of more importance than the perfect decanting of claret?" No. Thackeray applauds, adding, "Why, such a man's livery is a uniform of honour. The crest on his button is a badge of bravery." Thus, "Henry is a hero." This is not the standard of duty held up for Philip in his work as journalist or lawyer. The domestic virtue of placing first the welfare of one's own family and friends would have been, apparently, another prerogative of higher classes.

When Philip is helped by an inferior, an outsider, Mugford, the help comes through "pull" and influence; it is done "for the sake of Philip's young wife and child," and through the social arts of the wife of his friend Pendennis, who is, of course, a lady. Employer Mugford and his unladylike wife are kept in their place, since Philip is indulgently allowed to display his amusing contempt for their inferior pronunciation of English. Thackeray's version would ridicule the Samaritan for speaking Non-U. And the Samaritan would be led to have compassion just because "the conclaves and conspiracies of these women" (these Levites and Pharisees) "were endless in Philip's behalf" (xxi, 478, 516, 485). It is a matter of connections.

Apparently it never occurred to Thackeray that the very point of the word "Samaritan" in *Luke* is that it means "not a born Jew," and would be the equivalent in Victorian England to "not a born gentleman." Profound Biblical scholarship was not needed to see this. If he had *reread* the parable to which he makes repeated reference and from which he uses many phrases, surely he would have noticed that

---

[14] "On a Chalk-Mark on the Door," xxiii, 285-286. Thackeray seems to have forgotten that, as Lewis Mumford says, "insolence battens on servility" (*The City in History*, New York, 1961, p. 370); and this is relevant to the fact that the "good" people in *Philip* think its insolent hero is charming.

it is given as an answer to the question, *"Who* is my neighbor?" The question is not, "Can a man in need depend on his own people?" But if that had been the question, it is clear that the parable's answer would be No; and the answer of *Philip* is Yes. The glow of his *Yes* made Thackeray feel at the end of his life that he had turned away from earlier "cynicism"; whereas from the point of view of the younger Thackeray it would seem that the complacency and snobbery of *Philip* are more cynical. And who is my neighbor? Christ is designating someone who is *not* near to us, *not* "one of ours," but a despised colonial, a half-breed. In this novel, the "Samaritan" would have to be the mulatto with the punning name, Mr. Woolcomb. Not content to ignore the humanity of the parable, Thackeray has ridiculed it, in the last chapter of the novel, in an election campaign where the mulatto, running for Parliament, is made to say, "Vote for me! Am I not a Man and a Brudder?" Even the pronunciation of "brother" is wrong; and how could Christ have tolerated that?

For the middle of the nineteenth century, a real parallel to Christ's Good Samaritan would be for Thackeray to tell to Southern slave-holders and English ladies and gentlemen a story of The Good Nigger. But this is the opposite of the attitude expressed. In describing Wool-comb he rather bitterly scolds England for not having the prejudice against a mulatto that would be found in the slave states, and he recommends a Jim-Crow example: "a dark complexion, and hair so *very* black and curly, that I really almost think in some of the Southern States of America he would be likely to meet with rudeness in a railway-car. But in England we know better. In England Grenville Woolcomb is a man and a brother" (xx, 184). This may be compared—or contrasted—with the *Book of Snobs* where he voices his "savage" scorn for intermarriage between the families of a wealthy businessman and of "an old aristocrat, swelling with pride of race, the descendant of illustrious Norman robbers, whose blood has been pure for centuries, and who looks down upon common Englishmen as a free-born American does on a nigger" (Ch. viii, xi, 331).

As his earlier novels show the misery of girls who marry to rise in social rank, this shows the misery of a girl who lowers herself to marry a man who had some negro blood, when she might have married Philip (who is himself the descendant of an illustrious "thief," his father, and of several noble families). Thackeray demonstrates, by the events of the story, his endorsement of the remark made, for him, by a very minor character, "Serves her right! What did an English lady mean by marrying such a fellow?" (xxi, 630). Obviously the only motive that could tempt an English lady to marry a dark, curly-haired fellow would be money. And so our "showman of Vanity Fair," his hand almost too quick for the eye to follow, has shifted the lights and put the focus on another moral issue entirely; while, in passing, he rejects Shakespeare's humane treatment of race, and also the forgiving spirit of the parable of the Prodigal Son. A girl *ought* to have decent respect for Philip's unearned income:

> A young doctor's son, with a thousand a year for a fortune, may be considered a catch in some circles, but not, *vous concevez*, in the upper regions of society. And dear woman—dear, angelic, highly accomplished, respectable woman—does she not know how to pardon many failings in our sex? Age? psha! She will crown my bare old poll with the roses of her youth. Complexion? What contrast is sweeter and more touching than Desdemona's golden ringlets on swart Othello's shoulder! A past life of selfishness and bad company? Come out from among the swine, my prodigal, and I will purify thee!
>
> This [i.e., opposition to such benevolence] is what is called cynicism, you know. Then I suppose my wife is a cynic, who clutches her children to her pure heart, and prays gracious Heaven to guard them from selfishness, from worldliness, from heartlessness, from wicked greed. (xx, 185)

The selfishness, heartlessness, and worldliness of a Desdemona? What he is really admiring is his lady's Pharisaic purity. That quotation is from the end of a chapter entitled "Will Be Pronounced to be Cynical by the Benevolent." Only the "pure heart" of the lady can ultimately protect the Chosen or Best People from contamination by curly-haired Samaritans who might mispronounce "brother." In the final chapter Thackeray goes far out of his way to arrange further digs at the mulatto and his wife Agnes, that wicked Desdemona, though, just before, he has admitted that he may not have been fair to the outsiders. Of "our story" he says apologetically, "It interests itself about a little clique of people here below—their griefs, their trials, their weaknesses, their kindly hearts. People there are in our history who do not seem to me to have kindly hearts at all; and yet perhaps, if a biography could be written from their point of view, some other novelist might show how Philip and *his* biographer were a pair of selfish worldlings." And the novelist does actually seem not to know that he has already shown this! But he is bothered.

> I protest as I look back at the past portions of this history, I begin to have qualms, and ask myself whether the folks of whom we have been prattling have had justice done to them: whether Agnes Twysden is not a suffering martyr justly offended by Philip's turbulent behaviour, and

whether Philip deserves any particular attention or kindness at all . . .
Perhaps I do not understand the other characters round about him so
well, and have overlooked a number of their merits, and caricatured and
exaggerated their little defects. (XXI, 616–617)

Yet in the next sentence he uses again the word "Samaritans" and does
not apply it to any of these outsiders but to another member of what
he has just called Philip's "little clique."

IV

Literary criticism, and even scholarship, sometimes seems to proceed
on the assumption that if a great genius wrote several splendid master-
pieces, as did Thackeray, we should therefore accept uncritically everything else he wrote—except perhaps some juvenilia. Surely this is a
mistake. Indeed, the more profound our admiration for his greatest
achievements, the more clear-sighted should be our criticism of his
descent into something lower. In the earlier novels, Thackeray, as I
have shown in a former essay, made powerful new applications of an
ethical tradition that goes as far back as Christ and even Plato.[15]
Moreover, he had looked at the first nation of our world in which a
thoroughly developed capitalism served a thoroughly developed class
system, and he helped teach a century to hate the result. He had said
things about pride of class which we are only now catching up with;
and they have not been said better by political democrats, by American
sociologists, or by angry young British playwrights. He gave the word
"snob" its devastating meaning. All this he accomplished by a literary
art unsurpassed in English prose, with a creative vision more poetic
than most poetry. Some of his artistry he retained to the end, and
some of it was employed in writing *Philip*. This makes it all the worse,
as a repudiation of his own deepest insights and of the very humanity
he had taught us to value.

By the time he wrote *Philip*, he was anxious to recoup his own
fortune while nevertheless spending heavily on worldly goods. He felt
it a moral duty to make of his daughters well-to-do English ladies.
Should these facts mollify our estimate of the novel, or make it more
strict? Autobiographically he has put as much of his own life into
Philip as into *Pendennis*. But the trenchant and amused detachment

---

[15] *"Vanity Fair* and the Celestial City," *Nineteenth-Century Fiction,* Sept. 1955, pp.
89–98.

has been replaced by excuses and applause, and by exhortations to the reader to be blind. The lily has festered. There is a comment on *Philip* by Newman that I must quote, partly because those who care little for the novel have seldom gone so far: of Thackeray he wrote, "He himself is the greatest instance of the text of which he was so full, *Vanitas vanitatum, omnia vanitas.* I wonder whether he has known his own decay, for a decay I think there has been. I thought his last novel betrayed lassitude and exhaustion of mind." [16] But there is a still sadder comment to be made. I wonder whether we should revise our estimate of his earlier and greater novels by asking if they too carry implications that are only in *Philip* made explicit? I confess that I am reluctant to seek the answer to that question.

Aristotle at the beginning of *Nichomachaean Ethics,* in making a very damaging criticism of a concept basic to the thought of his master Plato, says, it is "our duty . . . to honor truth above our friends." Thackeray, surely, would prefer to sing, as the drinking song puts it,

> Ein Freund, ein guter Freund,
> das ist das schönste was es gibt.

[16] *Letters and Correspondence of John Henry Newman,* ed. Anne Mozley (London, 1891), II, 479 (27 Dec. 1863), quoted by Tillotson, *Thackeray the Novelist,* p. 265.

Chronology of Important Dates

1811   Born in Calcutta (July 18) to Richmond and Anne Becher Thackeray.

1815   Death of father.

1817   Sent to England for school. Mother marries Maj. Henry Carmichael-Smyth in India.

1819   Carmichael-Smyths return to England.

1822   School at Charterhouse.

1829   Trinity College, Cambridge.

1830–31   Leaves Cambridge; travels in Germany.

1831–32   Studies law in London.

1834–35   Studies art in Paris.

1836   Appointed Paris correspondent of *The Constitutional*. Marries Isabella Shawe in Paris.

1837   Daughter Anne born in London. *The Constitutional* fails; Carmichael-Smyths move to Paris. Thackeray begins to write in *Fraser's Magazine* and other journals.

1837–38   *The Yellowplush Correspondence (Fraser's)*.

1839   Second daughter, Jane, dies in infancy.

1839–40   *Catherine (Fraser's)*.

1840   *A Shabby Genteel Story (Fraser's)*. *The Paris Sketch Book*. Third daughter, Harriet Marian (Minny) born. Thackeray's wife becomes insane.

1841   *The Great Hoggarty Diamond (Fraser's)*. *Comic Tales and Sketches* (collected in 2 vols.).

1842   Begins contributing to *Punch*, and in 1844 to the *Morning Chronicle*.

1843   *The Irish Sketch Book.*

1844   *The Luck of Barry Lyndon (Fraser's).* Visits Mediterranean and Palestine.

1846–47   *The Snobs of England (Punch).*

ca. 1847   Begins Platonic affair with Jane Octavia Brookfield, wife of Rev. William Brookfield.

1847–48   *Vanity Fair* (monthly numbers).

1847   *Punch's Prize Novelists.*

1848–50   *The History of Pendennis* (monthly numbers, interrupted for 3 months by illness in 1849).

1850   *Rebecca and Rowena.*

1851   Quarrel with Brookfield and break with Jane Brookfield.

1852   *The History of Henry Esmond.*

1852–53   First American tour.

1853   *The English Humourists of the Eighteenth Century* (lectures first delivered in 1851).

1853–55   *The Newcomes* (monthly numbers).

1855   *The Rose and the Ring.*

1855–56   Second American tour.

1857–59   *The Virginians* (monthly numbers).

1859–62   Editor of *Cornhill Magazine.*

1860   *Lovel the Widower (Cornhill).*

1860–63   *Roundabout Papers (Cornhill).*

1860   *The Four Georges* (*Cornhill*; lectures first delivered in 1855).

1861–62   *The Adventures of Philip (Cornhill).*

1863   Dies (December 24).

1864   *Denis Duval* (unfinished, published posthumously in *Cornhill*).

Notes on the Editor and Contributors

ALEXANDER WELSH, editor of this volume, is Professor of English at the University of Pittsburgh and author of *The Hero of the Waverley Novels*.

G. K. CHESTERTON, the English polemicist and man of letters, made significant contributions to Victorian studies, notably in books on Dickens and Browning, as well as *The Victorian Age in Literature*.

PERCY LUBBOCK, best known today for *The Craft of Fiction*, was an essayist and novelist, and the editor of Henry James's letters.

JOHN W. DODDS, author of *The Age of Paradox: A Biography of England, 1841–1851* and other books, is Emeritus Professor of English and Humanities at Stanford University.

J. Y. T. GREIG was Professor at the University of the Wittersand, Johannesburg. He edited *The Letters of David Hume* and wrote a biography of Hume; also *The Psychology of Laughter and Comedy* and, under the pseudonym John Carruthers, a little book called *Scheherazade; or, the Future of the English Novel*.

MARIO PRAZ is Professor of English Language and Literature at the University of Rome. Among his books that have been translated into English, besides *The Hero in Eclipse*, are *The Romantic Agony, Seventeenth-Century Imagery, The Flaming Heart*, and *The House of Life*.

JULIET SUTTON, Assistant Professor of English at the University of Alberta, Edmonton, is working on a book on Thackeray.

KATHLEEN TILLOTSON, Professor of English in Bedford College, University of London, has written *Novels of the Eighteen-Forties, Dickens at Work* (with John Butt), and *Mid-Victorian Studies* (with Geoffrey Tillotson).

G. ARMOUR CRAIG, Professor of English at Amherst College, Massachusetts, has written articles on a number of novelists and is working on a book on the nineteenth-century novel.

JOHN LOOFBOUROW, the author of *Thackeray and the Form of Fiction*, is Associate Professor of English at Boston College.

GEORG (or GYÖRGY) LUKÁCS, an Hungarian, is the foremost Marxist critic and theorist today. A few of his works are now available in English, including *The Historical Novel, Studies in European Realism*, and his *Essay on Thomas Mann*.

JOHN E. TILFORD, JR., Professor of English and Dean of the College of Arts and Sciences at Jacksonville University, Florida, has written articles on Thackeray, George Borrow, and others.

GORDON N. RAY is President of the Guggenheim Memorial Foundation and Professor at New York University. His splendid biography, criticism, and editorial labors (see Bibliography) have made it possible to know more of Thackeray than the novelist's own contemporaries could know.

JOSEPH E. BAKER, the author of *The Novel and the Oxford Movement* and editor of *Reinterpretations of Victorian Literature,* is Professor of English at the University of Iowa.

Selected Bibliography

The editions of Thackeray's works most frequently cited by scholars are the Biographical Edition, with biographical introductions by Anne Thackeray Ritchie (13 vols., New York and London: Harper and Brothers, 1898–99) and the Oxford Thackeray, ed. George Saintsbury (17 vols., London, 1908). These are supplemented by *The Letters and Private Papers of William Makepeace Thackeray*, ed. Gordon N. Ray (4 vols., Cambridge: Harvard University Press, 1945–46); *Contributions to the Morning Chronicle*, ed. Gordon N. Ray (Urbana: University of Illinois Press, 1955); and the edition of *Vanity Fair* by Geoffrey and Kathleen Tillotson (Boston: Houghton Mifflin Company, 1963). The definitive biography of Thackeray is by Gordon N. Ray in two volumes, *Thackeray: The Uses of Adversity, 1811–1846* and *Thackeray: The Age of Wisdom, 1847–1863* (New York: McGraw-Hill Book Company, 1955, 1958). A short biography of independent interest is Lambert Ennis, *Thackeray: The Sentimental Cynic* (Evanston: Northwestern University Press, 1950). A chronological bibliography of Thackeray's published writings can be found in Lewis Melville, *William Makepeace Thackeray* (2 vols., London: The Bodley Head, 1910), II, 143–376. Two guides to Thackeray criticism are the chapter by Lionel Stevenson in *Victorian Fiction: A Guide to Research*, ed. Lionel Stevenson (Cambridge: Harvard University Press, 1964) and Dudley Flamm, *Thackeray's Critics: An Annotated Bibliography of British and American Criticism, 1836–1901* (Chapel Hill: University of North Carolina Press, 1967). *Thackeray: The Critical Heritage*, ed. Geoffrey Tillotson and Donald Hawes (New York: Barnes & Noble, Inc., 1968) is an anthology of nineteenth-century reviews and other essays. There follows a selected list of twentieth-century Thackeray criticism. Contributions printed in whole or in part in the present collection are not listed below.

Auchincloss, Louis. "The Two Ages of Thackeray," in *Reflections of a Jacobite*. Boston: Houghton Mifflin Company, 1961.

Brogan, Howard O. "Rachel Esmond and the Dilemma of the Victorian Ideal of Womanhood." *Journal of English Literary History*, XIII (1946), 223–232.

Brownell, W. C. "Thackeray," in *Victorian Prose Masters*. New York: Charles Scribner's Sons, 1902.

Cecil, Lord David. "William Makepeace Thackeray," in *Early Victorian Novelists*. London: Constable & Co., Ltd., 1934. Reprinted as *Victorian Novelists*, Chicago: University of Chicago Press, 1958.

Colby, Robert A. "Barry Lyndon and the Irish Hero." *Nineteenth-Century Fiction*, XXI (1966), 109–130.

Dyson, A. E. "*Vanity Fair*: An Irony against Heroes." *Critical Quarterly*, VI (1964), 11–31.

Elton, Oliver. *A Survey of English Literature, 1830–1880*. 2 vols. London: Edward Arnold (Publishers), Ltd., 1920. II, 231–257.

Fido, Martin. "*The History of Pendennis*: A Reconsideration." *Essays in Criticism*, XIV (1964), 363–379.

Fraser, Russell A. "Pernicious Casuistry: A Study of Character in *Vanity Fair*." *Nineteenth-Century Fiction*, XII (1957), 137–147.

Goodell, Margaret Moore. *Three Satirists of Snobbery: Thackeray, Meredith, Proust*. Britannica, XVII (Hamburg, 1939), 7–25, 56–113.

Harden, Edgar F. "The Fields of Mars in *Vanity Fair*." *Tennessee Studies in Literature*, X (1965), 123–132.

Johnson, E. D. H. "*Vanity Fair* and *Amelia*: Thackeray in the Perspective of the Eighteenth Century." *Modern Philology*, LIX (1961), 100–113.

Kettle, Arnold. "Thackeray: *Vanity Fair*," in *An Introduction to the English Novel*. 2 vols. London: Hutchinson University Library, 1951. Reprinted, New York: Harper Torchbooks, 1960, I, 156–170.

Las Vergnas, Raymond. *W. M. Thackeray: l'homme, le penseur, le romancier*. Paris: Librairie Ancienne Honoré Champion, 1932.

Lester, John A., Jr. "Thackeray's Narrative Technique." *PMLA*, LXIX (1954), 392–409. Reprinted in *Victorian Literature: Selected Essays*, ed. Robert O. Preyer, New York: Harper Torchbooks, 1966, pp. 159–181.

Pacey, W. C. D. "Balzac and Thackeray." *Modern Language Review*, XXXVI (1941), 213–224.

Rader, Ralph Wilson. "Thackeray's Injustice to Fielding." *Journal of English and Germanic Philology*, LVI (1957), 203–212.

Ray, Gordon N. *The Buried Life: A Study of the Relation between Thackeray's Fiction and his Personal History*. Cambridge: Harvard University Press, 1952.

———. "*Vanity Fair*: One Version of the Novelist's Responsibility." *Essays by Divers Hands*, n.s. XXV (1950), 87–101. Reprinted in *Victorian Literature: Modern Essays in Criticism*, ed. Austin Wright, New York: Oxford Galaxy Books, 1961, pp. 342–357.

Solomon, Eric. "Thackeray on War." *Victorian Newsletter*, No. 23 (Spring, 1963), 6–11.

Spilka, Mark. "A Note on Thackeray's *Amelia*." *Nineteenth-Century Fiction*, X (1955), 202–210.

Stewart, David H. "Thackeray's Modern Detractors." *Papers of the Michigan Academy of Science, Arts, and Letters*, XLVIII (1963), 629–638.

Talon, Henri-A. "Thackeray's *Vanity Fair* Revisited: Fiction as Truth," in *Of Books and Humankind: Essays and Poems Presented to Bonamy Dobrée*, ed. John Butt. London: Routledge & Kegan Paul, Ltd., 1964.

————. "Time and Memory in Thackeray's *Henry Esmond.*" *Review of English Studies*, XIII (1962), 147–156.

Taube, Myron. "The Character of Amelia in the Meaning of *Vanity Fair.*" *Victorian Newsletter*, No. 18 (Fall, 1960), 1–8.

Taylor, A. Carey. "Balzac et Thackeray." *Revue de littérature comparée*, XXXIV (1960), 354–369.

Tillotson, Geoffrey. *Thackeray the Novelist*. Cambridge: Cambridge University Press, 1954.

Touster, Eva Beach. "The Literary Relationship of Thackeray and Fielding." *Journal of English and Germanic Philology*, XLVI (1947), 383–394.

Van Ghent, Dorothy. "On *Vanity Fair*," in *The English Novel: Form and Function*. New York: Holt, Rinehart & Winston, Inc., 1953. Reprinted, New York: Harper Torchbooks, 1961.

Wells, Chauncey W. "Thackeray and the Victorian Compromise." *University of California Publications in English*, I (1929), 179–199.

TWENTIETH CENTURY VIEWS

American Authors